P9-EML-535

EVERY ONE A WITNESS

THE STUART AGE

EVERY ONE A WITNESS

The Stuart Age

COMMENTARIES OF AN ERA

A. F. SCOTT

WHITE LION PUBLISHERS
London and New York

CONTENTS

CONTENTS

LIST OF ILLUSTRATIONS

The author and publisher acknowledge with thanks permission to reproduce the illustrations listed below.

ACKNOWLEDGEMENTS

The author and publishers are grateful to the authorities named for permission to use copyright material. Furthermore, the publishers have tried to trace the owners of all copyright material, and apologise for any omissions. Should these be made known to us proper acknowledgements will be made in future editions.

PREFACE
by Sir John Wolfenden

Thousands of readers are already deeply indebted to Mr Scott. With apparently inexhaustible energy he continues to give us books which combine in an unusual degree scholarship with readability.

This present volume is the second in his series of anthologies 'Every One a Witness'. The first dealt with the Georgian Age, and we now move backwards in time to the Stuarts.

The purpose and the method of the two are the same. The purpose is to give you and me a picture of the everyday life of everyday people like us – what they wore, what they ate, how they travelled about, how they earned a living, how they treated their children, how they died. Many of us find the ordinary lives of ordinary people more interesting than the exceptional lives of the great ones. And certainly they give us a far more accurate and lively picture of an age. Besides, we are healthily inquisitive.

The method is to use nothing but contemporary sources, both in the text and in the illustrations. This is first-hand evidence, set out in direct quotation, without any 'interpretation' from any later historian. So we get a double benefit, an insight into lives and at the same time an insight into the way in which those lives were described by contemporary writers and artists.

The amount of work which must have gone into the selection is prodigious. But, more than that, Arthur Scott is an anthologist of taste, experience and rare judgment. He knows the kind of thing we want to know about those who lived three hundred years ago, and he knows exactly where to put his finger on the contemporary evidence.

We are now still more deeply in his debt, and we eagerly await further gatherings of similar flowers from earlier ages.

J.F.W.

Royalty

Elizabeth I died at Richmond on 24 March 1603. She was succeeded by her Scots cousin James VI, the grandson of Henry VIII's sister Margaret.

James I showed himself to be 'very facile using no great solemnities in his accesses, but witty to conceive, and ready of speech'. His sense of humour, always coarse, matched his personal habits once called 'a fluorescence of obscenity'.

On spindly legs, he was often shambling from room to room, leaning on the shoulder of a Court favourite. He was better on horseback, for he rode well and was passionately fond of hunting. Rarely drunk, his thick Scots accent, restless movement of his head, and rolling eyes made him appear so.

Already learned, he spoke with authority on many subjects, including religion and witchcraft and tobacco. He possessed that sense of dignity of Kingship later seen in his son and grandsons. Giving thought to his possible death, blown up with Parliament assembled, James declared, 'It should never have been spoken or written in ages succeeding that I had died ingloriously in an Ale-house, a Stews, or such vile place, [but] that mine end should have been in that most honourable and fittest place for a King to be in, for doing the terms most proper to his office.'

James died at Theobalds on 27 March 1625. Sully described him as 'the wisest fool in Christendom'. 'He was indeed', said Macaulay, 'made up of two men – a witty, well-read scholar, who wrote, disputed, and harangued, and a nervous, drivelling idiot who acted.'

Charles I is the martyr-king of Van Dyck's portraits. When the Italian sculptor Bernine saw Van Dyck's 'Charles I in Three Positions' in 1637 he declared: 'Never have I beheld a countenance more unfortunate.'

Charles retained a stammer, but outgrew the weakness of his ankles. He became an accomplished horseman, a skilful tilter and marksman, a sound scholar, diligent in the study of theology. In the words of

1

Rubens, he was 'the greatest amateur of paintings among the princes of the world'.

His manners were perfect, and he had a sweetness of disposition which unhappily he could not communicate to the nation. William Laud said, 'a mild and gracious prince who knew not how to be, or be made, great'. Charles thought himself above all ordinary laws, so he broke promises and showed himself faithless to enemies and friends. His wife Henrietta Maria, a Roman Catholic, was sister of the French king Louis XIII. She was *chic, petite, difficile* and *dévote*. They had for each other continuing love and faith.

Charles never enjoyed the act of ruling. He felt himself to be a man of honour, pursued by misfortune. After he had raised his standard at Nottingham in 1642, direct action on his part would have won the Civil War. But suspicious dealing and hesitation led to trial and execution. The army not parliament stood behind the judges. The courage and dignity of Charles, his evident sincerity before God, were the basis of 'a martyrology unprecedented in English history'.

Charles II entered London in triumph on 29 May 1660, his birthday. Evelyn writes, 'with a triumph of above 20,000 horse and foot, brandishing their swords and shouting with inexpressible joy; the ways strawed with flowers, the bells ringing, the streets hung with tapestry, fountains running with wine . . . so as they were seven hours in passing the city, even from two in the afternoon till nine at night. I stood in the Strand, and beheld it, and blessed God.'

He towered above most of his contemporaries, had his father's long, slender face, and a graceful, tireless stride. Charles had dark eyes, almost black hair, swarthy complexion and a wide, rather ugly, mouth. 'A tall, black man, six foot two inches high', ran the 'wanted' notices in 1651. His affable, disarming manner and love of sport – riding, dancing, hunting, swimming and tennis – endeared him to ordinary men.

In many ways his marriage to Catherine of Braganza was a disaster, though he treated her in public with marked courtesy. His taste in women ranged from the delicate beauty of the Duchess of Richmond to the high-spirited charms of Nell Gwynn. Louise de Kéroualle (with the pet name of Fubbs) held his affections for many years. James, Duke of York, remarked in 1682 that Charles was 'very well pleased with his new yacht, the "Fubbs", she outsailing all the old ones.' (Old ones were the *Cleveland* and *Portsmouth*.)

Burnet wrote of Charles, 'He has a strange command of himself; he can pass from business to pleasure and from pleasure to business in so easy a manner that all seem alike to him; he has the greatest art of concealing himself of any man alive.' This king was superficially content, with an easy air of command. He said to Burnet, 'All appetites are free, and God will never damn a man for allowing himself a little pleasure.'

Shrewd, supple, 'an exact knower of mankind', Charles was at heart a Catholic and an absolute monarch. In his last illness he made the famous remark, 'Let not poor Nelly starve.' John Drummond wrote, 'He died as he lived, the admiration of all men for his piety, his contempt of this world, and his resolution against death.'

At coronations, superstition had the fullest play. John Aubrey recorded what he saw, 'When King James II was Crowned (according to the Ancient Custom, the Peers go to the Throne, and kiss the King): The Crown was almost kiss'd off his Head. An Earl did sett it right: and as he came from the Abbey to Westminster Hall, the Crown totter'd extremely. . . .

'Nor was this all. Upon Saint Mark's day, were prepared stately fire-works on the Thames. It happened, that they took fire all together, and it was so dreadful, that several Spectators leap'd into the River, choosing rather to be drown'd than burn'd.'

James exposed his chief weaknesses – a narrow, rigid mind and lack of imagination. Lauderdale summed him up:

> This good prince has all the weakness of his father without his strength. He loves, as he saith, to be served in his own way, and he is as very a papist as the pope himself, which will be his ruin . . . [and] if he had the empire of the whole world he would venture the loss of it, for his ambition is to shine in a red letter after he is dead.

Naturally extremely gloomy, his warped judgement lost him the throne. He escaped to France and found his way to Versailles. A member of the French court said, 'When you listen to him you realise why he is here.'

William III and Mary II were crowned jointly as King and Queen regnant. William was a King in England, a Stadtholder in Holland, and his preference lay for his homeland. Mary echoes his feeling, 'He could not restrain [himself, and] as soon as we were alone we both shed tears of joy to meet, and of sorrow for meeting in England, both wishing it might have been in Holland, both bewailing the loss of the liberty we had left behind.'

William was thin and solemn, with fierce eyes and 'a constant deep cough'. In him was something of his grandfather, Charles I – self-assurance and aloof demeanour. But he had determination and an exact judgment of men. Mary displayed gaiety, and under the trials of the time their love grew. She wrote it was 'a passion that cannot end but with my life'; this and her graciousness helped her husband, one of the least popular of all English kings.

It has been said that Queen Anne, like Victoria, was the quintessence of ordinariness. The Duchess of Marlborough wrote of her: 'a person and appearance not at all ungraceful, till she grew exceeding gross and corpulent. There was something of majesty in her look, but mixed with a sullen and constant frown, that plainly betrayed a gloominess of soul and a cloudiness of disposition within.'

Anne had strong affections and hatreds. William III was 'Mr Caliban'; the Marlboroughs, 'Mr and Mrs Freeman'; Godolphin, 'Mr Montgomery'. She and the prince, George of Denmark, were 'Mr and Mrs Morley'. They prematurely grew middle-aged together. Anne's long succession of pregnancies unfortunately produced no heir to the throne. She had deserted her father James II, and saw this as punishment from God.

Quarrels among her ministers kept the poor Queen in a state of constant unrest. Then, widowed and friendless, the last of the Stuart monarchs died.

On the same day, when King George was proclaimed, some fellows of the Privy Council protested, saying the Queen was not dead. They were silenced by the words, 'Dead! She is as dead as Julius Caesar.'

THE NEW KING – JAMES I

About 10 o'clock King *James* was proclaimed in *Cheapside* by all the Council with great joy and triumph. I went to see and hear. This peaceable coming-in of the King was unexpected of all sorts of people. Within three days we returned to *Clerkenwell* again. A little after this Queen *Elizabeth's* corpse came by night in a barge from *Richmond* to *Whitehall*, my Mother and a great company of ladies attending it, where it continued a great while standing in the Drawing Chamber, where it was watched all night by several lords and ladies, my Mother sitting up with it two or three nights, but my Lady would not give me leave to watch, by reason I was held too young. At this time we used to go very much to *Whitehall*, and walked much in the garden which was frequented by lords and ladies, my Mother being all full of hopes, every man expecting mountains and finding molehills, excepting Sir *R. Cecil* and the house of the *Howards*, who hated my Mother and did not much love my Aunt *Warwick*. About this time my *Lord Southampton* was enlarged of his imprisonment out of the *Tower*. When the corpse of Queen *Elizabeth* had continued at *Whitehall* as the Council had thought fit, it was carried with great solemnity to *Westminster*, the lords and ladies going on foot to attend it, my Mother and my Aunt of *Warwick* being mourners, but I was not allowed to be one, because I was not high enough, which did much trouble me then, but yet I stood in the church at *Westminster* to see the solemnities performed. A little after this my Lady and a great deal of other company as Mrs *Eliz. Bridges*, Lady *Newtin*, and her daughter Lady *Finch*, went down with my Aunt *Warwick* to *North Hall*, and from thence we all went to *Tibbalds* to see the King who used my Mother and Aunt very graciously, but we saw a great change between the fashions of the Court as it is now and of that in the Queen's time, for we were all lousy by sitting in the chamber of Sir *Thomas Erskine*. As the King came out of Scotland, when he lay at *York*, there was a strife between my Father and Lord *Burleigh* (who was the President) who should carry the sword, but it was adjudged on my Father's side because it was an office by inheritance and so it lineally descended to me.   Lady Anne Clifford, *Diary*, 1616–1619

JAMES I

The people of all sorts rode and ran, their eyes flaming nothing but sparkles of affection, their mouths and tongues uttering nothing but sounds of joy. . . discovering a passionate longing and earnestness to meet and embrace their new sovereign.

And this is what James I was like:

He was of a middle stature, more corpulent through his clothes than in his body, yet fat enough, his clothes ever being made large and easy, the doublets quilted for stiletto proof, his breeches in great pleats and full stuffed. He was naturally of a timorous disposition, which was the reason for his quilted doublets; his eyes large, ever rolling after any stranger came in his presence, insomuch as many for shame have left the room, as being out of countenance. His beard was very thin, his tongue too large for his mouth, which ever made him speak full in the mouth, and made him drink very uncomely, as if eating his drink, which came out into the cup of each side of his mouth. His skin was as soft as taffeta sarsnet, which felt so because he never washed his hands, only rubbed his finger ends slightly with the wet end of a napkin. His legs were very weak, having had (as was thought) some foul play in his youth, or rather before he was born, that he was not able to stand at seven years of age; that weakness made him ever leaning on other men's shoulders. His walk was ever circular. . . .

He was very temperate in his exercises and in his diet, and not intemperate in his drinking: however, in his old age and Buckingham's jovial suppers, when he had any turn to do with him, made him sometimes overtaken, which he would the very next day remember, and repent with tears. It is true he drank very often, which was rather

1.   Portrait of James I, painted in 1625 when he was 59 years old.

out of a custom than any delight, and his drinks were of that kind for strength, as Frontiniack, Canary, High Country wine, Tent Wine and Scottish ale, that had he not had a very strong brain, might daily have been overtaken, although he seldom drank at any one time above four spoonfuls, many times not above one or two. . . .

In his diet and apparel and journeys he was very constant; in his apparel so constant as by his good will he would never change his clothes until worn out to very rags: his fashion, never, insomuch as one bringing to him a hat of a Spanish block, he cast it from him, swearing he neither loved them nor their fashions. Another time, bringing him roses on his shoes, he asked if they would make him a ruff-footed Dove; one yard of six-penny ribbon served that turn. His diet and journeys were so constant that the best observing courtier of our time was wont to say, were he asleep seven years and then awakened, he would tell where the King every day had been and every dish he had had at his table. . . .

He would make a great deal too bold with God in his passion, both in cursing and swearing, and one strain higher verging on blasphemy, but would in his better temper say he hoped God would not impute them as sins and lay them to his charge, seeing they proceeded from passion. . . .

Sir Anthony Weldon, Court and Character of James I, 1650

CHARLES I

His deportment was very majestic, for he would not let fall his dignity, no, not to the greatest foreigners that came to visit him at his court; for though he was far from pride, yet he was careful of majesty and would be approached with respect and reverence. His conversation was free, and the subject matter of it (on his own side of the court), was most commonly rational, or if facetious, not light. With any artist or good mechanic, traveller or scholar he would discourse freely, and as he was commonly improved by them, so he often gave light to them in their own art or knowledge. For there were few gentlemen in the world that knew more of useful or necessary learning than this prince did; and yet his proportion of books was but small, having like Francis the first of France learnt more by the ear than by study. His way of arguing was very civil and patient, for he seldom contradicted another by his authority, but by his reason; nor did he by any petulant dislike quash another's arguments, and he offered his exception by this civil intro-duction, *By your favour, Sir, I think otherwise on this or that ground:* yet he would discountenance any bold or forward address unto him. . . .

His exercises were manly, for he rode the great horse very well, and on the little saddle he was not only adroit, but a laborious hunter or field-man: and they were wont to say of him that he failed not to do any

2. Charles I's children, painted in 1637. *Left to right:* Mary (to be mother of William III); James, Duke of York (later James II); Charles, Prince of Wales (later Charles II), aged seven; Elizabeth; and Anne.

of his exercises artificially, but not very gracefully, like some well-proportioned faces which yet want a pleasant air of countenance. . . .

His exercises of religion were most exemplary, for every morning early, and evening not very late, singly and alone, in his own bed-chamber or closet he spent some time in private meditation – (for he durst reflect and be alone) – and through the whole week, even when he went a hunting, he never failed before he sat down to dinner, to have part of the Liturgy read unto him and his menial servants, came he never so hungry or so late in. And on Sundays and Tuesdays he came (commonly at the beginning of Service) to the Chapel, well attended by his Court-Lords and chief attendants, and most usually waited on by many of the nobility in town who found those observances acceptably entertained by him. . . .

    Sir Philip Warwick, *Memoirs of the Reign of Charles I,* 1676–1677

CHARLES I
Archbishop William Juxon said in his Sermon on the Death of Charles I:
Observe his great temperance, his exemplary chastity . . . a refined purity from all lasciviousness of either gesture or speech. His abstinence in his feeding gave unto him constancy in health and readiness

into action, and his sobriety in drinking (whom the sun nor all the sons of men ever saw overcome or disguised by ingurgitation of strong liquors) made him unconquerable by wine or woman.

OLIVER CROMWELL

I have no mind to give an ill character of Cromwell, for in his conversation towards me he was ever friendly, though at the latter end of the day, finding me ever incorrigible and having some inducements to suspect me a tamperer, he was sufficiently rigid. The first time that ever I took notice of him was in the very beginning of the Parliament held in November 1640, when I vainly thought myself a courtly young gentleman (for we courtiers valued ourselves much upon our good clothes). I came one morning into the House well clad, and perceived a gentleman speaking (whom I knew not) very ordinarily apparelled, for

3. A contemporary Dutch engraving of Cromwell indicating his ambition for the royal crown.

it was a plain-cloth suit, which seemed to have made by an ill country tailor: his linen was plain and not very clean, and I remember a speck or two of blood upon his little band, which was not much larger than his collar. His hat was without a hat-band. His stature was of good size, his sword stuck close to his side, his countenance swollen and reddish, his voice sharp and untunable, and his eloquence full of fervour, for the subject matter would not bear much of reason, it being in behalf of a servant of Mr Prynne's, who had dispersed libels against the Queen for her dancing and such like innocent and courtly sports: and he aggravated the imprisonment of this man by the Council-Table unto that height that one would have believed the very government itself had been in great danger by it. I sincerely profess it lessened much my reverence unto that great council, for he was very much hearkened unto. And yet I lived to see this very gentleman, whom out of no ill will to him I thus describe, by multiplied good successes and by real (but usurped) power (having had a better tailor and more converse among good company) in my own eye, when for six weeks together I was a prisoner in his sergeant's hands and daily waited at Whitehall, appear of a great and majestic deportment and comely presence. Of him therefore I will say no more, but that verily I believe he was extraordinarily designed for those extraordinary things which one while most wickedly and facinorously he acted, and at another as successfully and greatly performed.

Sir Philip Warwick, *Memoirs of the Reign of Charles I*, 1676–1677

CHARLES II

Charles II's mother, Henrietta Maria, was writing, after his birth, to Madame St George, her governess and friend, and said, 'At present he is so black that I am ashamed of him.'

Two years later she still declared, 'He is so ugly I am ashamed . . . but his size and fatness supply what he lacks in beauty. He is so serious in all he does that I cannot help fancying him far wiser than myself.'

He is somewhat taller than the middle stature of Englishmen; so exactly formed that the most curious eye cannot find any error in his shape. His face is rather grave than severe, which is very much softened whensoever he speaks; his complexion is somewhat dark, but much enlightened by his eyes, which are quick and sparkling. Until he was near twenty years of age the figure of his face was very lovely, but he is since grown leaner, and now the majesty of his countenance supplies the lines of beauty. His hair, which he hath in great plenty is of a shining black, not frizzled, but so naturally curling into great rings that it is a very comely ornament. His motions are so easy and graceful that they do very much recommend his person when he either walks,

4. A portrait of Charles II in marble, signed by a French sculptor, Honore Pelle, and dated 1684.

dances, plays at pall mall, at tennis, or rides the great horse, which are his usual exercises. To the gracefulness of his deportment may be joined his easiness of access, his patience in attention, and the gentleness both in the tune and style of his speech; so that those whom either the veneration for his dignity or majesty of his presence have put into an awful respect are reassured as soon as he enters into the conversation.   Sir Samuel Tuke, *A Character of Charles II*, 1660

JAMES II

I will digress a little to give an account of the Duke's character, whom I knew for some years so particularly, that I can say much upon my own knowledge. He was very brave in his youth, and so much magnified by Monsieur *Turenne*, that, till his marriage lessened him he really clouded the King, and pass'd for the superior genius. He was naturally candid and sincere, and a firm friend, till affairs and his religion wore out all his first principles and inclinations. He had a great desire to understand affairs: And in order to that he kept a constant journal of all that pass'd, of which he shewed me a great deal. The Duke of *Buckingham* gave me once a short but severe character of the two brothers. It was the more severe, because it was true: The King (he said) could see things if he would, and the Duke would see things if he could. He had no true judgment, and was soon determined by those whom he trusted: But he was obstinate against all other advices. . . . He was perpetually in one amour or other, without being very nice in his choice: Upon which the King said once, he believed his brother had his mistresses given him by his Priests for penance.

Bishop Burnet, *History of His Own Time*, 1633–1701

MARY OF MODENA

Mary Beatrice d'Este of Modena was 'tall and admirably shaped, her complexion was of the last degree of fairness, her hair black as jet, so were her eyebrows and her eyes, but the latter so full of light and sweetness as they did dazzle and charm too'. She was a most bigoted Catholic, and when James married her in 1673 his conversion privately in 1668 was now widely known. It was not only 'Lillibullero' which 'danced James II out of three kingdoms'.

WILLIAM III

Thus lived and died William the Third, King of Great Britain, and Prince of Orange. He had a thin and weak body, was brown haired, and of a clear and delicate constitution: he had a Roman eagle nose, bright and sparkling eyes, a large front, and a countenance composed to gravity and authority; all his senses were critical and exquisite. He was always asthmatical, and the dregs of the smallpox falling on his lungs, he had a constant deep cough. His behaviour was solemn and serious, seldom cheerful, and but with a few: he spoke little and very slowly, and most commonly with disgusting dryness, which was his character at all times, except in a day of battle; for then he was all fire, though without passion; he was then everywhere and looked to everything. He had no great advantage from his education; De Wit's discourses were of great use to him, and he, being apprehensive of the observation of those who were looking narrowly into everything he said or did, had brought himself under a habitual caution that he could never shake off, though in another scene it proved as hurtful, as it was then necessary to his affairs: he spoke Dutch, French, English, and German equally well; and he understood the Latin, Spanish, and Italian, so that he was well fitted to command armies composed of several nations. He had a memory that amazed all about him, for it never failed him: he was an exact observer of men and things: his strength lay rather in a true discerning and a sound judgment, than in imagination or invention: his designs were always great and good; but it was thought he trusted too much to that, and that he did not descend enought to the humours of his people, to make himself and his notions more acceptable to them: this, in a government that has so much of freedom in it as ours, was more necessary than he was inclined to believe; his reservedness grew on him, so that it disgusted most of those who served him; but he had observed the errors of too much talking, rather than those of too cold a silence.   Bishop Burnet, *History of My Own Time*, 1723

ANNE

Though her reign was a glorious part of our history, Queen Anne herself had few talents. Charles II once said of her husband, Prince George of Denmark: 'I have tried him drunk and tried him sober, but there is nothing in him either way.' Still, rare among the Stuarts, their marriage brought lifelong affection.

Her person was middle-sized and well-made, but after she bare children, corpulent; her hair dark brown, her complexion sanguine and ruddy; her features strong but regular; and the only blemish in her face was owing to the diffluxion she had in her infancy on the eyes, which left a contraction in the upper lids, that gave a cloudy air to her countenance. . . . What was most remarkable in her personal accomplishments was a clear harmonious voice, particularly conspicuous in her graceful delivery of her speeches to Parliament.

Abel Boyer, *History of the Life and Reign of Queen Anne*, 1722

5.   An engraving of the City of London 1714, after the rebuilding by Christopher Wren.

London

LONDON

> But now behold,
> In the quick forge and working-house of thought,
> How London doth pour out her citizens.

This is what Shakespeare said. Frederick, Duke of Würtemberg, at about the same time, gave a foreigner's opinion.

London is a large, excellent and mighty city of business, and the most important in the whole Kingdom. Most of the inhabitants are employed in buying and selling merchandise, and trading in almost every corner of the world, since the river is most useful and convenient for this purpose, considering that ships from France, the Netherlands, Sweden, Denmark, Hamburg and other Kingdoms, come almost up to the city, to which they convey goods and receive and take away others in exchange.

It is a very populous city, so that one can scarcely pass along the streets, on account of the throng.

The inhabitants are magnificently apparelled, and are extremely proud and overbearing; and because the greater part, especially the tradespeople, seldom go into other countries, but always remain in their houses in the city attending to their business, they care little for foreigners, but scoff and laugh at them. And moreover one dare not oppose them, else the streetboys and apprentices collect together in immense crowds and strike to the right and left unmercifully without regard to person; and because they are the strongest, one is obliged to put up with the insult as well as the injury.

The women have much more liberty than perhaps in any other place; they also know well how to make use of it, for they go dressed out in exceedingly fine clothes, and give all their attention to their ruffs and stuffs, to such a degree indeed, that as I am informed, many a one does not hesitate to wear velvet in the streets, which is common with them, whilst at home perhaps they have not a piece of dry bread. All the English women are accustomed to wear hats upon their heads, and gowns cut after the old German fashion – for indeed their descent is from the Saxons.

HOG LANE
John Stow, writing of Hog Lane in 1603, said:
. . . within these forty years, had on both sides fair hedgerows of elm trees, with bridges and easy stiles to pass over into the pleasant fields, very commodious for citizens therein to walk, shoot, and otherwise to re-create and refresh their dull spirits in the sweet and wholesome air, which is now within a few years made a continual building throughout, of garden houses and small cottages. And the fields on either side be turned into garden plots, teynter yards [for stretching cloth], bowling alleys, and such like, from Houndsditch in the West, so far as Whitechapel, and further towards the East.

THE TOWER OF LONDON
This tower is a citadel, to defend or command the city: a royal place for assemblies, and treaties. A prison of estate, for the most dangerous offenders: the only place of coinage for all England at this time: the armoury for warlike provision: the treasury of the ornaments and jewels of the crown, and general conserver of the most records of the King's Courts of Justice at Westminster.   John Stow, *c.* 1603

THE BUSY STREETS
Thomas Dekker, the playwright and contemporary of Shakespeare, was born and lived in London, and is the first great writer of London street life. Here he describes the rush and hurry of traffic, and the general bustle of people at every corner.
In every street, carts and coaches make such a thundering as if the world ran upon wheels. At every corner men, women and children meet in such shoals, that posts are set up on purpose to strengthen the houses, lest with jostling one another they should shoulder them down. Besides hammers are beating in one place, tubs hooping in another, pots clinking in a third, water tankards running at tilt in a fourth. Here are porters sweating under burdens, there merchants' men bearing bags of money. Chapmen (as if they were at leap frog) skip out of one shop into another. Tradesmen (as if they were dancing galliards) are lusty at legs and never stand still. All are as busy as country attorneys at an assizes.
                Thomas Dekker, *The Seven Deadly Sinnes of London,* 1606

THE GROWTH OF LONDON
Our trades do meet in Companies, our Companies at halls, and our

halls become monopolies of freedom, tied to London: where all our Crafts and Mysteries are so laid up together, that outrunning all the wisdom and prudence of the land, men live by trades they never learned, nor seek to understand. By means whereof, all our creeks seek to one river, all our rivers run to one port, all our ports join to one town, all our towns make but one city, and all our cities but suburbs to one vast, unwieldy and disorderly Babel of buildings, which the world calls London.   Thomas Milles, *The Customer's Alphabet*, 1608

LONDON TAVERNS

The Gentry to the *King's Head*,
  The Nobles to the *Crown*,
The Knights unto the *Golden Fleece*,
  And to the *Plough*, the Clown.
The Churchman to the *Mitre*,
  The Shepherd to the *Star*,
The Gardener hies him to the *Rose*,
  To the *Drum* the man of war.
To the *Feathers* Ladies you! The *Globe*
  The Seaman doth not scorn!
The Usurer to the *Devil*; and
  The Townsman to the *Horn*.
The Huntsman to the *White Hart*,
  To the *Ship* the Merchants go:
But you that do the Muses love,
  The *Swan*, called river Po.
The Bankrupt to the *World's End*.
  The Fool to the *Fortune* hie;
Unto the *Mouth*, the Oyster Wife;
  The Fiddler to the *Pie*.

Thomas Heywood, *c.* 1610

COACHES

Coaches were not allowed to ply for hire till 1634, when they stood in a line by the maypole in the Strand in London.
Coaches are not to be hired anywhere but only at London, and the ways far from London are so dirty as hired coachmen do not ordinarily take any long journeys. Sixty or seventy years ago coaches were very rare in England, but at this day pride is far increased as there be few gentlemen of any account who have not their coaches, so as the streets of London are almost stopped up with them.

Fynes Moryson, *Itinerary*, 1617

6. London Bridge painted by a Dutch artist, Claude de Jongh, 1630. Wood panel at Kenwood, Hampstead. The bridge was built between 1176 and 1209 and rebuilding of one part or another occurred many times after that.

LONDON BRIDGE

The first stone bridge was not completed till 1209 and was frequently rebuilt after that. A chapel was built on it where travellers could pray and make an offering for the upkeep of the bridge. Houses and shops were built on either side, tenants paying rent to the bridge-master. In spite of accidents, London Bridge was the pride of all London citizens.

The bridge at London is worthily to be numbered among the miracles of the world, if men respect the building and foundation laid artificially and stately over an ebbing and flowing water upon 21 piles of stone, with 20 arches, under which barks may pass, the lowest foundation being (as they say) packs of wool, most durable against the force of water, and not to be repaired but upon great fall of the waters and by artificial turning or stopping the recourse of them; or if men respect the houses built upon the bridge, as great and high as those of the firm land, so as a man cannot know that he passeth a bridge, but would judge himself to be in the street, save that the houses on both sides are combined in the top, making the passage somewhat dark, and that in some few open places the river of Thames may be seen on both sides.

Fynes Moryson, Itinerary, 1617

ROGUES AND VAGABONDS

In 1630 John Taylor wrote these lines showing how many trouble-makers still existed.

> In London, and within a mile I ween,
> There are of jails or prisons full eighteen,
> And sixty whipping-posts, and stocks and cages.

CHEAPSIDE

'Tis thought the way through this street is not good, because so broad and so many go in it; yet though it be broad, it's very straight, because without any turnings. It is suspected here are not many sufficient able men, because they would sell all: and but little honesty, for they show all, and, some think, more sometime than their own: they are very affable, for they'll speak to most that pass by: they care not how few be in the streets, so their shops be full: they that bring them money, seem to be used worst, for they are sure to pay soundly. There are a great company of honest men in this place, if all be gold that glisters: their parcel-gilt [partly gilded] plate is thought to resemble themselves, most of them have better faces than heart; their monies and coins are used as prisoners at sea, kept under hatches. One would think them to be good men, for they deal with the purest and best metals and every one strives to work best, and stout too, for they get much by knocking and especially by leaning on their elbows. Puritans do hold it for a fine street but something addicted to popery, for adoring the cross too much. The inhabitants seem not to affect the standard; the kings and queens would be offended with, and punish them, knew they how these batter their faces on their coins. Some of their wives would be ill prisoners, for they cannot endure to be shut up; and as bad nuns, the life is solitary. There are many virtuous and honest women, some truly so, others are so for want of opportunity. They hold that a harsh place of scripture: That women must be no goers or gadders abroad. In going to a lecture [sermon by wandering preacher without cure, called a 'lecturer'] many use to visit a tavern: the young attendant must want his eyes, and change his tongue, according as his mistress shall direct, though many times they do mistake the place, yet they will remember the time an hour and half, to avoid suspicion. Some of the men are cunning launders [washermen] of plate, and get much by washing that plate they handle, and it hath come from some of them, like a man from the broker's that hath cashiered his cloak, a great deal the lighter. Well, if all the men be rich and true, and the women all fair and honest, then Cheapside shall stand by Charing Cross for a wonder, and I will make no more characters.

Donald Lupton, *London and the Countrey Carbonadoed*, 1632

THE THAMES

Donald Lupton was touched not only with the fascination of London streets but also of the Thames, 'the maintainer of a great company of watermen'.

This is a long, broad slippery fellow; rest he affects not, for he is always in motion: he seems something like a carrier, for he is still either going or coming, and once in six or eight hours, salutes the sea his mother and then brings tidings from her. He follows the disposition of the wind, if that be rough, so is the water; if that calm, so is this: and he loves it, because when the wind is at highest then the water will best show her strength and anger: it is altogether unsteady, for it commonly is sliding away. . . .

Merchandise he likes and loves; and therefore sends forth ships of traffic to most parts of the earth: his subjects and inhabitants live by oppression like hard landlords at land, the greater rule, and many times devour the less: the city is wondrously beholden to it, for she is furnished with almost all necessaries by it. He is wondrously crossed, he is the maintainer of a great company of watermen. He is a great labourer, for he works as much in the night as the day. He is led by an unconstant guide the moon: he is clean contrary to Smithfield, because that is all for flesh, but this for fish: his inhabitants are different from those upon land, for they are most without legs: fishermen seem to offer him much wrong, for they rob him of many of his subjects: he is seldom without company, but in the night or rough weather. He meets the sun but follows the moon: he complains at the bridge, because it hath intruded into his bowels, and that makes him roar at that place. To speak truth of him, he is the privileged place for fish and ships, the glory and wealth of the city, the highway to the sea, the bringer in of wealth and strangers, and his business is all for water, yet he deals much with the land too: he is a little sea, and a great river.

> Donald Lupton, *London and the Countrey Carbonadoed*, 1632

PURE WATER
Sir Hugh Myddleton was the first man to bring pure water to London. From the Hertfordshire springs, a channel thirty-eight miles long, the New River, brought water to Clerkenwell. The Reservoir was formally opened in 1613. James I knighted Myddleton for this successful project and the King willingly forgot the occasion when riding to Theobalds he fell into the New River.

WATER SUPPLY
John Taylor, the 'water-poet', after being pressed for the navy, became a Thames waterman, and added to his earnings by rhyming. He went on many journeys on foot, once even sailed in a brown-paper boat, wrote about many different subjects with odd titles, and diverted both 'Court and City'.

> Some ten years since, fresh water there was scant,
> But with much cost they have supplied that want.
> By a most exc'lent water-work that's made,
> And to th' Town in Pipes it is conveyed,

Wrought with most artificial engines, and
Performed by th' Art of the Industrious hand
Of Mr William Maltby Gentleman.
So that each man of note there always can
But turn a Cock within his house, and still
They have fresh water always at their will.
This have they all, unto their great content,
For which they each do pay a yearly rent.

John Taylor, *Carrier's Cosmography*, 1634

THE MILITIA

The city hath many courts of guard, with new barricaded posts, and
they strongly girded with great chains of iron . . . the daily musters and
shows of all sorts of Londoners here were wondrous commendable.

William Lithgow, *The Present Surveigh of London*, 1643

MONKEYS AND APES AT ST MARGARET'S FAIR

*John Evelyn, the model English country gentleman, tells the history of his life
in his diary, and touches upon many of the customs and occurrences of his
day.*

13 September 1660 – I saw in Southwark at St Margaret's Fair,
monkeys and apes dance and do other feats of activity on the high
rope; they were gallantly clad *à la mode*, went upright, saluted the
company, bowing and pulling off their hats. They saluted one another
with as good a grace as if instructed by a dancing-master. They turned
heels over head with a basket having eggs in it, without breaking any;
also with lighted candles in their hands and on their heads without
extinguishing them, and with vessels of water without spilling a drop. I
also saw an Italian wench dance and perform all the tricks on the high
rope to admiration. All the Court went to see her. Likewise here was a
man who took up a piece of iron cannon of about 400 lb. weight with
the hair of his head only. John Evelyn, *Diary*

THE GREAT PLAGUE

*The Great Plague of 1665 was a bubonic plague brought in by black rats and
carried by their fleas. It was exceptionally severe and widespread. In London
68,000 people died of it in six months. It flourished in slums on the waterfront,
in dark attics and overcrowded cellars, in dirt and squalor.*

31 August 1665. Up; and after putting several things in order to my
removal to Woolwich; the plague having a great increase this week
beyond all expectation of almost 2,000, making the general Bill 7,000,
odd 100; and the plague above 6,000. Thus this month ends with great

sadness upon the public, through the greatness of the plague every-where through the Kingdom almost. Every day sadder and sadder news of its increase. In the City died this week 7,496, and of them 6,102 of the plague. But it is feared that the true number of the dead this week is near 10,000; partly from the poor that cannot be taken notice of, through the greatness of the number, and partly from the Quakers and others that will not have any bell ring for them.

Samuel Pepys, Diary

THE GREAT FIRE

This fire extended from east to west, from the Tower to the Temple Church and northward to Holborn Bridge. It lasted four days and destroyed eighty-seven churches including St Paul's Cathedral. Many public buildings were destroyed, among them the Royal Exchange, the Custom House and the Guildhall. Some 13,200 houses were in ruins and 400 streets.

At the rebuilding the churches were replaced by fifty-two, all designed and constructed by Christopher Wren.

2 September 1666. Jane called us up about three in the morning, to tell us of a great fire they saw in the City. . . . By and by Jane comes and tells me that she hears that above 300 houses have been burned down tonight by the fire we saw, and that it is now burning down all Fish-street, by London Bridge. So I made myself ready presently, and walked to the Tower. The Lieutenant of the Tower tells me that it began this morning in the King's baker's house in Pudding-lane, and that it hath burned down St Magnes Church and most part of

7.   An engraving of the Great Fire of London, 1666.

LONDONS fier began September the second, 1666.

To be sold by Tho: Parkhurst: Nath: Ranew and Jonath: Robinson.

8. A dramatic engraving of the Fire of London, 1666. Over thirteen thousand houses and many public buildings were destroyed. Only six people were killed.

9. A receipt for £2.13.9, money collected from the village of Cowfold, Sussex, to help those in distress after the fire.

Fish-street already. So I down to the waterside, and there got a boat, and through bridge, and there saw a lamentable fire. Poor Michell's house, as far as the Old Swan, already burned that way, and the fire running further, that in a very little time it got as far as the Steele-yard, while I was there. Everybody endeavouring to remove their goods, and flinging into the river, or bringing them into lighters that lay off. Poor people staying in their houses as long as till the very fire touched them, and then running into boats, or clambering from one pair of stairs by the waterside to another.

. . . When we could endure no more upon the water, we to a little ale-house on the Bankside, over against the Three Cranes, and there stayed till it was dark almost, and saw the fire grow. And as it grew darker, appeared more and more, and in corners and upon steeples, and between churches and houses, as far as we could see up the hill of the City, in a most horrid, malicious flame, not like the fine flame of an ordinary fire. Barbary and her husband away before us. We stayed till, it being darkish, we saw the fire as only one entire arch of fire from this to the other side of the bridge, and in a bow up the hill for an arch of above a mile long: it made me weep to see it. The churches, houses, and all on fire, and flaming at once; and a horrid noise the flames made, and the cracking of houses at their ruin.   Samuel Pepys, *Diary*

THE BELLMAN

Streets were not lit. There was no police force. In some parts of London citizens paid a Bellman. He acted as night-watchman, patrolling the streets at night, and calling the hours. Isaac Ragg, Bellman in the Holborn district of London, wrote these verses:

Time, Master, calls your bellman to his task
To see your doors and windows are all fast
And that no villainy or foul crime be done
To you or yours in absence of the sun.

If any base lurker I do meet,
In private alley or in open street,
You shall have warning by my timely call,
And so God bless you and give rest to all.
                    Luttrell Collection of Broadsides, 1683–1684

FIRST COFFEE-HOUSE IN LONDON
Oldys, the antiquarian, tells us what happened in 1652:
A Mr Edwards, a Turkey merchant, brought from Smyrna to London
one Pasqua Rosee, a Ragusan youth, who prepared this drink for him
every morning. But the novelty thereof drawing too much company to
him, he allowed his said servant . . . to sell it publicly, and they set up the
first coffee-house in London, in St Michael's Alley in Cornhill. The sign
was Pasqua Rosee's own head.

A PUBLIC LIBRARY IN LONDON
*In the seventeenth century private libraries were growing more common, from
the fine collection of Samuel Pepys to the armful of books in a merchant's house.
There was certainly a demand for public libraries; one was established by
Tenison, later Archbishop of Canterbury.*
15 February 1684. Dr Tenison communicated to me his intention of
erecting a library in St Martin's parish, for the public use, and desired
my assistance with Sir Christopher Wren about the placing and struc-
ture thereof. A worthy and laudable design. He told me there were
thirty or forty young men in Orders in his parish, either governors to
young gentlemen or chaplains to noblemen, who being reproved
by him on occasion for frequenting taverns or coffee-houses, told
him they would study or employ their time better, if they had books.
This put the pious doctor on his design. And indeed a great reproach
it is that so great a city as London should not have a public library
becoming it. There ought to be one at St Paul's; the west end of that
church (if ever finished) would be a convenient place.
                                                  John Evelyn, *Diary*

THE THAMES QUITE FROZEN, 1684
*John Evelyn, the diarist, describes the Frost Fair on the Thames when the river
was quite frozen in 1684, and coaches, carts and horses passed over, and
bull-baiting took place on the ice.*
1683–4. 1st January. The weather continuing intolerably severe, streets
of booths were set upon the Thames; the air was so very cold and thick,
as of many years there had not been the like.
    6th. The river quite frozen.

9th. I went across the Thames on the ice, now become so thick as to bear not only streets of booths, in which they roasted meat, and had several shops of wares, quite across as in a town, but coaches, carts, and horses passed over. So I went from Westminster-stairs to Lambeth, and dined with the Archbishop, where I met my Lord Bruce, Sir George Wheeler, Colonel Cooke and several divines. After dinner and discourse with his Grace till evening prayers, Sir George Wheeler and I walked over the ice from Lambeth-stairs to the Horse-ferry.

16th. The Thames was filled with people and tents, selling all sorts of wares as in the City.

24th. The frost continuing more and more severe, the Thames before London was still planted with booths in formal streets, all sorts of trades and shops furnished, and full of commodities, even to a printing-press, where the people and ladies took a fancy to have their names printed, and the day and year set down when printed on the Thames: this humour took so universally, that it was estimated the printer gained £5 a day, for printing a line only, at sixpence a name, besides what he got by ballads, &c. Coaches plied from Westminster to the Temple, and from several other stairs to and fro, as in the streets, sleds, sliding with skates, a bull-baiting, horse and coach-races, puppet-plays and interludes, cooks, tippling, and other lewd places, so that it seemed to be a bacchanalian triumph, or carnival on the water, whilst it was a severe judgment on the land, the trees not only splitting as if lightning-struck, but men and cattle perishing in divers places, and the very seas so locked up with ice, that no vessels could stir out or come in. The fowls, fish, and birds, and all our exotic plants and greens, universally perishing. Many parks of deer were destroyed, and all sorts of fuel so dear, that there were great contributions to preserve the poor alive. Nor was this severe weather much less intense in most parts of Europe, even as far as Spain and the most southern tracts. London, by reason of the excessive coldness of the air hindering the ascent of the smoke, was so filled with the fuliginous steam of the sea-coal, that hardly could one see across the streets, and this filling the lungs with its gross particles, exceedingly obstructed the breast, so as one could scarcely breathe. Here was no water to be had from the pipes and engines, nor could the brewers and divers other tradesmen work, and every moment was full of disastrous accidents.

4th February. I went to Sayes Court to see how the frost had dealt with my garden, where I found many of the greens and rare plants utterly destroyed. The oranges and myrtles very sick, the rosemary and laurels dead to all appearance, but the cypress likely to endure it.

5th. It began to thaw, but froze again. My coach crossed from Lambeth to the Horse-ferry at Milbank, Westminster. The booths were

almost all taken down; but there was first a map or landscape cut in
copper representing all the manner of the camp, and the several
actions, sports, and pastimes thereon, in memory of so signal a frost.

John Evelyn, *Diary*

THE ROYAL COFFEE-HOUSE OLD MAN'S

This was Man's or the Royal Coffee-house, situated behind Charing Cross,
near Scotland Yard. It was, indeed, the most fashionable coffee-house in
London, and was kept by one Alexander Man. To distinguish it from a
neighbour of the same name it was sometimes called Old Man's and the other
Young Man's.

In one sense the coffee-houses were the inheritors of the news and gossip
imparted in Paul's Walk; in another they were forerunners of the London
clubs.

By this time we were come to the door of the most eminent Coffee-
house at this end of the town, which my friend had before propos'd to
give me a sight of. Accordingly we blunder'd thro' a dark entry, where
the blackguard of quality were playing their unlucky tricks and damn-
ing each other in their master's dialect. They were arm'd with flam-
beaus against the approaching night, that the grandeur of the great
and fortunate may not be hid in darkness, but shine in their proper
sphere above lesser mortals, who bow their heads to my Lord's distin-
guishable lustre. At the end of the entry we ascended a pair of stairs
which brought us into an old fashion'd room of a cathedral tenement,
where a very gaudy crowd of odoriferous Tom-essences were walking
backwards and forwards with their hats in their hands, not daring to
convert 'em to their intended use, lest it should put the fore-tops of
their wigs into some disorder.

We squeez'd thro' the fluttering assembly of snuffing peripatetics till
we got to the end of the room, where, at a small table, we sat down, and
observ'd that tho' there was abundance of guests, there was very little to
do, for it was as great a rarity to hear anybody call for a dish of
Politician's porridge [coffee], or any other liquor, as it is to hear a
sponger in a company ask what's to pay, or a beau call for a pipe of
tobacco. Their whole exercise was to charge and discharge their
nostrils, and keep the curls of their periwigs in their proper order. The
clashing of their snuff-box lids, in opening and shutting, made more
noise than their tongues, and sounded as terrible in my ears as the
melancholy ticks of so many Death-watches.

Bows and cringes of the newest mode were here exchang'd 'twixt
friend and friend, with wonderful exactness. They made a humming
like so many hornets in a country chimney, not with their talking, but
with their whispering over their new minuets and bories, with their

hands in their pockets, if freed from their snuff-boxes, by which you might understand they had most of them been travellers into the Seven Provinces [the Netherlands].

Ned Ward, *The London Spy*, 1698–1709

BRIDEWELL: THE FIRST REFORMATORY

Henry I built a palace on the site of Roman and Saxon buildings. It was rebuilt by Wolsey and given by Edward VI to Queen Mary as a refuge for the homeless. Later used as a prison, it became the first reformatory.

We then turn'd into the gate of a stately edifice which my friend told me was Bridewell. At my first entrance, it seem'd to me rather a Prince's palace than a House of Correction, till, gazing round me, I saw in a large room a parcel of ill-looking mortals stripped to their shirts like haymakers, pounding a pernicious weed, which I had thought from their unlucky aspects seemed to threaten their destruction. 'These,' I said to my friend, 'I suppose, are the offenders at work. Pray what do you think their crimes may be?' 'Truly,' said he, 'I cannot tell you; but if you have a mind to know, ask any of them their offence, and they will soon satisfy you.'

'Prithee, friend,' said I to a surly bull-necked fellow, who was thumping as lazily at his wooden anvil as a ship-carpenter at a log in the Queen's Yard at Deptford, 'what are you confined to this labour for?' My hempen operator, leering over his shoulder, cast at me a hanging look which so frightened me that I stepped back, for fear he should have knocked me on the head with his beetle. 'Why, if you must know, Mr Tickletail;' says he, taking me, as I believe (being in black) for some country pedagogue, 'I was committed here by Justice Clodpate, for saying I had rather hear a blackbird whistle *Walsingham** or a peacock scream against foul weather, than a parson talk nonsense in a church, or a fool talk Latin in a coffee-house. And I'll be judged by you, that are a man of judgement, whether in all I said there be one word of treason to deserve a whipping-post.'

The impudence of this canary bird so dashed me out of countenance, together with this unexpected answer, that, like a man surfeited with his mistress's favours, I had nothing to say, but heartily wished myself well out of their company. As we were turning back to avoid their further sauciness another calls to me, 'Hark you, master in black, of the same colour with the devil, can you tell me how many thumps of this hammer will soften the hemp so as to make a halter fit easy if a man should have occasion to wear one?' A third cried out, 'I hope,

*This was a very old and popular song, beginning:
    'As I went to Walsingham, to the Shrine with Speed
    I met with a jolly palmer, in a pilgrim's weed.'

gentlemen, you will be so generous as to give us something to drink, for you don't know but that we may be hard at work for you.'

Ned Ward, The London Spy, 1698–1709

LONDON THE NOISY CAPITAL

In this description of early eighteenth-century London, we find noisy turbulence and riotous behaviour. Remarkable elements formed this mighty city.

. . . London is a world by itself; we daily discover in it more new centuries and surprising singularities than in all the universe besides. There are among the Londoners so many nations differing in manners, customs, and religions, that the inhabitants themselves don't know a quarter of 'em. Imagine, then, what an Indian would think of such a motley herd of people, and what a diverting amusement it would be to him to imagine with a traveller's eye all the remarkable things of this mighty city. A whimsy takes me in the head to carry this stranger all over the town with me: no doubt but his odd and fantastical ideas will furnish me with variety, and perhaps with diversion. . . .

I will therefore suppose this Indian of mine dropped perpendicularly from the clouds, to find himself all of a sudden in the midst of this prodigious and noisy city, where repose and silence dare scarce show their heads in the darkest night. At first dash the confused clamours near Temple Bar stun him, fright him, and make him giddy.

He sees an infinite number of different machines, all in violent motion, with some riding on the top, some within, others behind, and Jehu on the coach-box, whirling towards some dignified villain who has got an estate by cheating the public. He lolls at full stretch within, with half a dozen brawny, bulk-begotten footmen behind. . . .

Some carry, others are carried. 'Make way there,' says a gouty-legged chairman, that is carrying a punk of quality to a morning's exercise; or a Bartholomew baby-beau, newly launched out of a chocolate-house, with his pockets as empty as his brains. 'Make room there,' says another fellow, driving a wheelbarrow of nuts that spoil the lungs of the city 'prentices and make them wheeze over their mistresses as bad as the phlegmatic cuckolds, their masters, do when called to family duty. One draws, the other drives. 'Stand up there, you blind dog,' says a carman, 'will you have the cart squeeze your guts out?' One tinker knocks, another bawls, 'Have you brass-pot, iron-pot, kettle, skillet or frying-pan to mend?' Another son of a whore yelps louder than Homer's stentor, 'Two a groat, and four for sixpence, mackerel.' One draws his mouth up to his ears and howls out, 'Buy my flounders,' and is followed by an old burly drab that screams out the sale of her 'maids' and her 'soul' at the same instant.

Here a sooty chimney-sweeper takes the wall of a grave alderman, and a broom-man jostles the parish parson. There a fat greasy porter runs a trunk full-butt upon you, while another salutes your antlers with a basket of eggs and butter. 'Turn out there, you country putt,' says a bully with a sword two yards long jarring at his heels, and throws him into the kennel. By and by comes a christening, with the reader screwing up his mouth to deliver the service *a la mode de Paris*, and afterwards talks immoderately nice and dull with the gossips, the midwife strutting in the front with young original sin as fine as fippence; followed with the vocal music of 'Kitchen-stuff ha' you maids,' and a damned trumpeter calling in the rabble to see a calf with six legs and a top-knot. . . .

Tom Brown, *Amusements, Serious and Comical Calculated for the Meridian of London*, 1700

A TRIP UP THE THAMES

The safest and quickest form of transport to any outlying spot was by river-boat on the Thames. Watermen in great numbers were at your service, scattering 'verbal wild-fire on every side of them'.

. . . the next that we met was a jolly parson, skudding from Lambeth House in a skuller. 'Rare game, master,' cries our navicular spokesman, and thus he accosted the man of scripture as soon as within hearing. 'Well met, holy father; I'll warrant in your time you have drawn as many tithe pigs in at your mouth . . . as would have stocked Bartholomew Fair for a whole season, or else you could never have shown such a fat gut to your lean parishioners. Ah, doctor, 'tis a sign the

10.   A print of Westminster.

church is at a low ebb, or else a long scarf and a rose hatband would never be so humble as to be seen lolling in a skuller, in such a pious age too, when every Wapping under-strapper that has but a congregation of old women to hold himself forth to scorns to have no less than oars, though he crosses but the water to administer comfort to a holy sister.'

'Thou art a wicked reprobate, I'll warrant thee,' replied the priest: 'Prithee desire the minister of your parish to teach thee the Lord's prayer and the Ten Commandments, that thou may'st not go out of this world in thy old age like a heathen, and be damned in the next for the sin of wilful ignorance.'

Tom Brown, *Amusements, Serious and Comical Calculated for the Meridian of London*, 1700

LONDON'S MAY FAIR

The name comes from a fair held in May from the time of Charles II till 1809. Part of the site is now occupied by Shepherd Market which was built round about 1735.

By the help of a great many slashes and hey-ups, and after as many jolts and jumbles, we were dragg'd to the fair, where the harsh sound of untunable trumpets, the catterwauling scrapes of thrashing fiddlers, the grumblings of beaten calves-shins, and the discording toots of broken organs set my teeth on edge, like the filing of a hand-saw. We order'd the coach to drive through the body of the Fair, that we might have the better view of the tinsey heroes and of the gazing multitude, expecting to have seen several corporations of strolling vagabonds, but there proved but one company, amongst whom Merry Andrew was very busy in coaxing the attentive crowd into a good opinion of his fraternities and his own performances. Beyond these were a parcel of scandalous boosing-kens, where soldiers and their trulls were skipping and dancing about to most lamentable music perform'd upon a crack'd crowd by a blind fiddler. In another hut, a parcel of Scotch peddlars and their moggies, dancing a highlander's jig to a hornpipe. Over against 'em the Cheshire Booth, where a gentleman's man was playing more tricks with his heels in a Cheshire Round than ever were shown by a Mad Coffee Man at Sadler's Music House.

A contemporary of Ned Ward, *c.* 1700

BEDLAM

Bedlam, a corruption of Bethlehem, is applied to the Hospital of St Mary of Bethlehem in Bishopsgate, London, founded in 1247. In 1402 it was known as a hospital for lunatics. In 1675 a new hospital, still for lunatics, was built in Moorfields. If bull-baiting was a popular sport, a cheaper one was to watch and tease these unhappy people after paying one penny for admission.

The hospital is now at Monks Orchard, Eden Park, Beckenham.
Bedlam is a pleasant place, that it is, and abounds with amusements. The first is the building so stately a fabric for persons wholly insensible of the beauty and the use of it; the outside is a perfect mockery to the inside, and admits of two amusing queries, whether the persons that order the building of it, or those that inhabit it, were the maddest? But what need I wonder at that, since the whole is but one entire amusement? Some were preaching, and others in full cry a-hunting; some were praying, others cursing and swearing; some were dancing, others groaning; some singing, others crying; and all in perfect confusion. A sad representation of the greater chimerical world! Only in this there's no whoring, cheating, or fleecing, unless after the Platonic mode, in thought, for want of action. . . . Is your wife or your daughter mad, for something that shall be nameless? Send 'em hither to be made sober. Or has one relation, male or female, that's over-bashful? Let not either him or her despair of a cure, for here are guests enough to teach 'em to part with their modesty.

Here are persons confined that having no money nor friends, and but a small stock of confidence run mad for want of preferment; a poet that, for want of wit and sense, ran mad for want of victuals; and a hard-favoured citizen's wife, that lost her wits because her husband had so little as to let her know that he kept a handsome mistress. In this apartment is a common lawyer pleading; in another a civilian sighing; a third encloses a Jacobite, ranting against the Revolution; and a fourth, a morose, melancholy Whig, bemoaning his want of an office and complaining against abuses at court, and mismanagements. A fifth has a comical sort of a fellow, laughing at his physician, Doctor Tyson, for his great skill in taciturnity; and a sixth a Cantabrigian organist for its tenant, that had left sonnet and madrigal for philosophy, and had lost his senses while he was in pursuit of knowledge.

Tom Brown, *Amusements, Serious and Comical Calculated for the Meridian of London*, 1700

OUTSIDE THE EXCHANGE
The pillars at the entrance of the front Porticum were adorned with sundry memorandums of old age and infirmity, under which stood here and there a Jack in a Box, like a parson in a pulpit, selling cures for your corns, glass eyes for the blind, ivory teeth for broken mouths, and spectacles for the weak sighted; the passage to the gate being lined with hawkers, gardeners, mandrake sellers, and porters. After we had crowded a little way amongst the miscellaneous multitude, we came to a pippin monger's stall, surmounted with a chemist's shop, where drops, elixirs, cordials, and balsams had justly the pre-eminence of apples,

chestnuts, pears and oranges, showing a view of the motley group of
costermongers without.   Ned Ward, *The London Spy, c.* 1707

THE MOHOCKS

*The word comes from Mohawk, the name of a North American Indian tribe,
once thought to be cannibals. In the early eighteenth century it applied to
aristocratic ruffians infesting London streets at night.*

Did I tell you of a race of rakes called the Mohocks, that play the devil
about this town every night, slit peoples noses, and bid them, etc. . . .
Young Davenant was telling us at Court how he was set upon by the
Mohocks, and how they ran his [sedan] chair through with a sword. It is
not safe being in the streets at night with them. The Bishop of
Salisbury's son is said to be of the gang. They are all Whigs; and a great
lady sent to me, to speak to her father and to lord treasurer, to have a
care of them, and to be careful likewise of myself; for she heard they
had malicious intentions against the Ministers and their friends . . . I
walked in the Park this evening, and came home early to avoid the
Mohocks. . . . Here is the devil and all to do with these Mohocks. My
man tells me, that one of the lodgers heard in a coffee-house, publicly,
that one design of the Mohocks was upon me, if they could catch me;
and though I believe nothing of it, I forbear walking late. Lord
Treasurer advised me not to go in a chair, because the Mohocks insult
chairs more than they do those on foot. They think there is some
mischievous design in those villains. I heard at dinner, that one of them
was killed last night. Lord Winchelsea told me at Court today, that two
of the Mohocks caught a maid of old Lady Winchelsea's at the door of
their house in the Park, with a candle, and had just lighted out
somebody. They cut all her face, and beat her without any provocation.
                Jonathan Swift, *Journal to Stella*, 12 March 1711–12

OUR STREETS

Our streets are filled with Blue Boars, Black Swans, and Red Lions not
to mention Flying Pigs and Hogs in Armour, with many other crea-
tures more extraordinary than any in the deserts of Africa.
                    Joseph Addison, *The Spectator*, 1711

Towns, Gardens and Buildings

TOWNS

At the beginning of the seventeenth century the population of England and Wales was over four million, and had risen to over five million at the end. London had a population rising from 200,000 to 400,000 during this period. It has been said that one-fifth of the total population lived in the valley of the Thames.

The most populous towns after London were Norwich, with about 30,000 inhabitants, Bristol, the second largest port, York, and Newcastle upon Tyne. Leeds, Liverpool, Manchester, and Birmingham were large villages. Thomas Wilson said in 1600 that there were twenty-five cities and 641 'great towns' in the kingdom. In those days a 'great town' might have about five thousand inhabitants.

As Maurice Ashley says, 'Big towns are the product of concentrated industries and – with a few exceptions – industry was still organised largely on a loose domestic basis, work being commissioned by middlemen, who bought the raw materials and disposed of the finished goods. Many industrial workers would have a cottage and a little land, perhaps as much as six acres: the spinning wheels and looms on which, for example, Yorkshire kerseys, Lancashire fustians, and Norfolk worsteds were manufactured would be found in the operatives' own homes. . . . Most work was performed by small family units: apprentices lived and fed with their masters. No real factory system yet existed.'

We must remember that agriculture, including sheep farming, was, at this time, the most usual occupation, and here four-fifths of the whole population was engaged.

GARDENS

Gardens were usually formal, laid out geometrically, with clipped hedges and shaped trees. Terraces, neatly constructed, were adorned with huge vases, stone and lead statues, intricate wrought ironwork. Hampton Court is a typical example. Pepys describes Evelyn's garden 'containing among other rarities, a hive of bees making their honey and combs mighty pleasantly'. Towards the end of the century Celia

Fiennes tells us of a splendid house in England. 'The gardens are very fine with many gravel walks with grass squares set with fine brass and stone statues, fish-ponds and basins with figures in the middle, spouting out water, dwarf trees of all sorts and a fine flower garden, much wall fruit'.

Fruits and vegetables are no longer neglected. New countries bestowed new products as William Harrison tells us in 1587, 'It is a world also to see how many strange herbs, plants and unusual fruits are daily brought unto us from the Indies, Americas, Taprobane, Canary Isles and all parts of the world'. A gardener's bill dated 1692 at Knole tells us of 'sweet yerbs, pawsley, sorrill, spinnig, spruts, leeks, sallat, horse rydish, jerusalem hawty-chorks'.

BUILDINGS

Inigo Jones brought a great change to architecture in England. With him the architect was the single controlling mind, dominating the whole process of building exterior and interior alike. He became a vitally important figure, and the Queen's House, the Banqueting House, Whitehall, and the Queen's Chapel at St James's reveal his quality. William, Third Earl of Pembroke, and Philip, Fourth Earl – 'the incomparable pair of brethren' to whom Shakespeare dedicated

11.   A perspective view of the Great Model of St Paul's Cathedral, 1673.

12.   The interior of St Paul's Cathedral soon after the building was completed.

13.   Engraving by Fourdrinier of south-east view of St Paul's Cathedral, *c.* 1709.

the first Folio of his plays – called on Inigo Jones to transform Wilton House. The rich form of interior decoration in the famous Double Cube Room matched the intricate formal gardens laid out in 1633 by de Caux. Ham House, planned as an H, originally built in 1610 by Sir Thomas Vavasor, became the most lavish example of interior decoration of the Restoration period.

The later Renaissance was not established till after 1660 under the great Sir Christopher Wren. He used a classic style in St Paul's Cathedral and in many of the London churches which he built to replace those destroyed in the Great Fire. Chatsworth, the most distinguished private house of the age of Wren, stands baroque in stress of mass in the austere landscape of Derbyshire. Set in the Yorkshire Dales is Bolton Hall. This was built in 1678 by the first Duke of Bolton, a strange man 'who would not speak until late in the day when he considered the air to be purer'.

At Blenheim Palace, the birthplace of Sir Winston Churchill, John Vanbrugh achieved heroic architecture. Here the scale is vast, and the forms are massive in a building presented by Queen Anne to the Duke of Marlborough as a sign of the nation's gratitude.

In this century there is also much fine ironwork in the style of the Huguenot, Jean Tijou. State rooms had painted ceilings with

14. The choir stalls by Grinling Gibbons, in St Paul's Cathedral.

15.   An engraving of Sir Christopher Wren's St Paul's Cathedral.

allegorical scenes. These elaborate decorations by Antonio Verrio, Louis Laguerre, Sir James Thornhill were done at Windsor Castle, Hampton Court, Petsworth, Greenwich Hospital, Chatsworth, and Blenheim.

SURVEY OF SHEFFIELD, 1615
It appeareth that there are 2,207 people, of whom 725 are unable to live without charity; 160 households, though they beg not, could not abide the storm of a fortnight's sickness, and 1,222 children and servants of these said householders are constrained to live on small wages, working sore to provide themselves with necessities.

THE BUILDINGS IN ENGLAND
Now at London the houses of the citizens (especially in the chief streets) are very narrow in the front towards the street, but are built five or six roofs high, commonly of timber and clay with plaster, and are very neat and commodious within: and the building of citizens' houses in other cities is not much unlike this. But withal understand, that in London many stately palaces, built by noblemen upon the river Thames, do make a very great shew to them that pass by water; and that there be many more like palaces, also built towards land, but scattered and great part of them in back lanes and streets. . . .

Great part of the towns and villages are built like the citizens' houses in London, save that they are not so many stories high nor so narrow in the front towards the street. Others of them are built in like sort of unpolished small stones, and some of the villages in Lincolnshire and some other countries are of mere clay, and covered with thatch; yet even these houses are more commodious within for cleanliness, lodging and diet, than any stranger would think them to be. Most of the houses in cities and towns have cellars under them, where for coolness they lay beer and wine.

Gentlemen's houses for the most part are built like those in the cities, but very many of gentlemen's and noblemen's palaces, as well near London as in other countries, are stately built of brick and freestone, whereof many yields not in magnificence to like buildings of other kingdoms, as Homby, built by Sir Christopher Hatton; Tybals lately belonging to the Earl of Salisbury, seated near London; and the Earl of Exeter his house near Stamford: by which palaces lying near the highway a stranger may judge of many other like stately buildings in other parts. The King's palaces are of such magnificent building, so curious art, and such pleasure and beauty for gardens and fountains, and are so many in number, as England need not envy any other

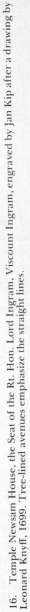

16. Temple Newsam House, the Seat of the Rt. Hon. Lord Ingram, Viscount Ingram, engraved by Jan Kip after a drawing by Leonard Knyff, 1699. Tree-lined avenues emphasize the straight lines.

kingdom therein. Among them being many a stranger may see near London: the King's palaces of Hampton Court, of Richmond, of Greenwich, of Nonsuch, of Oatlands, of Sheen, of Windsor, and in London the palace of Whitehall.   Fynes Moryson, *Itinerary*, 1617

SMALL TENEMENTS
The parish of St Margaret Lothbury complained in 1637 that Ralph Harrison, draper, was
possessed of divers small tenements, five in number all in one passage called the Dark Entry . . . being so noisome and unhealthful a place as few the like in London, some . . . having been divided of late years and the rents of them much raised by the said Ralph Harrison all . . . being inhabited by poor and needy people which are a continual burden and charge to the said parish.

HARROGATE
Spent in charges at Harrogate, when my wife and I and Nan Barber, with John Pullaine, John Taylor and Mat Tillsley and Will Kendell the coachman, when we went to drink the spa waters, having four coach horses, and two riding horses, we laid at Mr Hansitts from Tuesday the 18th day of June, till Friday the 28th day of June 1672, and we laid one night at Barmbow as we came home, our charges in all for ourselves and horses, with advice of doctors, etc. . . . £12.0.0.
Sir Miles Stapleton, *The Household Books of Sir Miles Stapleton, Bart.*, 1658–1705

THE GARDEN AT SWALLOWFIELD
22 October 1685 – I accompanied my Lady Clarendon to her house at Swallowfield in Berks . . . this house is after the ancient building of honourable gentlemen's houses, when they kept up ancient hospitality, but the gardens and waters as elegant as it is possible to make a flat by art and industry, and no mean expense, my lady being so extraordinarily skill'd in the flowery part, and my lord, in diligence of planting; so that I have hardly seen a seat which shows more tokens of it than what is to be found here, not only in the delicious and rarest fruits of a garden, but in those innumerable timber trees in the ground about the seat, to the greatest ornament and benefit of the place. There is one orchard of 1000 golden, and other cider pippins; walks and groves of elms, limes, oaks, and other trees. The garden is so beset with all manner of sweet shrubs, that it perfumes the air. The distribution also of the quarters, walks, and parterres, is excellent. The nurseries, kitchen-garden full of the most desirable plants; two very noble orangeries well furnished; but, above all, the canal and fishponds, the

one fed with a white, the other with a black running water, fed by a quick and swift river, so well and plentifully stored with fish, that for pike, carp, bream, and tench, I never saw any thing approaching it. We had at every meal carp and pike of size fit for the table of a Prince, and what added to the delight was, to see the hundreds taken by the drag, out of which, the cook standing by, we pointed out what we had most mind to, and had carp that would have been worth at London twenty shillings a-piece. The waters are flagged about with *Calamus aromaticus,* with which my lady has hung a closet, that retains the smell very perfectly. There is also a certain sweet willow and other exotics: also a very fine bowling-green, meadow, pasture, and wood; in a word, all that can render a country-seat delightful.   John Evelyn, *Diary*

A GROTTO IN THE GARDEN AT WILTON NEAR SALISBURY

Garnished with many fine figures of the goddesses, and about two yards off the door is several pipes in a line that with a sluice spouts water up to wet the strangers – in the middle room is a round table and a large pipe in midst, on which they put a crown or gun or a branch, and so it spouts the water through the carvings and points all round the room at the artist's pleasure to wet the company – there are figures at each corner of the room that can weep water on the beholders.

The Journeys of Celia Fiennes, 1685

BATH AND BUBBLING SPRINGS

When you would walk about the bath I used to have a woman guide or two to lead me, for the water is so strong it will quickly tumble you down; and then you have two of the men guides go at a distance about the bath to clear the way. At the sides of the Arches are rings that you may hold by and so walk a little way, but the springs bubble up so fast and so strong and are so hot against the bottoms of one's feet, especially in that they call the Kitching in the King's bath, which is a great Cross with seats in the middle and many hot springs riseth there; the King's bath is very large, as large as the rest put together, in it is the hot pump that persons are pumped at for lameness or on their heads for palsies.

The Journeys of Celia Fiennes, 1687

BUILDINGS

Houses in cities, that were heretofore usually of wood, are now built of good stone or brick, and covered with slate or tile; the rooms within, formerly wainscotted, are now hung with tapestry, or other convenient stuff, and are ceiled with plaster, excellent against the rage of fire, against the cold, and to hinder the passage of all dust and noise.

17. The Sheldonian Theatre, Oxford; built by Christopher Wren, 1662–1663.
Engraving by D. Loggan.

The modern buildings have been far more slight, and of less continuance than the ancient.

The houses of the nobles and rich are abundantly furnished with
pewter, brass, fine linen, and plate: the mean mechanics and ordinary
husbandmen want not silver spoons, or some silver cups in their
houses.

The windows everywhere glazed, not made of paper or wood, as is
usually in Italy or Spain. Chimneys in most places, no stoves, although
the far more southern parts of Germany can hardly subsist in the
Winter without them.

E. Chamberlayne, *Angliae Notitia, or the Present State
of England*, 1687

NOTTINGHAM AND THE WEAVING OF STOCKINGS

Nottingham is the neatest town I have seen, built of stone and delicate,
large and long streets much like London and the houses lofty and well
built, the Market Place is very broad – out of which runs two very large
streets much like Holborn but the buildings finer, and there is a Piazza
all along one side of one of the streets, with stone pillars for walking
that runs the length of the street, which is a mile long. . . .

They make brick and tile by the town; the manufacture of the town consists in weaving of stockings, which is a very ingenious art. There was a man that spun glass and made several things in glass, birds and beasts. I spun some of the glass and saw him make a swan presently, with divers coloured glass he makes buttons which are very strong and will not break. Nottingham is famous for good ale so for cellars they are all dug out of the rocks and so are very cool.

The Journeys of Celia Fiennes, 1697

PONTEFRACT: GARDENS FULL OF LIQUORISH

Thence to Pomffret [Pontefract] three miles, which looks very finely in the approach.... It's a fruitful place, fine flowers and trees with all sorts of fruit, but that which is mostly intended is the increasing of liquorish [liquorice], which the gardens are all filled with, and any body that has but a little ground improves it for the produce of liquorish, of which there is vast quantities, and it returns several hundred pounds yearly to the town.   *The Journeys of Celia Fiennes*, 1697

AN APOTHECARY'S AT BURY ST EDMUNDS

In Bury St Edmunds ... this high house is an apothecary's, at least sixty steps up from the ground and gives a pleasing prospect of the whole town ... except this the rest are great old houses of timber and mostly in the old form of the country which are long peaked roofs of tiling; this house is the new mode of building, four rooms of a floor pretty sizeable and high, well furnished, a drawing room and chamber full of china and a damask bed embroidered, two other rooms, camlet [Eastern fabric] and mohair beds, a pretty deal of plate in his wife's chamber, parlours below and a large shop; he is esteemed a very rich man; he shewed me a curiosity of an herbal all written out with every sort of tree and herb dried and cut out and pasted on the leaves – it was a Doctor of Physic work that left it him as legacy at his death, it was a fine thing and would have delighted me several days.

The Journeys of Celia Fiennes, 1698

WATER SUPPLY IN NORWICH

The street that I entered in first was very broad for two coaches or carts to pass on either side, and in the middle was a great well house with a wheel to wind up the water for the good of the public; a little farther is a large pond walled up with brick a man's height with an entrance on one end, a little farther was a building on which they were at work designed for a Water house to supply the town by pipes into their houses with water.   *The Journeys of Celia Fiennes*, 1698

COLCHESTER AND BAIZE
... in this street is the Market Cross and Town Hall and a long building like stalls on purpose to lay their baize when exposed to sale, great quantities are made here and sent in bales to London that is 44 miles distant. The whole town is employed in spinning, weaving, washing, drying and dressing their baize, in which they seem very industrious; there I saw the card they use to comb and dress the baize, which they call them teazels which are a kind of rush tops or something like them which they put in frames or laths of wood. The town looks like a thriving place by the substantial houses, secured by stumps of wood and is convenient for three to walk together. Their buildings are of timber, of loam and lathes and much tiling, the fashion of the country runs much in long roofs and great cantilevers and peaks; out of these great streets run many little streets but not very narrow, mostly old buildings except a few houses built by some Quakers that are brick and of the London mode.

The Journeys of Celia Fiennes, 1698

NEWCASTLE: FULL OF THIS COAL
As I drew nearer and nearer to Newcastle I met with and saw abundance of little carriages with a yoke of oxen and a pair of horses together, which is to convey the coal from the pits to the barges on the river; this is the sea-coal which is pretty much small coal though some is round coal, yet none like the cleft coal; that is what the smiths use and it cakes in the fire and makes a great heat.... This country all about is full of this coal the sulphur of it taints the air and it smells strongly to strangers; upon a high hill two mile from Newcastle I could see all about the country which is full of coal pits.

The Journeys of Celia Fiennes, 1698

LIVERPOOL: LONDON IN MINIATURE
Liverpool which is in Lancashire is built just on the river Mersey, mostly new built houses of brick and stone after the London fashion. The first original was a few fisherman's houses and now is grown to a large fine town and but a parish and one church, though there be twenty-four streets in it. There is indeed a little chapel and there are a great many dissenters in the town; it's a very rich trading town, the houses of bricks and stone built high and even, that a street quite through looks very handsome, the streets well pitched; there are abundance of persons you see very well dressed and of good fashion; the streets are fair and long, it's London in miniature as much as ever I saw any thing.

The Journeys of Celia Fiennes, 1698

18.   Trinity College Library, Cambridge, built by Christopher Wren, 1676–1684. From David Loggan, *Cantabrigia Illustrata*.

LEEDS AND THE YORKSHIRE CLOTH
Leeds is a large town, several large streets, clean and well pitched and good houses all built of stone, some have good gardens and steps up to their houses and walls before them; this is esteemed the wealthiest town of its bigness in the country, its manufacture is the woollen cloth, the Yorkshire Cloth in which they are all employed and are esteemed very rich and proud.   *The Journeys of Celia Fiennes*, 1698

TAUNTON AND WEST COUNTRY ROCKETS
Taunton is a large town having houses of all sorts of buildings both brick and stone but mostly timber and plaster; it's a very neat place and looks substantial as a place of good trade; you meet all sorts of country women wrapped up in mantles called West Country rockets [rochets], a large mantle doubled together of a sort of serge, some are linseywolsey, and a deep fringe or fag at the lower end; these hang down some to their feet, some only just below the waist, in the summer they are all in white garments of this sort, in the winter they are in red ones; I call them garments because they never go out without them and this is the universal fashion in Somerset and Devonshire and Cornwall.
                    The Journeys of Celia Fiennes, 1698

SCOTLAND
The House of the Commonalty are very mean, mud-wall and thatch the best; but the poorer sort live in such miserable huts as never eye beheld; men, women and children ligg [lie] altogether in a poor mouse-house of mud, heath, and such like matter, in some parts where turf is plentiful; they build up little cabins thereof, with arched roofs of turf, without a stick of timber in it; when the house is dry enough to burn, it serves them for fuel, and they remove to another. The habit of the people is very different, according to the qualities or the places they live in, as low-land or high-land men. The low-land gentry go well enough habited, but the poorer sort go (almost) naked, only an old cloak, or a part of their bed-clothes thrown over them. The highland-ers wear slashed doublets, commonly without breeches, only a plaid tied about their waists, etc., thrown over one shoulder, with short stockings to the gartering place, their knees and part of their thighs being naked; others have breeches and stockings all of a piece of plaid wear, close to their thighs; in on[e] side of their girdle sticks a curk or skean [dagger], about a foot or half a yard long, very sharp, and the back of it filed into divers notches, wherein they put poison, on the other side a brace (at least) of brass pistols; nor is this honour sufficient, if they can purchase more, they must have a long swinging sword.
     The women are commonly two handed tools, strong posted timber,

they dislike English men because they have no legs, or (like themselves) posts to walk on; the meaner go bare-foot and bare-head, with two black elflocks on either side of their faces; some of them have scarce any clothes at all, save part of their bed-clothes pinned about their shoulders, and their children have nothing else on them but a little blanket; those women that can purchase plaids, need not bestow much upon other clothes, these coversluts being sufficient. Those of the best sort are very well habited in their modish silks, yet must wear a plaid over all for the credit of their country.

The people are proud, arrogant, vain-glorious boasters, bloody, barbarous, and inhuman butchers. Couzenage and theft is in perfection amongst them, and they are perfect English-haters, they shew their pride in exalting themselves and depressing their neighbours.

Their meat is carrion when 'tis killed, but after it has been a fortnight a-perfuming with the aromatic air, strained through the calmy trunks of flesh flies, then it passes the trial of fire under the care of one of those exquisite artists, and is dished up in a sea of sweet Scotch butter. . . . Their nobility and gentry have tables plentifully enough furnished, but few or none of them have their meat better ordered: To put one's head into their kitchen-doors, is little less than destructive.

. . . The poorer sort live of haddock, whiting, and sour milk, which is cried up and down their streets (Whea buys sour milk) and upon the stinking fragments that are left at their Laird's table. . . .

Their drink is ale made of beer-malt, and tunned up in a small vessel, called a coque; after it has stood a few hours, they drink it out of the coque, yeast and all; the better sort brew it in larger quantities; and drink it in wooden queighs, but it is sorry stuff, yet excellent for preparing birdlime, but wine is the great drink with the gentry, which they pour in like fishes, as if it were their natural element; the glasses they drink out of, are considerably large, and they always fill them to the brim, and away with it; some of them have arrived at the perfection to tope brandy at the same rate. . . .

Music they have, but not the harmony of the spheres, but loud terrant noises, like the bellowing of beasts; the loud bagpipe is their chief delight, stringed instruments are too soft to penetrate the organs of their ears that are only pleased with sounds of substance.

A Trip to Barbarous Scotland by an English Gentleman, *c.* 1708

In Review, *25 June 1709, Defoe divides the population of England:*
1. The great, who live profusely.
2. The rich, who live very plentifully.
3. The middle sort, who live well.
4. The working trades, who labour hard but feel no want.

5. The country people, farmers, etc., who fare indifferently.
6. The poor, that fare hard.
7. The miserable that really pinch and suffer want.

THE ART OF GARDENING
The theory and practice of gardening; wherein is fully handled all that relates to fine gardens, commonly called Pleasure-Gardens, as parterres, groves, bowling-greens, etc., containing divers plans, and general dispositions of gardens; new designs of parterres, groves, grass plots, mazes, banqueting-rooms, galleries, porticos and summer-houses of arbour-work; terraces, stairs, fountains, cascades, and the like ornaments, of use in the decoration and embellishment of gardens. With the manner of laying out the ground, cutting the terraces, and of drawing and executing all sorts of designs, according to the principles of geometry. The method of planting and raising, in little time, all the plants requisite in fine gardens. Also that of discovering water, conveying it into gardens, and of making basins and fountains for the same. . . . Done from the French original, printed at Paris, Anno 1709. By John James of Greenwich. . . .   *Post Boy*, 4–7 October 1712

TUNBRIDGE WELLS
The court set out . . . to pass nearly two months in the most simple and rustic, but at the same time the most agreeable and entertaining place in all Europe.

Tunbridge is at the same distance from London as Fontainbleau from Paris. All the handsome and gallant of both sexes meet here in the season for drinking the waters. The company is always numerous and always select: and as those who seek only to amuse themselves are always numerically in ascendancy over those who resort thither only from necessity, everything breathes pleasure and joy.

The visitors lodge in little dwellings, clean and convenient, separated from one another and scattered everywhere within half a league of the Wells. In the morning they assemble at the spot where the springs are situated. There is a fine avenue of shady trees, beneath which the visitors walk while they drink the waters. At one side of this avenue stretches a long row of shops, furnished with all sorts of elegant trifles, lace, stockings, and gloves, where you may amuse yourself as at the Fair. On the other side of the avenue the market is held; and as every one goes there to choose and buy his own provisions, you see nothing exposed for sale which could occasion disgust. Here are young countrywomen, fair and fresh-looking, with white linen, little straw hats, and neat shoes and stockings, who sell game, vegetables, flowers, and fruit.

You may here enjoy as good living as you wish.

Here is playing for high stakes, and love-making in abundance. When evening comes, every one quits his little place to assemble in the bowling-green. There in the open air is dancing for those who like it upon turf smoother than the finest carpet in the world.

Anthony Hamilton, *Memoirs of Count Gramont*, 1713

Family Life

This was the great age of the family. In Stuart England the family of the nobility might consist of forty relatives – from grandfathers to third and fourth cousins. The household would also include servants in large numbers. The gentry also lived in large families. They needed big houses, extensive gardens, to give each family real importance.

The greater part of the gentry lived in the country, and each big house would dominate the village. The owner would build, furnish, and decorate the house in imitation of the most splendid country homes of the day. Foreign influences would be evident – Dutch cabinets, French upholstery, Flemish wall-hangings, Venetian glass. Here we see the tone of style in England set by the peers, who were admired, envied, imitated by the gentry. As Peter Laslett has said, 'the high taste of the few became the fashion of the many'.

The ideal family life of the period has been recorded in the *Memoirs of the Verney Family*. Their household at Claydon in Buckinghamshire represented 'all that was best in the Puritan and Cavalier way of life'. Here was a great house that 'provisioned itself with little help'. 'The inhabitants', as their historian tells us,

> brewed and baked, they churned and ground their meal, they bred up, fed and slew their beeves and sheep, and brought up their pigeons and poultry at their own doors. Their horses were shod at home, their planks were sawn, their rough ironwork was forged and mended. Accordingly the mill-house, the slaughter-house, the blacksmith's, carpenter's and painter's shops, the malting and brewhouse, the woodyard full of large and small timber, the sawpit, the out-houses full of all sorts of odds and ends of store, iron and woodwork and logs cut for burning – the riding house, the laundry, the dairy with a large churn turned by a horse, the stalls and styes for all manner of cattle and pigs, the apple and root chambers, show how complete was the idea of self-supply.

In this large and affectionate family no one was idle.

> Among the employments of the female part of the household at Claydon were spinning at wool and flax, fine and coarse needlework, embroidery, fine cooking, curing, preserving, distillery, preparing medicines from herbs at the prescription of the doctor or by family tradition, and last but not least

the making of fruit syrups and home-made wines from currants, cowslips and elder, which played a great part in life before tea and coffee began to come in at the Restoration. [G. M. Trevelyan]

It was becoming easier now to climb the social ladder. Yeomen and farmers, traders and merchants were rising to the gentry once they had acquired wealth and distinction. With this promotion they had to accept and fulfil the social responsibilities of their position. Their interests in politics, education, taste, expanded. The family had to move to further success. Hence younger sons went to the colonies, entered commerce, or turned to parliament.

Artisans and labourers had a much harder life. Many lived in small cottages with pressed earth floors, no rooms upstairs, dark interiors. There was, however, always the chance to be servants and become part of a family, when this could be both satisfying and dignified. Perhaps Sir Tobie Matthew, a courtier of Charles I, points to a reason when he says in the preface to his *Letters* that the English had a monopoly of 'a certain thing called Good Nature'.

SOME ENGLISH CUSTOMS

Touching customs, England keeps the old calendar, begins the day at midnight, and the year upon the 25th of March. . . . Strangers blame two customs of the English: first, that a man telling of a tale or speaking to others at table, if any of them drink, will be silent till they have drunk, which may be good manners if the speech démand or require present answer, but otherwise is needless . . . secondly that we put off hats too often at table with offence of shedding loose hairs and the like, and too little at other meetings as at ordinaries, where some, as in a place of equal expense, will enter without salutation, and generally think it needless towards familiar friends, and base towards unknown men.

England excels all other countries in the goodness and number of ambling nags and geldings, and no other nation hath so many and easy pads to ride upon, nor in any measure chairs and stools so frequently bombasted and richly adorned. But strangers seeing most of our gentlemen ride upon hard northern saddles, wonder they should use them abroad, who desire to sit so soft at home.

The custom for each parish to keep a register of all children christened, whereby any man may prove his age (being a thing important for many cases of law and otherwise) was first begun in England in the time of Henry the Eighth. . . .

England hath three very old and very laudable customs, used in no other kingdom that I know. First for children at morning and evening to ask their parents' blessing, and extraordinarily their godfathers' when they meet them. Secondly that all malefactors are followed from village to village by public officers with hue and cry. Thirdly that when any man is at the point of death, a great bell is tolled, to warn all men to pray for him while he yet liveth, and when the party is dead, by a number of several strokes at the bell, notice is given whether the party dead be a man, woman, or child, and then the bell is rung out. As likewise at the burial all the bells of the church for some hours are rung out.

Touching bells, England hath many singularities, as in the general greatness of them, some one (as that of Lincoln Minster) requiring the help of many men to toll it, and some dozen or twenty men to ring it out. Also in the incredible number of them. . . .

Besides that most churches have each of them three, five, or seven bells of differing bigness, which men commonly ring out in musical tunes for recreation, which I never observed to be done in any other country.   Fynes Moryson, *Itinerary*, 1617

CHRISTMAS DAY
It is now Christmas, and not a cup of drink must pass without a carol; the beasts, fowl, and fish, come to a general execution; and the corn is ground to dust for the bakehouse, and the pastry. Cards and dice purge many a purse, and the youth shew their agility in shoeing of the wild mare. Now 'Good cheer' and 'Welcome', and 'God be with you', and 'I thank you', and 'Against the new year', provide for the presents. The Lord of Misrule is no mean man for his time, and the guests of the high table must lack no wine. The lusty bloods must look about them like men, and piping and dancing puts away much melancholy. Stolen venison is sweet, and a fat coney is worth money. Pit-falls are now set for small birds, and a woodcock hangs himself in a gin. A good fire heats all the house, and a full alms-basket makes the beggars' prayers. The masquers and mummers make the merry sport: but if they lose their money, their drum goes dead. Swearers and swaggerers are sent away to the ale-house, and unruly wenches go in danger of judgement. Musicians now make their instruments speak out, and a good song is worth the hearing. In sum, it is a holy time, a duty in Christians for the remembrance of Christ, and custom among friends for the maintenance of good fellowship. In brief, I thus conclude of it: I hold it a memory of the heaven's love and the world's peace, the mirth of the honest, and the meeting of the friendly.
                    Nicholas Breton, *Fantastickes*, 1626

OLD ENGLISH HOSPITALITY
This true noble hearted fellow is to be dignified and honoured, wheresoever he keeps the house. It's thought that pride, puritans,

19. Jugs in the seventeenth century were made of leather. This
one known as a 'leather-jack' is at
Montacute House, Somerset.

coaches and covetousness hath caused him to leave our land. There are
six upstart tricks come up in great houses of late which he cannot
brook: peeping windows for the ladies to view what doings there are in
the hall, a buttery hatch that's kept locked, clean tables and a French
cook in the kitchen, a porter that locks the gates in dinner time, the
decay of black-jacks [leather bottles] in the cellar and blue-coats [ser-
vants] in the hall. He always kept his greatness by his charity: he loved
three things, an open cellar, a full hall, and a sweating cook: he always
provided for three dinners, one for himself, another for his servants,
the third for the poor.

Any one may know where he kept house, either by the chimney's
smoke, by the freedom at gate, by want of whirligig-jacks [spinning-
jacks] in the kitchen, by the fire in the hall or by the full furnished
tables. He affects not London, Lent, lackeys or bailiffs. There are four
sorts that pray for him, the poor, the passenger, his tenants and
servants. He is one that will not hoard up all, nor lavishly spend all, he
neither racks nor rakes his neighbours (they are sure of his company at
church as well as at home), and gives his bounty as well to the preacher
as to others whom he loves for his good life and doctrine. He had his
wine came to him by full butts, but his age keeps her wine-cellar in little

bottles. Lusty able men well maintained were his delight, with whom he would be familiar. His tenants knew when they saw him, for he kept the old fashion, good, commendable, plain. The poor about him wore upon their backs; but now since his death, landlords wear and waste their tenants upon their backs in French or Spanish fashions. Well, we can say that once such a charitable practitioner there was, but now he's dead, to the grief of all England: and 'tis shrewdly suspected that he will never rise again in our climate.

Donald Lupton, *London and the Countrey Carbonadoed*, 1632

A GENTLEMAN'S PURSUITS

. . . he had a great love of music, and often diverted himself with a viol, on which he played masterly; and he had an exact ear and judgement in other music; he shot excellently in bows and guns, and much used them for his exercise; he had great judgment in paintings, graving, sculpture, and all liberal arts, and had many curiosities of value in all kinds: he took great delight in perspective glasses, and for his other rarities was not so much affected with the antiquity as the merit of the

20. A portrait of the future James I at the age of eight holding a falcon.

work; he took much pleasure in improvement of grounds, in planting groves, and walks, and fruit-trees, in opening springs and making fish-ponds.

The Life of Mrs Lucy Hutchinson, written by herself – a fragment

HENRY HASTINGS (1551–1650)

. . . by his quality, being the son, brother, and uncle to the Earls of Huntingdon, and his way of living, had the first place amongst us. He was peradventure an original in our age, or rather the copy of our nobility in ancient days in hunting and not warlike times. He was low, very strong and very active, of a reddish flaxen hair, his clothes always green cloth, and never all worth when new five pounds. His house was perfectly of the old fashion, in the midst of a large park well stocked with deer, and near the house rabbits to serve his kitchen, many fish-ponds, and great store of wood and timber. . . .

He kept all manner of sport-hounds that ran buck, fox, hare, otter, and badger, and hawks long and short winged; he had all sorts of nets for fishing: he had a walk in the New Forest and the manor of Christ Church. This last supplied him with red deer, sea and river fish; and indeed all his neighbours' grounds and royalties were free to him, who bestowed all his time in such sports, but what he borrowed to caress his neighbours' wives and daughters, there being not a woman in all his walks of the degree of a yeoman's wife or under, and under the age of forty, but it was extremely her fault if he were not intimately acquainted with her. This made him very popular, always speaking kindly to the husband, brother, or father, who was to boot very welcome to his house whenever he came. There he found beef pudding and small beer in great plenty, a house not so neatly kept as to shame him or his dirty shoes, the great hall strewed with marrow bones, full of hawks' perches, hounds, spaniels, and terriers, the upper side of the hall hung with the fox-skins of this and last year's skinning, here and there a polecat intermixed, guns and keepers' and huntsmen's poles in abundance.

The parlour was a large long room, as properly furnished; on a great hearth paved with brick lay some terriers and the choicest hounds and spaniels; seldom but two of the great chairs had litters of young cats in them, which were not to be disturbed, he having always three or four attending him at dinner, and a little white round stick of fourteen inches long lying by his trencher, that he might defend such meat as he had no mind to part with to them. . . . An oyster-table at the lower end, which was of constant use twice a day all the year round, for he never failed to eat oysters before dinner and supper through all the seasons: the neighbouring town of Poole supplied him with them.

21. A gentleman smoking a long clay pipe in the seventeenth century. The clay pipe was popular for over two hundred years.

The upper part of this room had two small tables and a desk, on the one side of which was a church Bible, on the other the Book of Martyrs; on the tables were hawks' hoods, bells, and such like, two or three old green hats with their crowns thrust in so as to hold ten or a dozen eggs, which were of a pheasant kind of poultry he took much care of and fed himself; tables, dice, cards, and boxes were not wanting. In the hole of the desk were store of tobacco-pipes that had been used. On one side of this end of the room was the door of a closet, wherein stood the strong beer and the wine, which never came thence but in single glasses, that being the rule of the house exactly observed, for he never exceeded in drink or permitted it. On the other was a door into an old chapel not used for devotion; the pulpit, as the safest place, was never wanting of a cold chine of beef, pasty of venison, gammon of bacon, or great apple-pie, with thick crust extremely baked.

His table cost him not much, though it was very good to eat at, his sports supplying all but beef and mutton, except Friday, when he had the best sea-fish as well as other fish he could get, and was the day that his neighbours of best quality most visited him. He never wanted a London pudding, and always sung it in with 'my part lies therein-a'. He drank a glass of wine or two at meals, very often syrup of gilliflower in his sack, and had always a tun glass without feet stood by him holding a pint of small beer, which he often stirred with a great sprig of rosemary. He was well natured, but soon angry, calling his servants bastard and cuckoldy knaves, on one of which he often spoke truth to his own knowledge, and sometimes in both, though of the same man. He lived to a hundred, never lost his eyesight, but always writ and read without spectacles, and got to horse without help. Until past fourscore he rode to the death of a stag as well as any.

Earl of Shaftesbury, *Fragment of Autobiography, c.* 1675

GROWING-UP IN SHROPSHIRE

In the village where I lived the reader read the Common-Prayer briefly, and the rest of the day even till dark night almost, except eating time, was spent in dancing under a May-pole and a great tree, not far from my father's door; where all the town did meet together: And though one of my father's own tenants was the piper, he could not restrain him, nor break the sport: So that we could not read the Scripture in our family without the great disturbance of the tabor and pipe and noise in the street. Many times my mind was inclined to be among them, and sometimes I broke loose from conscience, and joined with them; and the more I did it the more I was inclined to it. But when I heard them call my father *Puritan* it did much to cure me and alienate me from them: for I considered that my father's exercise of reading the Scripture, was better than theirs, and would surely be better thought on by all men at the last; and I considered what it was for that he and others were thus derided. When I heard them speak scornfully of *others* as Puritans whom I never knew, I was at first apt to believe all the lies and slanders wherewith they loaded them: But when I heard my own father so reproached, and perceived the drunkards were the for-wardest in the reproach, I perceived that it was mere malice: For my father never scrupled Common-Prayer or ceremonies, nor spake against Bishops, nor ever so much as prayed but by a book or form, being not ever acquainted then with any that did otherwise: But only for reading Scripture when the rest were dancing on the Lord's Day, and for praying (by a form out of the end of the Common-Prayer Book) in his house, and for reproving drunkards and swearers, and for talking sometimes a few words of Scripture and the life to come, he was reviled commonly by the name of *Puritan, Precisian* and *Hypocrite*: and so were the godly conformable ministers that lived any where in the country near us, not only by our neighbours, but by the common talk of the vulgar rabble of all about us. By this experience I was fully convinced that godly people were the best, and those that despised them and lived in sin and pleasure, were a malignant unhappy sort of people: and this kept me out of their company, except now and then when the love of sports and play enticed me.

Richard Baxter, *Reliquiae Baxterianae,* 1664

GEORGE SITWELL'S COMPLAINT OF THE POSTAL SERVICE

For the gentlemen who take care of the letters at the Post Office in London

February 27th, 1663–64

Gentlemen,

This that I am about to say doth not . . . reflect upon you: I believe you are careful and faithful in your employment, for I have not had a letter failed that came into your hands this three or four years-past. But the 13th instant I lay at the Grayhound in Holborn and sent a letter into the country thus directed viz. – For Mr Francis Sitwell at Renishaw in Derbyshire near Chesterfield. Being careful of it I went myself to the stationer's shop at Gray's Inn Gate, who takes in letters and found none within but a boy. I delivered it to him; when he had written upon it, I asked him what he had written; he answered nothing but that he had added '3d' to the 'post paid'. I am confident he made it away for when I came home my son had heard nothing of it. . . . I doubt not but you will procure him to be whipped, for if he escape it may encourage him to play the knave again.

THE VENETIAN WASH

THE VENETIAN WASH, being a Most Excellent Water, to beautify and add loveliness to the face, by taking out all sorts of freckles, sun-brown and yellowness, 1s. the Bottle. A DENTIFRICE TO WHITEN THE TEETH; being an excellent powder of so singular a virtue, that teeth, though as black as ebony, being rubbed with it will to admiration, be as white as ivory. 6d. the Box.   *London Post*, 18–20 March 1702

MARRIAGE INSURANCE

Tomorrow, being the 10th of this instant January, will be opened the Two Royal Union Societies of Insurance on Marriages, up one pair of stairs in the last house in Petty-France, entering into Moor-Fields. In One, any person paying 5s. for Policy and Stamps, will be entitled to a Claim of 500 *l.* in fifteen days after marriage; in the Other, on paying 2s. for Policy and Stamps, will entitle to 200 *l.* in twelve days after marriage. . . .

Money for Marriages, Apprentices, and Children on their Births, and at 7, and at 14 years, is all completely performed at the First and Perpetual Office at London-Stone, by the Directions of the FIRST INVENTOR, WHOSE SONS ARE TO SUCCEED HIM. Last Wednesday, 8 new married, for 12s. had near 16 *l.* and next Wednesday, the Apprentices, for 4s. will receive above 4 *l.* The fairness and safety of this Office is confirmed by 12 Dividends of near 1000 *l.* to about 140 persons; and now by 18 months experience, and above 4500 entries. And notwithstanding an exorbitant number of interlopers daily setting up; yet since the 1st of the last month, near 300 Tickets of Assurance at 8s. per quarter [by the Friendly Society] have been taken out. In the mean time, what may you expect from the great pretences of such as make no conscience so publicly to invade the lawful right and property of another.   *Post Boy*, 6–9 January 1710

Food

According to Fynes Moryson, 'The art of Cookery is much esteemed in England. . . . The English cookes . . . are much commended for roasted meates.' 'In general', he tells us, 'the English eat but two meals each day.' These meals were dinner at eleven and supper at five. Huge quantities were consumed in a leisurely way. The food left over would be sent down from the hall to the serving men. This would be in addition to their usual meals. In turn they would take what remained to the poor gathered at the gate.

Till the Restoration, people drank ale, commonly home brewed, and country wines in moderation. The well-to-do ate off silver plate, and drank out of silver or pewter tankards till glass came strongly into favour. 'Our gentility, as loathing those metals, because of their plenty, do now choose rather the Venice glasses.'

With the return of Charles II a change came. Drunkenness was common in the court and high circles. Pepys writes on 2 April 1661,

> then to the Privy Seal and signed some things, and then to the Dolphin to Sir W. Batten, and Pen, and other company; where strange how these men, who at other times are all wise men, do now, in their drink, betwitt and reproach one another. . . . But parted all friends at 12 at night after drinking a great deal of wine.

TIPPLING

Clowns and vulgar men only use large drinking of beer or ale. Gentlemen carouse only in wine, with which many mix sugar – which I never observed in any other place or kingdom to be used for that purpose. And because the taste of the English is thus delighted with sweetness, the wines in taverns (for I speak not of merchants' or gentlemen's cellars) are commonly mixed at the filling thereof, to make them pleasant. Thomas Coryat, *Crudities*, 1611

FOOD

The Devil, disguised as a novice, is told to say grace:

62

PRIOR Stand forth, and render thanks.
RUSH Hum, hum:

> For our bread, wine, ale and beer,
> For the piping hot meats here:
> For broths of sundry tastes and sort,
> For beef, veal, mutton, lamb, and pork:
> Green-sauce with calve's head and bacon,
> Pig and goose, and cramm'd-up capon:
> For pastries rais'd stiff with curious art,
> Pie, custard, florentine and tart.
> Bak'd rumps, fried kidneys, and lamb-stones,
> Fat sweet-breads, luscious marrowbones,
> Artichoke, and oyster pies,
> Butter'd crab, prawns, lobsters' thighs,
> Thanks be given for flesh and fishes,
> With this choice of tempting dishes:
> To which preface, with blithe looks sit ye,
> Rush bids this Convent, much good do't ye.

Thomas Dekker, *If It be not Good, the Devil is in It*, 1612

MEALS

The Italian Sansovino is much deceived, writing, that in general the English eat and cover the table at least four times in the day; for howsoever those that journey and some sickly men staying at home may perhaps take a small breakfast, yet in general the English eat but two meals (of dinner and supper) each day, and I could never see him that useth to eat four times in the day. And I will profess for myself and other Englishmen, passing through Italy so famous for temperance, that we often observed, that howsoever we might have a pullet and some flesh prepared for us, eating it with a moderate proportion of bread, the Italians at the same time, with a charger full of herbs for a salad, and with roots, like meats of small price, would each of them eat two or three penny-worth of bread. And since all fulness is ill, and that of bread worst, I think we were more temperate in our diet, though eating more flesh, than they eating so much more bread than we did.

Fynes Moryson, *Itinerary*, 1617

MORYSON DISCOVERS THE FORK

I observed a custom in all those Italian cities and towns through which I passed that is not used in any other country that I saw in my travels, neither do I think that any other nation of Christendom doth use it, but only Italy. The Italians . . . do always at their meals use a little fork when they cut their meat. . . . The reason for this their curiosity is because the

Italian cannot endure by any means to have his dish touched by fingers, seeing that all men's fingers are not alike clean.

Fynes Moryson, *Itinerary*, 1617

A RECIPE FOR HERRING PIE
Take salt herrings, being watered; wash them between your hands, and you shall loose the fish from the skin; take off the skin whole, and lay them in a dish; then have a pound of almond-paste ready; mince the herrings and stamp them with the almond-paste, two of the milts or roes, five or six dates, some grated manchet, sugar, sack, rose-water and saffron; make the composition somewhat stiff, and fill the skins; put butter in the bottom of your pie, lay on the herring, and on them dates, gooseberries, currants, barberries, and butter; close it up, and bake it; being baked, liquor it with butter, verjuice, and sugar.

A seventeenth-century cookery book, 1620

DAILY MEALS AT SCHOOL
Our breakfast in the morning is a little piece of bread not bulted [sieved], but with all the bran in it, and a little butter, or some fruit, according to the season of the year. To dinner we have herbs, or everyone a mess of porridge. Sometimes turnips, coleworts [cabbage], wheat and barley in porridge, a kind of delicate meat made of fine wheat, flour and eggs. Upon fish days, fleeted [skimmed] milk, in deep porrengers (whereout the butter is taken) with some bread put in it. Some fresh fish, if in Fish Street it can be had at a reasonable price. If not, salt fish, well watered. After pease-pudding, or beans . . . small beer or a little watered wine.

Schoolboy in a London school, 1621

A MINCE-PIE
Take a leg of mutton, and cut the best of the best flesh from the bone, and parboil it well: then put to it three pound of the best mutton suet, and shred it very small: then spread it abroad, and season it with pepper and salt, cloves and mace: then put in good store of currants, great raisins and prunes, clean washed and picked, a few dates sliced, and some orange-pills [orange peel] sliced: then being all well mixed together, put it into a coffin [pie], or into divers coffins, and so bake them: and when they are served up, open the lids, and strew store of sugar on the top of the meat, and upon the lid. And in this sort you may also bake beef or veal: only the beef would not be parboiled, and the veal will ask a double quantity of suet.

Gervase Markham, *The English Hus-wife*, 1623

LORD FAIRFAX GIVES INSTRUCTIONS TO THE SERVANTS OF HIS HOUSEHOLD, 1650

The Cupboard

Let no man fill beer or wine but the cupboard keeper, who must make choice of his glasses or cups for the company, and not serve them hand over head. He must also know which be for beer and which for wine: for it were a foul thing to mix them together.

'ADVICE' OR ADVERTISEMENT, 1657

The drink called Coffee. A very wholesome and physical drink: helpeth Digestion, quickeneth the Spirits, maketh the Heart lightsome: is good against Eyesores, Coughs, Colds, Rhumes, Consumptions, Headaches, Gout, Dropsy, Scurvy, and many others.

ANOTHER NEW BEVERAGE, 1658

That Excellent, and by all Physicians approved, *China* Drink, called by the *Chineans, Tcha,* by other Nations *Tay, alias Tee,* is sold at the *Sultaness-head,* a *Cophee house* in *Sweetings Rents* by the Royal Exchange, *London.*

REFINEMENTS AMONG THE WELL-TO-DO, 1660

We went to our house in Mugwell street which Mr Cripps hath made very handsome. I was led by his wife into all the rooms of it, and being come down we had a collation, viz., a dish of pickled oysters and glasses of old and new sack out of the butt. She gave us also a box of Spanish marmalade, and when she perceived that I was putting it up into a paper to keep what I could not eat, she gave unto me not only the remainder of the first box, but also another box, both which, about three days before were brought out of Spain.

Michael Woodward, Warden of New College, Oxford

22. This tea-pot was made at Yi-hsing in China in the late seventeenth century. Those who could not afford a silver pot accepted the red hard pottery that came from China with the tea. The belief grew that these pots brewed the best tea, and potters in Europe soon imitated them.

CHESHIRE CHEESE
Poor men do eat it for hunger, rich for digestion. It seems that the
Ancient British had no skill in the making thereof, till taught by the
Romans, and now the Romans may even learn of us more exactness
therein. This county doth afford the best for quantity and quality, and
yet their cows are not (as in other shires) housed in the winter, so that it
may seem strange that the hardiest kine should yield the tenderest
cheese. Some essayed in vain to make the like in other places, though
hence they fetched both their kine and dairymaids. It seems they
should have fetched their ground too (wherein surely some occult
excellency in this kind), or else so good cheese will not be made. I hear
not like commendation of the butter in this county, and perchance
these two commodities, are like stars of a different horizon, so that the
elevation of the one to eminency is the depression of the other.
                    Thomas Fuller, *The History of the Worthies of England*, 1662

CORNISH PILCHARDS
Plenty hereof are taken in these parts, persecuted to the shore by their
enemies, the tunny and hake, till in pursuance of their private revenge,
they all become a prey to the fisherman. The pilchard may seem
contemptible in itself, being so small, though the wit of the vulgar here
will tell you, they have seen many pilchards an ell-long, understand it
laid at length, head and tail together. Their numbers are incredible,
employing a power of poor people, in polling (that is, beheading)
gutting, splitting, powdering and drying them, and then (by the name
of *Fumadoes*) with oil and a lemon, they are meat for the mightiest don
in Spain. I wish, not only their nets, but fish may hold, suspecting their
daily decay, their shoals usually shifting coasts, and verging more
westward to Ireland. Other fish here be which turn to good account, all
welcome to fishermen's hooks, save the star-fish, esteemed contagious.
                    Thomas Fuller, *The History of the Worthies of England*, 1662

MAKING TEA
*On his return from China in 1664 a Jesuit told his friend Mr Walters that 'the
hot water should not stay upon the tea-leaves any longer than you can say the
Miserere Psalm very leisurely'.*

DINING AT THE BACK-STAIRS
25 July 1666. By and by the King to dinner, and I waited there his
dining; but Lord! how little I should be pleased, I think, to have so
many people crowding about me; and among other things it astonished
me to see my Lord Barkeshire waiting at table and serving the King
drink, in that dirty pickle as I never saw man in my life. Here I met Mr

Williams, who would have me to dine where he was invited to dine, at the Back-stairs. So after the King's meat was taken away, we thither; but he could not stay, but left me there among two or three of the King's servants, where we dined with the meat that come from his table; which was most excellent, with most brave drink cooled in ice.

Samuel Pepys, *Diary*

ORANGE MARMALADE

To make the best Orange Marmalade. Take the rinds of the deepest coloured oranges, boil them in several waters till they are tender, then mince them small, and to one pound of oranges, take a pound of pippins cut small, one pound of the finest sugar, and one pint of spring-water, melt your sugar in the water over the fire, and scum it, then put in your pippins, and boil them till they are very clear, then put in the orange rind, and boil them together, till you find by cooling a little of it, that it will jelly very well, then put in the juice of two oranges, and one lemon, and boil it a little longer; and then put it up in galley-pots.

Hannah Woolley, *The Queen-like Closet*, 1684

VERY GOOD CAKE

Take a peck of flour, four pound of currants well washed, dried and picked, four pounds of butter, one pound of sugar, one ounce of cinnamon, one ounce of nutmegs, beat the spices, and lay it all night in rosewater, the next day strain it out, then take one pint and a half of good ale-yeast, the yolks of four eggs, a pint of cream, put a pound of the butter into the warmed cream, put the rest into the flour in pieces, then, wet your flour with your cream, and put in your currants, and a little salt, and four or five spoonfuls of caraway-comfits and your spice, mix them all and the yeast well together, and let it lie one hour to rise, then make it up and bake it in a pan buttered: it may stand two hours.

Hannah Woolley, *The Queen-like Closet*, 1684

A NEW DIET TABLE APPROVED BY THE GOVERNING BODY OF ST BARTHOLOMEW'S HOSPITAL IN APRIL, 1687

Source: Sir Norman Moore, *The History of St Bartholomew's Hospital*, 1918

Sunday   10 ounces of Wheaten Bread
              6 ounces of Beefe boyled without bones
              1 pint and a halfe of Beef Broth
              1 pint of Ale Cawdell
              3 pints of 6 shilling Beere

Monday   10 ounces of Wheaten Bread
               1 pint of Milk Pottage
               6 ounces of Beefe
               1½ pints of Beefe Broth
               3 pints of Beere

Tuesday   10 ounces of Bread
               halfe a pound of Boyled Mutton
               3 pints of Mutton Broth
               3 pints of Beere

Wednesday 10 ounces of Bread
               4 ounces of Cheese
               2 ounces of Butter
               1 pint of Milk Pottage
               3 pints of Beere

Thursday   The same allowance as Sunday
               1 pint of Rice Milke

Friday   10 ounces of Bread
               1 pint of Sugar Soppes
               2 ounces of Cheese
               1 ounce of Butter
               1 pint of Water Gruell
               3 pints of Beere

Saturday   The same allowance as Wednesday

FOOD FOR FARM SERVANTS

. . . they feed on the variety of flesh and fish that cometh from their master's tables, when the poor tenants are glad of a piece of hanged bacon once a week, and some few that can kill a bull eat now and then a bit of hanged beef, enough to try the stomach of an ostrich. He is a rich man that can afford to eat a joint of fresh meat (beef, mutton or veal) once in a month or fortnight. If their sow pig or their hens breed chickens, they cannot afford to eat them, but must sell them to make their rent. They cannot afford to eat the eggs that their hens lay, nor the apples nor pears that grow on their trees (save some that are not vendible) but must make money of all. All the best of their butter and cheese they must sell, and feed themselves and children and servants, with skimmed cheese and skimmed milk and whey curds. And through God's mercy all this doth them no harm.

          Richard Baxter, *Poor Husbandman's Advocate to Rich Raçking
Landlords,* 1691

OAT CLAP BREAD MADE IN WESTMORLAND

They mix their flour with water so soft as to roll it in their hands into a ball, and then they have a board made round and something hollow in the middle . . . drive it [the dough] to the edge in a due proportion till drove it thin as a paper and still they clap it and drive it round, and then they have a plate of iron same size with their clap board, and so shove off the cake on it and so set it on coals and bake it; then enough on one side they slide it off and put the other side . . . they have no other sort of bread unless at market towns.   Celia Fiennes, *Journeys*, 1685–1703

ROBERT INWOOD'S SECRET INVENTION FOR CHOCOLATE

Whereas the author of the new invention for chocolate hath given a general satisfaction in making the finest and cleanliest in the world with that pleasure, that he can afford it 12d. a pound cheaper than the drugster, or any in London, if made from sound nuts, all Spanish nut, or all Martineco nuts, either rich or plain, or both sorts with sugar rich or plain, known by the rates often published in the *Daily Courant*. The author is an Englishman, notwithstanding there is no Jew or others will pretend to make chocolate their loathsome way upon a stone so fine or cleanly. The invention is to be seen [all bright cast iron], the working past is a secret. The chocolate is no where to be sold but by the author Mr Robert Inwood in Strapson's-court in White-Friars the third door behind the Green Dragon Tavern in Fleet-street, there is a Coach-way at the Golden Lion, a drugsters. Those that take but a pound shall have a dish liquid gratis, or allowance by the dozen.

Daily Courant, 25 March 1704

ACT TO REGULATE THE PRICE AND ASSIZE OF BREAD, 1710

. . . and that every Loaf be fairly Imprinted or Marked, several Letters for Knowing the Price and Sort thereof, as followeth, that is to say

	Finest or White	*Wheaten*	*Household*
On every Penny Loaf	I.F.	I.W.	I.H.
Two Penny Loaf	II.F.	II.W.	II.H.
Six Penny Loaf		VI.W.	VI.H.
Twelve Penny Loaf		XII.W.	XII.H.
Eighteen Penny Loaf		XVIII.W.	XVIII.H.

Dress

For the first thirty years of the seventeenth century Jacobean dress was a continuation of the late Elizabethan. Minor gentry were beginning to move into upper ranks in society. Woollen cloth in simple styles became more popular for day suits, though gentlewomen did not wear woollen dresses till much later. French influence was rapidly becoming more dominant. Doublet and breeches became more ornate. Cloaks were very fashionable, usually circular in cut, and often made of velvet. Neckwear was either the band (or collar) and the ruff; these were of lawn, linen and lace. Starch was widely used. In 1614 a complaint was made against a Stratford starchmaker whose work caused 'such a stink and ill-favour so that liege subjects are not able to come and go along the highway without great danger to their lives through the loathsome smell'.

On footwear the round toe remained till 1635; then the shape tapered to a square toe. From 1600 raised heels were worn. Boots were long, underwent changes, and about 1635 became known as 'bucket-tops'. In this century cloth stockings were replaced by knitted woollen or worsted ones. Silk stockings were commonly seen at court.

Up to about 1680 men wore hats indoors, even in church. Then wigs grew in size and hats were removed for comfort indoors. Hats had wide brims and moderate crowns. Men of fashion developed the cravat 'of lace elegantly fringed'. One is described in *London Amusements,* 1700: 'His cravat reached down to his middle and had stuff enough in it to make a sail for a barge. A most prodigious cravat-string peeped from under his chin.'

But, as C. Willett Cunnington says:

it was the periwig which transformed the wearer into a personage and gave the epoch a distinctive symbol of magnificence. Worn over a shaven head, the periwig no longer imitated the natural hair, but assumed the proportions of a gigantic head-dress. The large French wig, known as the 'full-bottomed', was a mass of curls framing the face and falling on to the shoulders. The Campaign or travelling wig, full but shorter, ended in one or two corkscrew curls or 'dildos' sometimes tied back on the neck in a queue.

70

23. Sleeveless leather jerkin, also a falling ruff. *c.* 1625. Painting by du Chapell.

The wig was a massive affair. Tom Brown in *Letters from the Dead to the Living*, 1702, tells us: 'His periwig was large enough to have loaded a camel and he bestowed upon it at least a bushel of powder.' This had its effect on hats, now with flattened crowns.

Women's fashions in late Elizabethan times were extravagant and exaggerated. William Harrison describes the exotic shades – 'goose-turd green, peas-porridge tawny, popinjay blue, lusty gallant, devil-in-the-head' – of doublet and hose and women's farthingales and galligascons. Soon the stiff farthingale gave way to the flowing gown, high-waisted with full sleeves. Long gloves, heavily perfumed, were now commonly worn. The ruff went out of fashion after 1630, and was replaced by a cape-like collar. Shoes had high heels made of cork.

The Restoration brought other changes in fashion. Tight-lacing became a marked feature, and the bodice was now long-waisted with low decolletage. The gown had a long skirt worn open over an embroidered underskirt. Curls were now *à la mode,* variously named: 'Confidants', 'Favourites', 'Heart-breakers'. Make-up was elaborate with paint, powder, patches, rouge, even artificial eyebrows made from mouse-skin.

24.   Hair style of the mid-seventeenth century, gown with circular decolletage. Artist unknown.

25. Short-skirted doublet, compound ruff and bombasted breeches. (*Bombace*, Old French for cotton; clothes padded, usually with cotton, for effect) *c.* 1605.

The taste for colour is shown in this description of a costume in 1709: 'A black silk petticoat with red and white calico border, cherry-coloured stomacher trimmed with blue and silver, and a red and dove-coloured damask gown flowered with large trees, and a yellow satin apron trimmed with white.'

TUFTED TAFFETAS
In 1604 we hear of
Master John Tyce, dwelling near Shoreditch Church, the first Englishman that devised and attained the perfection of making all manner of tufted taffetas, cloth of tissue, wrought velvet, branched satins, and all other kind of curious silk stuffs.

A DANDY
At last, to close up the lamentable tragedy of us ploughmen, enters our young landlord, so metamorphosed into the shape of a French puppet, that at the' first we started, and thought one of the baboons had marched in in man's apparel. His head was dressed up in white feathers like a shuttlecock, which agreed so well with his brain, being nothing but cork, that two of the biggest of the guard might very easily have tossed him with battledores, and made good sport with him in his majesty's great hall. His doublet was of a strange cut; and shews the

26.   Richard Sackville, Earl of Dorset, wearing a short-skirted doublet, sleeves
with wings. Trunk hose, nether stocks and shoe roses. Large miniature by Isaac
Oliver, 1616.

fury of his humour, the collar of it rose up so high and sharp as if it would have cut his throat by daylight. His wings, according to the fashion now, were as little and diminutive as a puritan's ruff, which shewed he ne'er meant to fly out of England, nor do any exploit beyond sea, but live and die about London, though he begged in Finsbury. His breeches, a wonder to see, were full as deep as the middle of winter, or the roadway between London and Winchester, and so large and wide withal, that I think within a twelve-month he might very well put all his lands in them; and then you may imagine they were big enough, when they would outreach a thousand acres. Moreover, they differed so far from our fashioned hose in the country, and from his father's old gascoins [loose breeches], that his back-part seemed to us like a monster; the roll of the breeches standing so low, that we conjectured his house of office, sir-reverence, stood in his hams. All this while his French monkey bore his cloak of three pounds a yard, lined clean through with purple velvet, which did so dazzle our coarse eyes, that we thought we should have been purblind ever after, what with the prodigal aspect of that and his glorious rapier and hangers [straps suspending the rapier] all bossed with pillars of gold, fairer in show than the pillars in Paul's or the tombs at Westminster. Beside, it drunk up the price of all my plough-land in very pearl, which stuck as thick upon those hangers as the white measles upon hogs' flesh. When I had well viewed that gay gaudy cloak and those unthrifty wasteful hangers, I muttered thus to myself: 'That is no cloak for the rain, sure; nor those no hangers for Derrick' [hangman of the period]: when of a sudden, casting mine eyes lower, I beheld a curious pair of boots of king Philip's leather, in such artificial wrinkles, sets and plaits, as if they had been starched lately and came new from the laundress's, such was my ignorance and simple acquaintance with the fashion, and I dare swear my fellows and neighbours here are all as ignorant as myself. But that which struck us most into admiration, upon those fantastical boots stood such huge and wide tops, which so swallowed up his thighs, that had he sworn as other gallants did, this common oath, 'Would I might sink as I stand!' all his body might very well have sunk down and been damned in his boots. Lastly he walked the chamber with such a pestilent gingle that his spurs oversqueaked the lawyer, and made him reach his voice three notes above his fee; but after we had spied the rowels of his spurs, how we blest ourselves! they did so much and so far exceed the compass of our fashion, that they looked more like the fore-runners of wheelbarrows. Thus was our young landlord accoutred in such a strange and prodigal shape that it amounted to above two years' rent in apparel.

Thomas Middleton(?), *Father Hubburds Tales*, 1604

27.   Winged jerkin with a sham hanging sleeve. Cloak-bag breeches
with tags, 1625. Painting by C. Jansen.

PORTRAIT OF A YOUNG CITY WIFE

I must be a Lady and I will be a Lady. I like some humours of the City dames well, to eat cherries only at an angel [gold coin] a pound, good; to dye rich scarlet black, pretty; to line a Grogarom gown clean through with velvet, tolerable; their pure linen, their smocks of 3 pound·a smock are to be borne withal. But your mincing niceries, taffeta pipkins, durance petticoats, and silver bodkins – God's my life, as I shall be a Lady I cannot endure it.

G. Chapman, B. Jonson, J. Marston, *Eastward Hoe,* 1605

CORKED SHOES

I came trip trip over the Market Hill, holding up my petticoats to the calves of my legs, to show my fine coloured stockings, and how trimly I could foot it in a new pair of corked shoes I had bought.

Anon., *Willy Beguiled,* 1623

DECLINE IN BEHAVIOUR

Your gallant is not man unless his hair be of the women's fashion, dangling and waving over his shoulders; your women nobody except (contrary to the modesty of her sex) she be half at least of the man's

28. A lady with breasts exposed, riding with a safeguard (a skirt both for warmth and to protect her dress from mud when travelling), *c.* 1620.

fashion; she jests, she cuts, she rides, she swears, she games, she smokes, she drinks, and what not that is evil?

Samuel Rowlands, 1628

NO LONG HAIR FOR THE KING IN OXFORD

1635. There is a Proctor for every house during the King's continuance in Oxford, and the chiefest thing that they will endeavour to amend is the wearing of long hair. The Principal protested that after this day he would turn out of his house [Magdalen Hall] whomsoever he found with hair longer than the tips of his ears. I believe this severity will last but a week.   Edmund Verney to his father

LADY BRILLIANA HARLEY TO HER SON AGED 15, 1639

Let your stockings be always of the same colour of your clothes. . . . If your tutor does not intend to buy you silk stockings to wear with your silk shirt send me word, and I will, if please God, bestow a pair on you.

FASHIONS GIVE 'LITTLE EASE'

Another foolish affection there is among young virgins though grown big enough to be wiser, but that they are led blindfold by custom to a fashion pernicious beyond imagination; who thinking a slender waist a great beauty, strive all that they possibly can by straight-lacing themselves, to attain into a wand-like smallness of waist, never thinking themselves fine enough until they can span their waist. . . . And while they ignorantly affect an august or narrow breast, and to that end by strong compulsion shut up their waists in a whale-bone prison or little-ease, they open a door to consumptions, and a withering rottenness.   John Bulwer, *The Artificial Changling*, 1650

A SILKEN FOP

It was a fine silken fop which I spied walking the other day through Westminster-Hall, that had as much ribbon about him as would have plundered six shops, and set up twenty country pedlars: all his body was dressed like a maypole, or a Tom-a-Bedlam's cap. A frigate newly rigged kept not half such a clatter in a storm, as this puppet's streamers did when the wind was in his shrouds; the motion was wonderful to behold, and the colours were red, orange, and blue, of well-gummed satin, which argued a happy fancy: but so was our gallant over charged . . . whether he did wear this garment, or (as a porter) bear it only, was not easily to be resolved.

John Evelyn, *Tyrannus or The Mode*, 1661

EFFEMINATE AGE OF FASHION

December 1663. A strange effeminate age when men strive to imitate women in their apparel, viz. long periwigs, patches in their faces, painting, short wide breeches like petticoats, muffs, and their clothes highly scented, bedecked with ribbons of all colours. And this apparel was not only used by gentlemen and others of inferior quality, but by soldiers especially those of the Life-Guard to the King, who would have spanners [to wind up the wheel-lock of pistol or musket] hanging on one side and a muff on the other, and when dirty weather some of them would relieve their guards in pattens [overshoe with wooden sole].

On the other side, women would strive to be like men, viz. when they rode on horseback or in coaches wear plush caps like monteros [Spanish hunter's cap], whether full of ribbons or feathers, long periwigs which men used to wear, and riding coat of a red colour all bedaubed with lace which they call vests, and this habit was chiefly used by the ladies and maids of honour belonging to the Queen, brought in fashion about anno 1662.

Life and Times of Anthony Wood, Antiquary of Oxford, 1632–1695,
described by himself

A COAT OF CLOTH

A close coat of cloth, pinked [adorned] with a white taffeta under the cut. This in length reached the calf of the leg, and upon that a surcoat cut at the breast, which hung loose and shorter than the vest six inches. The breeches, the Spanish cut, and the buskins, some of cloth, some of leather but of the same colour as the vest or garment, of never the like fashion since William the Conqueror.   T. Rugge, *Diurnal,* 1666

A STRANGE FASHION

I remember there was a fashion, not many years since, for women in their apparel to be so pent up by the straightness, and stiffness of the gown-shoulder-sleeves, that they could not so much as scratch their heads for the necessary remove of a biting louse; nor elevate their arms scarcely to feed themselves handsomely; nor carve a dish of meat at a table, but their whole body must needs bend towards the dish.

Thomas Mace, *Musick's Monument,* 1676

A WORKING GIRL'S OUTFIT, 1698

Ann Castleman [having finished her 'apprenticeship'] shall leave . . . apparelled with two new gowns, two new petticoats, one pair of boddys [stays], two pair of stockings, one pair of shoes, two new shifts, two new aprons, one straw hat, two suits [sets] of head clothes, and two handkerchiefs fit . . . for such an apprentice.

29.　Louise Renee de Penencouet de Keroualle, Duchess of Portsmouth, painted by Pierre Mignard in 1682.

ALL BEPATCHED

In England the young, old, handsome, ugly all are bepatched till they
are bed-rid. I have often counted fifteen patches, or more, upon the
swarthy wrinkled phiz of an old hag three-score and ten and upwards.
H. Misson, *Memories and Observations in his Travels over
England,* 1698

THE CRAVAT

His cravat reached down to his middle and had stuff enough in it to
make a sail for a barge. A most prodigious cravat-string peeped from
under his chin, the two corners of which in conjunction with a
monstrous periwig that would have made a Laplander sweat under the
North Pole, eclipsed three-quarters of his face.

Tom Brown, *London Amusements,* 1700

PERFUME FOR WIGS

The Royal Essence for the Hair of the Head and Periwigs, being the
most delicate and charming Perfume in Nature, and the greatest
Preserver of Hair in the World, for it keeps that of Periwigs (a much
longer time than usual) in the Curl, and fair Hair from fading or
changing colour, makes the Hair of the Head grow thick, strengthens
and confirms its Roots. . . . By its incomparable Odour and fragrancy it
strengthens the Brain, revives the Spirits, quickens the Memory, and
makes the Heart cheerful, never raises the Vapours in ladies, &c.,
being wholly free from Musk, Civet &c., 'tis indeed an unparalleled fine
Scent for the Pocket, and perfumes handkerchiefs excellently. To be
had only at Mr Allcraft's a Toyshop at the Bluecoat Boy by Popes-head-
Alley against the Royal Exchange, Cornhill, sealed up, at *2s. 6d.* a Bottle
with Directions.   *Daily Courant,* 10 March 1704

SHOE POLISH

The famous Spanish-Blacking for Gentlemen's shoes, that ever was
invented or used, it maketh them always look like new; never daubs the
hands in putting on or soils the stockings in wearing. Neither has it the
ordinary gloss of German-Balls, or the intolerable noisome stink of
size, but is of an agreeable scent. It makes the shoes look extremely
neat, and mightily preserves the leather. All that use it admire it, and
those that once try it, will never use anything else. Sold for *1s. 6d.* the
Pot, with directions (which will last 3 or 4 months) only at Mr John
Hannum's, a Toy-shop, at the 3 Angels near Foster-Lane in Cheapside.
Post Boy, 20–22 October 1713

Furnishings

Seventeenth-century furniture brings new woods, new techniques and new pieces. The wood, in particular, is walnut; the techniques from those new craftsmen, Huguenot refugees, are veneering, marquetry, japanning and gesso; the new specialized pieces are scrutoir, bureau, dressing-glass, candle-stand.

'Joyners, cabinet-makers, and the like who from very vulgar and pitiful artists', wrote Evelyn, 'are now come to produce works as curious for the filing, and admirable for their dexterity in contriving, as any we meet with abroad.' The 'contriving' is visible at the turn into the century. Men of Elizabeth's day could 'scant endewr to sitt upon' the hard plank forms and wainscot stools 'since great breeches were layd aside'. The padding 'layd aside' was now used to upholster the stools and benches and physical comfort was restored. On Cromwellian chairs strips of hide were strained over the seat and back and then secured by large brass-headed nails.

From the reign of Charles II, new methods and new materials increased. Walnut, 'pale brown' or 'the black wood' was brought from France and Virginia. Other decorative woods were olive, laburnum and kingwood. Marquetry was used for the decoration of the new veneered surfaces. By about 1675 it had replaced inlay. Table-legs and chair-legs were spiral turned. Frames of looking-glasses were now elaborately carved.

Oriental lacquer furniture was imported by the East India Company. Incised lacquer was known as 'Bantam work'; European imitations of oriental lacquer, a form of varnishing, became known as 'japan'. Gilt furniture, usually highly decorative side-tables, became popular. After 1690 gesso (carving done in a paste made of chalk and size) was used and then gilded.

Many French refugees were craftsmen and by learning from their skill English joiners became cabinet-makers. The new, popular William and Mary style, though intricate, was not extravagant. Furniture became simpler and more graceful. Chairs were padded, not carved nor caned, fitting more naturally into the domestic scene.

Queen Anne furniture showed further development in the age of walnut – a tendency towards greater simplicity. Startling designs were replaced by 'sea-weed' marquetry or by plain walnut veneer. Elaborate carving disappeared. The influence of Daniel Marot retained a consistent purity of style, direct and dignified.

EARL OF NORTHAMPTON'S INVENTORY, 1614

. . . a walnut-tree cupboard with a Turkey cupboard cloth . . . two small tables with two Turkey carpets . . . four Turkey cushions . . . two small Turkey carpets, whereof one is upon the ground . . . two large Persian carpets . . . 12 stools of Turkey work billeted red white and blue with crewel fringe.

INVENTORY

. . . the odd things in the room my mother kept herself, the iron closet, the little room between her bed's head and the backstairs, the little and great fripperies [hanging closets for gowns], your own green-wrought velvet furniture, the red velvet furniture, the looking-glasses (there should be at least four), leather carpets for the dining and drawing-rooms [probably wall hangings], the stools with nails gilt, the great cabinet like yours, the tapestry, the great branch candlestick, all such

30. This fireplace has panels of black marble with a design inlaid with coloured material called *scagliola, c.* 1640. It is in the queen's closet, Ham House, Surrey. The initials, interlaced, are 'J.E.L.' for John and Elizabeth, the Duke and Duchess of Lauderdale.

wrought work as my mother had from London and was not finished, the book of martyrs and other books in the withdrawing-room, the preserving room, the spicery with furnaces, brewing vessels, and a brass skillet; the plate left for the children's use, all the locks that are loose in the closet.

Sir Ralph Verney (to his wife), *Verney Papers*, 1645

THE RECTOR OF HORSTED KEYNES, SUSSEX, BUYS A CLOCK

16 September, 1656. I bought of Edward Barrett at Lewis a clock, for which I paid £2.10s., and for a new jack, at the same time, made and brought home, £1.5s. For 2 prolongers and an extinguisher 2d., and a pair of bellows 5s.

Revd Giles Moore, *Journal*

PROBATE INVENTORY OF RURAL LABOURER, 1662

An inventory of the goods and chattels and cattle of Bartholomew Burch, late of Shaddoxhurst in the county of Kent, deceased, taken and apprised by us whose names are hereunto subscribed the day and year above written:

Item in the hall: one table, one cupboard, one kneading trough, ten chairs, a pair of pothangers, a pair of tongs, a grid iron, a salt box

Item in the milk-house: five tongs, six bowls, three platters, a pair of scales

Item in the hall-chamber: one bed and bedstead, three bolsters, four blankets, one coverlet, one truckle bed, one linen treadle, one woollen treadle, four chests

Item in the drink-house: three tubs, two barrels, and other old lumber and a churn

Item: one hay-cutter, one hand-saw, and a mattock

Item: boards and shelves and old lumber

Item without doors: wood and hay and butts

Item: three cows

Item: one hog

Item: one birding-piece

Item: things unseen and forgotten

Nathaniel Manering, Thomas Yates,
Maidstone Record Office, PRC 11/21, 23 January 1662

A PENDULUM CASE

Sir Richard Legh of Lyme Hall, Cheshire, to his wife, c. 1675

I went to the famous pendulum maker Knibb, and have agreed for one, he having none ready but one dull stager which was at £19; for £5 more I have agreed for one finer than my father's, and it is to be better finished with carved capitals gold, and gold pedestals with figures of

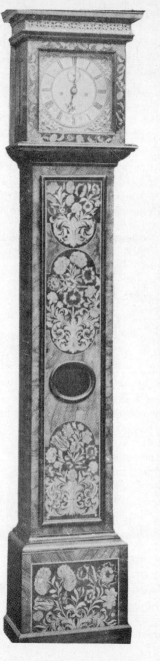

31. The Dutch introduced the pendulum.
Robert Hooke (a member of the Royal Society)
devised the slow-swinging pendulum that led to
the 'grandfather' clock. The movement of the
clock shown here is by William Clement of
London, made *c.* 1685.

boys and cherubims all brass gilt. I would have had it olive wood (the case I mean), but gold does not agree with that colour, so took their advice to have it black ebony which suits your cabinet better than walnut tree wood, of which they are mostly made. Let me have thy advice herein by the next.

To which the young wife answers:
My dearest soul; as for the pendulum case I think black suits anything.

CANE FURNITURE
That about the year 1664, cane chairs, etc., came into use in England, which gave so much satisfaction to all the nobility, gentry, and commonalty of this kingdom (for their durableness, lightness and cleanness from dust, worms and moths, which inseparably attend Turkey-work, serge, and other stuff-chairs and couches, to the spoiling

32.   Chinese patterns have influenced this curtain from a set of valances for a bedstead, worked in coloured wools on linen and cotton. On one of these valances appears the worker's name, Abigail Pett.

33.   This shows the oldest English silver tea-pot, engraved as follows: 'This silver tea-Pott
was presented to ye Comtte of ye East India Cumpany by ye Honoue George Lord
Berkeley of Berkeley Castle. A member of that Honourable & worthy Society and A true
Hearty Lover of them 1670.'

of them and all furniture near them) that they came to be much used in England, and sent to all parts of the world.

Petition to Parliament by the Cane-chair Makers in the 1680s

BED AND BED-CHAMBER
Bed-stocks, as bed posts, sides, ends, head and tester [canopy, especially over four-poster].
Mat, or sack-cloth bottom.
Cord, bed staves, and stay for the feet.
Curtain rods and hooks, and rings, either brass or horn.
Beds, of chaff, wool or flocks, feathers, and down in ticks or bed tick.
Bolsters, pillows.
Blankets, rugs, quilts, counterpane, caddows [rough woollen covering].
Curtains, valances [short curtain round frame of bedstead], tester head-cloth, all either fringed, laced or plain alike.
Inner curtains and valances, which are generally white silk or linen.
Tester bobs [knobs] or wood gilt, or covered suitable to the curtains.

34. A cup painted in colours, dated 1642, with the name Ann Chapman round the upper edge. The cup was made in London.

35. This container, made in 1621, is designed with lid and feet in the shape of scallop-shells. It was probably filled with that most valuable spice, pepper.

Tester top either flat, or raised, or canopy like, or half testered.
Basis, or the lower valance at the seat of the bed, which reaches to the ground, and fringed for state as the upper valance, either with inch fringe, caul [net] fringe, tufted fringe, snailing [spiralling] fringe, gimp [lace-like] fringe with tufts and buttons, etc.

Randle Holme, *Academy of Armory*, 1688

ITEMS OF DINING-ROOM, 1688
The room hung with pictures of all sorts, as history, landscapes, fancies, etc.
Long table in the middle, either square to draw out in leaves, or long, or round, or oval with falling leaves.
Side tables, or court cupboards, for cups and glasses to drink in, spoons, sugar box, phial and cruses for vinegar, oil and mustard pot.
Cistern of brass, pewter, or lead to set flagons of beer, and bottles of wine in.

A Turkey table cover, or carpet of cloth or leather printed.
Chairs and stools of Turkey work, Russia or calves leather, cloth or
stuff, or of needlework. Or else made all of joint work or cane chairs.
Fire grate, fire shovel, tongs, and land irons all adorned with brass bobs
and buttons. Flower pots, or alabaster figures to adorn the windows,
and glass well painted and a large seeing glass at the higher end of the
room.

Randle Holme, *Academy of Armory*, published at Chester, 1688

STRIKING CLOCKS
The clocks I now shall speak of, are such as by pulling a string, etc., do
strike the hour, quarter, or minute, at any time of the day and night.

These clocks are a late invention of one Mr Barlow, of no longer
standing than the latter end of King Charles II about the year 1676.

This ingenious contrivance (scarce so much as thought of before)
soon took air, and being talked of among the London artists, set their
heads to work, who presently contrived several ways to effect such a

36.   A variety of embroidery called 'stump-work'; many different varieties of stitch are
included, and figures in the picture are padded to gain a realistic effect. The man in the
tent may be James II as the date is 1686.

37. Wine bottles were made of a cheap greenish glass. Many had on them a glass seal. The unusual device on this one is a merchant's mark, of the type used from 1400 to 1700. The date here is 1698.

38. An ingenious, highly decorative seventeenth-century lock. The small dials on the left record the number of times the lock has been opened.

39. This exquisite and complicated sampler, dated 1649, reveals the skill of children in the art
of needlework. In the second row
from the top appear the initials of
the maker, S.I.D.

performance. And hence arose the different ways of *repeating work*, which so early might be observed to be about the Town, every man almost practising, according to his own invention.

William Derham, *The Artificial Clock-maker*, 1696

CRAFTSMEN

We daily find that when once they [English craftsmen] arrive to a thorough inspection and address in their trades, they paragon, if not exceed even the most exquisite of other countries, as we may see in that late reformation and improvement of our locksmiths' work, joiners, cabinet-makers and the like, who from very vulgar and pitiful artists, are now come to produce works as curious for the filing [smoothness]; and admirable for their dexterity in contriving, as any we meet with abroad.

John Evelyn, *An Account of Architects and Architecture*, 1696

FURNISHINGS

1698, July 16 . . . My dear sister Norton sent me towards furnishing my bare walls. A large fine tortoiseshell cabinet, which now stands in my best chamber, valued at near a hundred pounds. With some fine china for the top of it. My dear sister Austin sent me towards my house furniture five great china jars for my best chamber (now in my closet carefully laid up by Eliz. Freake). And a new long cane squab – now stands in the great parlour.

About the same time I bought for myself a new green damask bed, and all my tapestry hangings for the parlour and two chambers and the dining room; with two great glasses. And a new damask coach lined with a damask and scarlet silk, cosy for myself, with several other necessaries to about the value of three hundred and fifty pounds.

Mrs Elizabeth Freake, *Diary*, 1671–1714

CELIA FIENNES WROTE OF THE QUEEN'S CLOSET AT HAMPTON COURT

. . . the hangings, chairs, stools, and screen the same, all of satin stitch done in worsteds, beasts, birds, images, and fruits all wrought very finely by Queen Mary and her Maids of Honour.

Education

Children were taught by using the hornbook – a single leaf of paper containing the alphabet, Roman numerals, and the Lord's Prayer, protected by a thin piece of translucent horn, and mounted on wood with a projecting handle. The term is used by Thomas Dekker in *The Guls Horne-booke*, his satirical book of manners, published in 1609. Henry Peacham maintained that education should stand on a knowledge of grammar, taught by translating Latin into English, and English into Latin. He supported the study of geometry, geography, poetry and history. Education suffered during the Civil War. The Restoration brought to this country great admiration for the fashions, manners, arts of the French. Antony Wood said: 'There is not a gentleman of a considerable estate in England but must have a French man or woman to breed up their children after their way.' Ladies were expected to be accomplished rather than formally educated. Lucy Hutchinson at the age of seven had eight tutors to teach her music, dancing, needlework, writing and languages.

The famous schools of the time were Eton, Winchester, St Paul's, Westminster, and Merchant Taylors'. Many children had private tutors, first at home, then at school and university. Tutors would accompany their pupils on the 'finishing journey' abroad.

Boarding schools scattered up and down the country frequently had dull, incompetent ushers. It was said that young ladies in such places 'learn to quaver instead of singing; hop for dancing, take the guitar, rumble the virginals, and scratch and thumb the lute. To conclude, they learn nothing more gentle, but only to be so gentle that they commonly run away with the first serving-man or younger brother who makes love to them.'

MIDDLE SORT OF PARENTS
Richard Mulcaster, high-master of St Paul's School, spoke well of middle sort of parents

which neither welter in too much wealth, nor wrestle with too much want seemeth fittest of all ... to bring forth that student who must serve his country best.

TO ETON
In 1607, a boy of the Irish clan of O'Neill captured by the English was sent to Eton. The school bill of his expenses shows: the 'healing of his knee, being sore', cost 4d.; the purchase of candles for the term cost 1s. 6d.; '6 arrows, 2 strings, bowcase and gut', cost 2s. 4d.

METHODS IN 'ORDINAIRE' GRAMMAR SCHOOLS
These things may be effected in good sort ... if the masters ... will take meet pains: and the scholars being set to school, so soon as they shall be meet, be kept to learning daily, without loitering, having books and other necessary helps and encouragements: and by their parents' care caused to do their exercises at home, and be ever kept in meet awe, and submission to their masters. ... That so all scholars of any towardness and diligence, may be made good grammarians, and every way fit for the University by fifteen years of age, or at least by that time that they shall be meet by discretion and government, which is commonly sixteen or seventeen. And all this to be done with delight and certainty, both to masters and scholars; with strife and contention amongst the scholars themselves, without that usual terror and cruelty, which hath been practised in many places, and without so much as severity amongst good natures.

John Brinsley, the Elder, *A Consolation for our Grammar Schooles*, 1622

THE GOOD SCHOOLMASTER
There is scarce any profession in the commonwealth more necessary, which is so slightly performed. The reasons whereof I conceive to be these:

First, Young scholars make this calling their refuge; yea, perchance, before they have taken any degree in the University, commence schoolmasters in the country, as if nothing else were required to set up this profession but only a rod and a ferula.

Secondly, Others who are able, use it only as a passage to better preferment, to patch the rents in their present fortune, till they can provide a new one, and betake themselves to some more gainful calling.

Thirdly, They are disenheartened from doing their best with the miserable reward which in some places they receive, being masters to the children, and slaves to their parents.

Fourthly, Being grown rich, they grow negligent, and scorn to touch the school, but by the proxy of the usher.

Thomas Fuller, *The Holy State and the Profane State*, 1642

THE FOUNDING OF HARVARD COLLEGE IN 1636

After God had carried us safe to New England and we had builded our houses, provided necessaries for our livelihood, reared convenient places for God's worship, and settled the civil government, one of the next things we longed for and looked after was to advance learning and perpetuate it to posterity, dreading to leave an illiterate ministry to the churches when our present ministers shall lie in the dust. And as we were thinking and consulting how to effect this great work, it pleased God to stir up the heart of one Mr Harvard ... to give the one half of his estate (it being in all about £1,700) towards the erecting of a college, and all his library. After him another gave £300, others after them cast in more, and the public hand of the State added the rest. The college was by common consent appointed to be at Cambridge (a place very pleasant and accommodate) and is called (according to the name of the first founder) Harvard College.   *New England's First Fruits*, 1643

TO KEEP CHILDREN AT SCHOOL

James Howell, writing in the Fleet prison, 1647, said:
Every man strains his fortunes to keep his children at school. The cobbler will clout it till midnight, the porter will carry burdens till his bones crack again, the ploughman will pinch both back and belly to give his son learning, and I find that this ambition reigns nowhere so much as in this island.

VILLAGE SCHOOLMASTERS

In the village where I was born there was four readers successively in six years, ignorant men, and two of them immoral in their lives, who were all my schoolmasters. In the village where my father lived, there was a Reader of about eighty years of age that never preached, and had two churches about twenty miles distant. His eyesight failing him, he said Common Prayer without book: but for reading of the Psalms and chapters, he got a common thresher and day labourer one year, and a tailor another year: (for the clerk could not read well) and at last he had a kinsman of his own (the excellentest stage-player in all the country, and a good gamester and a good fellow) that got Orders and supplied one of his places. After him another younger kinsman, that could write and read, got Orders. And at the same time another neighbour's son that had been a while at school turned minister, and ... when he had been a preacher about twelve or sixteen years he was fain to give it over, it being discovered that his Orders were forged by the first ingenious stage-player. After him another neighbour's son took Orders. When he had been a while an attorney's clerk, and a common drunkard, and tipled himself into so great proverty that he had no other to live. . . . These were the schoolmasters of my youth (except two of them) who read Common Prayer on Sundays and holy days, and taught school and tipled on the week-days, and whipped the boys when they were drunk, so that we changed them very oft.

Richard Baxter, Autobiography (1615–1691), c. 1670

CHRIST'S HOSPITAL

I went this evening to see the boys and children at Christ's Hospital. There were near 800 boys and girls so decently clad, cleanly lodged, so wholesomely fed, so admirably taught, some the Mathematics, especially the forty of the late King's Foundation, that I was delighted to see the progress some little youths . . . had made. Some [boys] are taught for the Universities, others designed for seamen, all for trades and callings.

John Evelyn, Diary, 10 March 1686–7

FREE SCHOOLS

[Shrewsbury] . . . here are three free schools together all built of free stone, 3 large rooms to teach the children with several masters: the first has 150£ a year the second 100£ the third 50£ a year and teach children from reading English till fit for the University, and it's free for children not only of the town but for all over England if they exceed not the numbers . . . here is a very good school for young Gentlewomen for learning work and behaviour and music.

The Journeys of Celia Fiennes, 1697 and 1698

THE EASY WAY TO EVERYTHING

The way to get wealth; or, an easy and cheap way to make 23 sorts of wine, equal to that of France, and to make cyder, mead, rum, rack, brandy, cordial waters, pickles, vinegars. The mystery of a confectioner, physical receipts, the servant maids instructor for japan work, to back wood and gild, to make coffee, tea, chocolate, to help a bad memory, so that you may remember all you read or do; to keep rain though never so great showers from wetting through your clothes. A help to discourse, and many other curiosities. By the Author of the Way to save Wealth by Living well on 2d. a day, and the Author of 1,000 notable things, price 1s. 6d. Sold by G. Conyers at the Gold Ring in Little Brittain.

Post Man, 7–10 March 1702

CHEMISTRY COURSE

A Course of Chymistry consisting of near 100 Operations, will begin the 20th of this present January, perform'd by Mr Wilson at his Elaboratory in Well-yard by St Bartholomew's Hospital in Smithfield. The terms are 2 Guineas and a half, one Guinea Entrance, and one Guinea and a half at the beginning of the Course.

Daily Courant, 17 January 1704

OXFORD AND CAMBRIDGE

In 1622 the number of University men in proportion to the population was quite high. Oxford had 18 colleges, 7 halls with 2,850 students. Cambridge had 16 colleges with 3,050 students.

UNIVERSITY STUDENTS

A young gentleman of the university is one that comes there to wear a gown, and to say hereafter he has been at the university. His father sent him thither, because he heard there were the best fencing and dancing schools; from these he has his education, from his tutor the over-sight. The first element of his knowledge is to be shewn the Colleges, and initiated in a tavern by the way, which hereafter he will learn of himself. The two marks of his seniority is the bare velvet of his gown and his proficiency at tennis, where when he can once play a set, he is a fresh-man no more. His study has commonly handsome shelves, his books neat silk strings, which he shews to his father's man, and is loth to untie or take down, for fear of misplacing. Upon foul days, for recreation, he retires thither, and looks over the pretty book his tutor reads to him, which is commonly some short history, or a piece of 'Euphormio'; for which his tutor gives him money to spend next day. His main loitering is at the library, where he studies arms and books of honour, and turns a gentleman-critic in pedigrees. Of all things he endures not to be mistaken for a scholar, and hates a black suit though it be of satin. His companion is ordinarily some stale fellow, that has been notorious for an ingle to gold hatbands, whom he admires at first, afterwards scorns. If he have spirit or wit, he may light of better company and may learn some flashes of wit, which may do him knight's service in the country hereafter. But he is now gone to the Inns of Court, where he studies to forget what he learned before – his acquaintance and the fashion.   John Earle, *Micro-cosmographie,* 1628

AT CAMBRIDGE

We go twice a day to the chapel; in the morning about 7, and in the evening about 5. After we come from chapel in the morning, which is towards 8, we go to the butteries for our breakfast, which usually is 5 farthings; a halfpenny loaf and butter and a cize [portion] of beer.

John Strype to his mother, 1662

AT OXFORD
Writing of St John's College, Oxford, Ralph Thoresby says, 24 May 1684, 'the skeletons and stuffed skins in the Anatomy School suited my melancholy temper'.

The Arts

'The Englishman Italianate is the Devil Incarnate' was a popular saying in the sixteenth century. Noblemen travelled abroad and came back with new ideas and the enthusiasm of the Renaissance. These ideas about form, colour, design, freely used, became the fashion.

The whole mind of the Renaissance, backed by the wealth and influence of the aristocracy, became a specialized study of the arts. The craftsman followed the dictates of fashion. The first quarter of the seventeenth century moved forward with high hopes. It was a time of exploration, expansion, adventure. Travel in Europe brought into England a widening flow of ideas, starting with the grand idea of man as lord of creation: the study for man is man.

From India and the East Indies, from Africa and the New World, came new interpretations of colour, shapes, patterns, ornaments. These were vividly expressed in dress, fabrics, silver, glass, painting, sculpture, furniture. These forms of artistic expression were almost obliterated by the austerity of Puritan rule. This period, however, provided a brief resting space before confidence and exuberance returned.

In country districts the English tradition of design persisted, and things for everyday use retained their sturdy shapes. But what may be called the Golden Age of English design began at the Restoration. John Gloag describes it:

> and almost immediately a gay, spontaneous exuberance was apparent in the design of all kinds of things. Everywhere men with skill and ingenuity were at work, breathing again the air of freedom, without fanatical overseers glowering their disapproval: goldsmiths and silversmiths, weavers and clock-makers, cabinet-makers and chair-makers, joiners and glass-makers; and, controlling all the activities of such people with intelligence and highly civilised standards of taste, were new and incredibly accomplished architects. Inigo Jones had prepared the way . . . and early in his reign Charles II appointed as Assistant to the Surveyor General a man whom John Evelyn had described as 'that miracle of a youth': his name was Christopher Wren.

LITERATURE

In the Jacobean Age we move from the Forest of Arden to the rogues of Bartholomew Fair and the thieves of Thames Side. Ben Jonson, a vigorous personality, emphasizes the weaknesses and moral failings of human nature. Many other dramatists – Thomas Dekker, Thomas Heywood, John Webster, Cyril Tourneur – pursue the same realism, often revealing corruption and cruelty. John Fletcher and Francis Beaumont writing in happy collaboration, with great ingenuity present artificial courtly life.

With the Civil War the greatest period of English drama closes. A shadow of that splendour appeared in the masques of the Stuart Courts, written by Jonson, Chapman, Carew, with elaborate designs by Inigo Jones.

With the Restoration the theatres reopened, and now the comedy of manners emerged, the work of George Etherege, William Wycherley, and William Congreve. Their plays are elegant, mocking, and satirical. Congreve excels the others in the brilliance of his dialogue, and Millaman' is a lasting triumph on the English stage. John Vanbrugh and George Farquhar follow, ignoring the attack made by Jeremy Collier in the *Short View of the Immorality and Profaneness of the English Stage.*

The two great poets at the beginning of the seventeenth century, Ben Jonson and John Donne, exert considerable influence on the development of poetry. Jonson was the most learned of the humanists, and principally through him Neo-Classicism was introduced, leading to the work of Dryden. Donne's work has been spoken of as 'the battle ground between the difficulty, of belief and the reluctance to doubt'. He gave lyrical expression to the complex workings of his mind. Herbert, Crashaw, Vaughan, all marked by the 'metaphysical' poetry of Donne are, too, religious poets, accepting God with 'unimpeded devoutness'. Religion, more especially Puritanism, completed the work of the Renaissance, and in the poetry of Milton the two meet and fuse, though not without an inner conflict. *Paradise Lost*, published in 1667, is one of our greatest poems. Andrew Marvell also lived through the troubled days of the Commonwealth and the Restoration. His poetry has wit, tough reasonableness and lyric grace – the quality of a 'sophisticated literature'.

With the Restoration there came a new mental outlook – one of reflection. The King and his Court set the fashions for the new order. The exiles brought back with them as models the manners and the literary fashions of France. In this atmosphere of exclusiveness and refinement there was time for analysis and critical thought. Satire, as in

Samuel Butler's *Hudibras,* is the weapon which denounces tyranny, hypocrisy, and cant. Dryden is now the central figure. Not only does he adapt the heroic couplet to satire, but he inaugurates literary criticism. In *Annus Mirabilis* he writes of the Fire of London and the Dutch War. *Absalom and Achitophel* satirizes Shaftesbury and Monmouth.

The greatest fiction writer of the seventeenth century was John Bunyan. He is our supreme proletarian writer 'not concerned with the class-struggle but with the struggle for a man's soul'. *Pilgrim's Progress*

40. The title-page of *Leviathan* by Thomas Hobbes, 1651. 'The Leviathan' signifies sovereign power, which is finally responsible to God.

1819

Cromwell's

Bloody Slaughter-house;

OR,

His Damnable Defignes
laid and practifed by him and
his *Negro's*, in Contriving
the Murther of his Sacred
Majefty KING

CHARLES I.

DISCOVERED.

By a Perfon of Honor.

July   *LONDON:*
Printed for *James Davis*, and are to be
fold at the *Grey-hound* in St. Pauls
Church-yard. 1 6 6 o.

41. The title-page of *Crom-well's Bloody Slaughter-house,* 1660.

had instant success, and, as Q. D. Leavis says, 'its religious aims made it as indispensable to every respectable home as the Bible, till the Puritan conscience itself decayed'.

Locke and Newton, in a period of enlightened opinion, produce a philosophy of reason. South, Tillotson, Stillingfleet, show sensible argument in the pulpit. Evelyn and Pepys write detailed, precise prose. Clarendon is clear, elegant, ordered, in his *History of the Rebellion*; while Dryden's prose is almost modern in idiom and in its logical progression. Defoe was the brilliant journalist of the bourgeoisie; Addison endeavoured to cultivate and polish human life, to establish a taste of polite writing. Many steps now move towards the age of reason.

CORNISH MIRACLE-PLAYS

The guary-miracle, in English a miracle-play, is a kind of interlude compiled in Cornish out of some scripture history, with that grossness which accompanied the Romanes vetus commedia. For representing it, they raise an earthen amphitheatre in some open field, having the diameter of this inclined plain some forty or fifty feet. The country people flock from sides many miles off, to hear and see it, for they have devils and devices to delight the eye as the ear. The players con not their parts without book, but are prompted by one called the ordinary, who followeth at their backs with the book in his hand, and telleth them what to say.   R. Carew, *Survey of Cornwall*, 1602

THE LORD OF MISRULE, A KIND OF PAGEANT, 1603

. . . their pipers piping, their drummers thundering, their stumps dancing, their bells jingling, their handkerchiefs fluttering about their heads like mad men, their hobby horses and other monsters skirmishing amongst the throng, and in this sort they go to the church.

THE GALLANT IN THE PLAY-HOUSE

Sithence then the place [the theatre] is so free in entertainment, allowing a stool as well to the farmer's son as to your Templar; that your stinkard has the selfsame liberty to be there in his tobacco-fumes, which your sweet courtier hath; and that your carman and tinker claim as strong a voice in their suffrage, and sit to give judgment on the play's life and death, as well as the proudest Momus [Carper] among the tribe of critic: it is fit that he, whom the most tailors' bills do make room for, when he comes should not be basely (like a viol) cased up in a corner.

   Whether therefore the gatherers of the public or private play-house stand to receive the afternoon's rent, let our gallant, having paid it, presently advance himself up to the throne of the stage – on the very rushes where the comedy is to dance, yea, and under the state of Cambyses [proverbial for rant] himself, must our feathered ostrich, like a piece of ordnance, be planted valiantly, because impudently, beating down the mews and hisses of the opposed rascality.

   For do but cast up a reckoning; what large comings-in are pursed up by sitting on the stage? First a conspicuous eminence is gotten, by which means the best and most essential parts of a gallant (good clothes, a proportionable leg, white hand, the Parisian lock and a tolerable beard) are perfectly revealed.

   By sitting on the stage you have signed a patent to engross the whole commodity of censure, may lawfully presume to be a guider, and stand at the helm to steer the passage of scenes; yet no man shall once offer to hinder you from obtaining the title of an insolent overweening cox-comb. . . .

Before the play begins, fall to cards; you may win or lose, as fencers do in a prize, and beat one another by confederacy, yet share the money when you meet at supper. Notwithstanding, to gull the ragamuffins that stand aloof gaping at you, throw the cards, having first torn four or five of them, round about the stage, just upon the third sound, as though you had lost. . . .

Now sir; if the writer be a fellow that hath either epigrammed you, or hath had a flirt at your mistress, or hath brought either your feather, or your red beard, or your little legs, &c., on the stage; you shall disgrace him worse than by tossing him in a blanket, or giving him the bastinado [a thrashing] in a tavern, if, in the middle of his play, be it pastoral or comedy, moral or tragedy, you rise with a screwed and discontented face from your stool to be gone. No matter whether the scenes be good, or no; the better they are, the worse do you distaste them. And, being on your feet, sneak not away like a coward; but salute all your gentle acquaintance, that are spread either on the rushes, or on stools about you; and draw what troop you can from the stage after you. The mimics are beholden to you for allowing them elbow-room; their poet cries perhaps, 'A pox go with you'; but care not for that; there's no music without frets.

Marry; if either the company or indisposition of the weather bind you to sit it out, my counsel is then that you turn plain ape. Take up a rush, and tickle the earnest ears of your fellow gallants, to make other fools fall a laughing; mew at passionate speeches; blare at merry; find fault with the music; whew at the children's action; whistle at the songs; and, above all, curse the sharers, that whereas the same day you had bestowed forty shillings on an embroidered felt and feather, Scotch fashion, for your mistress in the court, or your punk in the city, within two hours after your encounter with the very same block on the stage, when the haberdasher swore to you the impression was extant but that morning.　　　　　　　　　Thomas Dekker, *The Guls Horne-booke*, 1609

BREECHES ON FIRE
A letter from Sir Henry Wotton to his nephew tells us that at the burning of the Globe in 1613 the only casualty beyond 'a few forsaken cloaks' was a man who had his breeches set on fire, but he 'by the benefit of a provident wit' put out the fire with bottled ale.

MASQUE
In honour of the marriage of Princess Elizabeth, daughter of James I, a masque held at Whitehall from 11–16 February 1613

And that night, in honour of this joyful nuptial, there was a very stately masque of lords and ladies, with many ingenious speeches, delicate devices, melodious music, pleasant dances, with other princely entertainments of time, all which were singularly well performed in the Banqueting-house. The four honourable Inns of Court, as well elders and grave benchers of each house as the towardly young active gallant gentlemen of the same houses, being of infinite desire to express their singular love and duteous affection to his Majesty, and to perform some memorable and acceptable service worthy of their reputation in honour of this nuptial. . . . They employed the best wits and skilfullest artisans in devising, composing and erecting their several strange properties, excellent speeches, pleasant devices and delicate music, brave in habit, rich in ornaments, in demeanour courtly, in their going by land and water very stately and orderly; all which, with their rare inventions and variable entertainments of time, were such as the like was never performed in England by any society, and was now as graciously accepted of by his Majesty, the Queen, the Prince, the bride and bridegroom, from whom they received all princely thanks and encouragement.   Edmond Howes, *Annales*, 1615

REALISM ON THE STAGE
Another will fore-tell of lightning and thunder that shall happen such a day, when there are no such inflammations seen, except men go to the Fortune in Golding-Lane, to see the tragedy of *Doctor Faustus*. There indeed a man may behold shag-haired devils run roaring over the stage with squibs in their mouths, while drummers make thunder in the tiring-house, and the twelve-penny hirelings make artificial lightning in their heavens.   *The Astrologaster, or the Figure-Caster, c.* 1620

STATIONERS
A mere stationer is he that imagines he was born altogether for himself, and exerciseth his mystery without any respect either to the glory of God or the public advantage. For which cause he is one of the most pernicious superfluities in a Christian government, and may well be termed the Devil's seedsman, seeing he is the aptest instrument to sow schisms, heresies, scandals and seditions through the world.

What book soever he may have hope to gain by, he will divulge, though it contain matter against his prince, against the state, or blasphemy against God. And all his excuse will be that he knew not it comprehended any such matter. For (give him his right) he scarcely reads over one page of a book in seven year, except it be some such history as the Wise men of Gotham, and that he doth furnish himself with some foolish conceits to be thought facetious.

He will fawn upon authors at his first acquaintance, and ring them to his hive by the promising sounds of some good advertisement; but as soon as they have prepared the honey to his hand, he drives the bees to seek another stall. If he be a printer, so his work have such appearance of being well done that he may receive his hire, he cares not how unworkmanlike it be performed, nor how many faults he let go to the author's discredit and the reader's trouble. If his employment be in binding books, so they will hold together but till his workmaster hath sold them, he desireth not they should last a week longer; for by that means a book of a crown is marred in one month which would last a hundred years if it had twopence more workmanship.

George Wither, *The Schollers Purgatory, c.* 1625

STRONG PURITAN FEELING

One Sunday, 27 September 1631, A Midsummer Night's Dream *was performed in a Bishop's house in London. The part of Bottom, the weaver, was played by Mr Wilson, who was later seized and punished for 'playing' on a Sunday.*
We do order that Mr Wilson, as he was a special plotter and contriver of this business, and did in such a brutish manner act the same with an ass's head, shall upon Tuesday next, from six o'clock in the morning till six o'clock at night, sit in the porter's lodge at my lord bishop's house, with his feet in the stocks, and attired with an ass's head, and a bottle [bundle] of hay before him, and this subscription on his breast:

Good people, I have played the beast,
And brought ill things to pass;
I was a man, but thus have made,
Myself a silly ass.

Quoted Chambers, *Book of Days*

PLAYERS AND PLAYHOUSES

Time, place, subject, actors and clothes either make or mar a play. The prologue and epilogue are like to an host or hostess, one bidding their guests welcome, the other bidding them farewell. The actors are like serving-men, that bring in the scenes and acts as their meat, which are liked or disliked, according to every man's judgment; the neatest drest and fairest delivered doth please most. They are as crafty with an old play, as bawds with old faces; the one puts on a new fresh colour, the other a new face and name. They practise a strange order, for most commonly the wisest man is the fool. They are much beholden to scholars that are out of means, for they sell them ware the cheapest. They have no great reason to love Puritans, for they hold their calling unlawful. New plays and new clothes many times help bad actions.

They pray the company that's in to hear them patiently, yet they would not suffer them to come in without payment. They say as scholars now use to say, there are so many, that one fox could find in his heart to eat his fellow. A player often changes: now he acts a monarch, to-morrow a beggar; now a soldier, next a tailor. Their speech is loud, but never extempore; he seldom speaks his own mind, or in his own name. When men are here, and when at church, they are of contrary minds; there they think the time too long, but here too short. Most commonly when the play is done, you shall have a jig or dance of all treads; they mean to put their legs to it, as well as their tongues. They make men wonder when they have done, for they all clap their hands. Sometimes they fly into the country; but 'tis a suspicion that they are either poor, or want clothes, or else company, or a new play: or do, as some wandering sermonists, make one sermon travel and serve twenty churches. All their care is to be like apes, to imitate and express other men's actions in their own persons. They love not the company of geese or serpents, because of their hissing. They are many times lousy, it's strange, and yet shift so often. As an ale-house in the country is beholden to a wild schoolmaster, so an whore-house to some of these, for they both spend all they get. Well, I like them well, if when they act vice they will leave it, and when virtue they will follow. I speak no more of them, but when I please I will come and see them.

> Donald Lupton, *London and the Countrey Carbonadoed*, 1632

STAGE-PLAYS ATTACKED

... popular stage-plays (the very pomp of the Devil which we renounce in baptism, if we believe the Fathers) . . . sinful, heathenism, lewd, ungodly spectacles, and most pernicious corruptions; condemned in all ages as intolerable mischiefs to churches, to republics, to the manners, minds, and souls of men.

> William Prynne, *Histrio-Mastix, the Players' Scourge*, 1635

ORDINANCE PASSED BY PARLIAMENT, 1642

Whereas public sports do not well agree with public calamities, nor public stage-plays with the seasons of humiliation. . . . It is therefore thought fit and ordained by the Lords and Commons in this Parliament assembled that while these sad causes and set times of humiliation continue, public stage-plays shall cease, and be forborne.

REMONSTRANCE AGAINST THE CLOSING OF LONDON THEATRES, 1642

Oppressed with many calamities and languishing to death under the burden of a long and (for aught we know) an everlasting restraint, we the comedians, tragedians and actors of all sorts and sizes belonging to the famous private and public houses within the city of London and the suburbs thereof, to you great Phoebus and your sacred Sisters, the sole patronesses of our distressed calling, do we in all humility present this our humble and lamentable complaint, by whose intercession to those powers who confined us to silence we hope to be restored to our pristine honour and employment. . . .

It is of all other our extremest grievance, that plays being put down under the name of public recreations, other public recreations of far more harmful consequences (are) permitted still to stand in statu quo prius, namely that nurse of barbarism and beastliness, the Bear-Garden, where upon their usual days those demi-monsters are baited by bandogs [band-dogs, tied up to make them fierce]; the gentlemen of stave and tail, namely boisterous butchers, cutting cobblers; hard-handed masons and the like rioting companions, resorting thither with as much freedom as formerly, making with their sweat and crowding a far worse stink than the ill-formed beasts they persecute with their dogs and whips; pickpockets, which in an age are not heard of in any of our houses, repairing thither, and other disturbers of the public peace which dare not be seen in our civil and well-governed theatres, where none use to come but the best of the nobility and gentry.

The Actors Remonstrance, 1643

WOMEN ON THE STAGE

3 January 1661. To the Theatre, where was acted 'The Beggars' Bush' it being very well done; and here the first time that ever I saw women come upon the stage.   Samuel Pepys, *Diary*

THE STAGE MORE GLORIOUS . . .

Pepys tells us in 1667:

That the stage is now . . . more glorious than heretofore. Now, wax-candles, and many of them; then, not above 3 lbs. of tallow; now, all things civil, no rudeness anywhere; then, as in a bear-garden: then, two or three fiddlers; now, nine or ten of the best: then, nothing but rushes upon the ground and everything else mean; now, all otherwise.

THE BATH, OR THE WESTERN LASS

At the Theatre Royal in Drury-Lane, to-morrow being Tuesday the 8th of December, will be reviv'd a Comedy call'd,

The Bath, or, The Western Lass.

Made shorter, and intermix'd with Vocal Musick and Dancing, particularly a Song beginning, Let the dreadful Engines, &c. perform'd by Mr Leveridge; a comical Dialogue by him and Mrs Lindsey, beginning with

Since the Times are so bad, &c. Another perform'd by Mr Laroone and Mr Hughes, beginning Sing, Sing, all ye Muses. With another new Scotch Song by Mr Leveridge. And a new Prologue, All in Honour of the Officers of the Army and Fleet, and to Welcome them home from Flanders and Vigo. With Dancing between every Act by a Devonshire Girl never seen on the Stage before, who performs 1st, a genteel Ground to the Harp alone. 2d, An Irish Humour call'd, The Whip of Dunboyne with her Master. 3d, Another genteel Dance by her alone. 4th, A Highland Lilt with her Master. 5th, A Country Farmer's Daughter singly; and all in natural Habits. To begin exactly at Five a Clock. The Boxes 5 s. the Pit 3 s. the middle Gallery 2 s. the upper Gallery 1 s. 6 d.   *Daily Courant*, 7 December 1702

MUSIC

In the first part of the seventeenth century, England was unrivalled in music. Chappell could declare in *Old English Popular Music*:

> Not only was music a necessary qualification for ladies and gentlemen, but even the city of London advertised the musical abilities of boys educated in Bridewell and Christs' Hospital, as a mode of recommending them as servants, apprentices, or husbandmen. Tinkers sang catches; milkmaids sang ballads; carters whistled; each trade, and even the beggars, had their special songs; the bass-viol hung in the drawing-room for the amusement of waiting visitors; and the lute, cittern, and virginals, for the amusement of waiting customers, were the necessary furniture of the barber's shop. They had music at dinner; music at supper; music at weddings; music at funerals; music at night; music at dawn; music at work; and music at play.

Dr John Case said:

> Every troublesome and laborious occupation useth musicke for solace and recreation. . . . And hence it is that manual labourers, and mechanical artificers of all sorts keepe such a chaunting and singing in their shoppes – the tailor on his bulk – the shoemaker at his last – the mason at his wall – the ship-boy at his oar – the tinker at his pan – and the tiler on the housetop.

Reputable musicians of the day were Byrd, Morley, Gibbons, Tomkins; all really vocal composers, though also for harpsichord, organ, and viols. Kirbye and Wilbye produced secular madrigals; Dowland, Campion, Rosseter wrote some of the world's finest songs. John Bull excelled on the keyboard and, like Dowland, on the flute. William Lawes, a tempestuous figure, was also a fine musician in this age of music. Weelkes at Chichester devoted himself to sacred music.

Conditions for amateur music remained favourable in early Stuart days. John Robinson expresses this in *Observations*, 1625:

> A follower of a great lord was wont to say that he had in effect as much as his lord, though he were owner of little or nothing, considering how he had the

use of his lord's garden and galleries to walk in, heard his music with as many ears as he did, hunted with him in his parks, and ate and drank of the same as he did, though a little after him; and so for the most part of the delights which his lord enjoyed.

Thomas Mace, a great teacher of the lute and the viol, tells us of the enjoyment of chamber music, of the widespread popularity of the cittern, spinet, hapsichord and virginal. Matthew Locke produces operatic music and John Blow puts church music in high esteem again.

Henry Purcell is the supreme genius of this age – renowned for songs, odes, scenas, dance suites, church anthems and opera. His *Dido and Aeneas* with its masterly skill and in Robert Donington's words 'uncanny Englishness' won the admiration of Europe.

WHEN JAMES I DINED AT MERCHANT TAYLORS' HALL IN 1607

John Bull, Doctor of Music, one of the organists of His Majesty's Chapel-royal, and free of the Merchant-taylors, being in a citizen's gown, cap, and hood, played most excellent melody upon a small pair of organs, placed there for that purpose only.

JOHN DOWLAND, FAMOUS AS A LUTENIST, RECEIVED MANY OFFERS

When I came to the Duke of Brunswick he used me kindly and gave me a rich chain of gold, £23 in money, with velvet and satin and gold lace to make me apparel, with promise that if I would serve him he would give me as much as any prince in the world. From thence I went to the Lantgrave of Hessen, who gave me the greatest welcome that might be for one of my quality, who sent a ring into England to my wife, valued at £20 sterling, and gave me a great standing cup with a cover gilt, full of dollars, with many great offers for my service. From thence I had great desire to see Italy and came to Venice and from thence to Florence, where I played before the Duke and got great favours.

SONGS OF THE COUNTRY PEOPLE

PISCATOR   I pray, do·us a courtesy that shall stand you and your daughter in nothing, and yet we will think ourselves something in your debt. It is but to sing a song that was sung by your daughter when I last passed over this meadow, about eight or nine days since.

MILK-WOMAN   What song was it, pray? Was it 'Come Shepherds, deck your herds'? or 'As at noon Dulcina rested'? or 'Phillida flouts me'? or 'Chevy Chace'? or 'Johnny Armstrong'? or 'Troy Town'?

PISCATOR   No, it is none of those; it is a song that your daughter sung
              the first part, and you sung the answer to it.
MILK-WOMAN Come, Maudlin, sing the first part to the gentleman with
              a merry heart; and I'll sing the second when you have
              done.
So the song is sung: 'Come live with me and be my love.'
When it is finished, *Venator* says:
Trust me, master, it is a choice song, and sweetly sung by honest
Maudlin. I now see that it was not without cause that our good Queen
Elizabeth did so often wish herself a milkmaid all the month of May.

                               Izaak Walton, *Compleat Angler*, 1653

VIOLS OR VIOLINS?

Jan. 1657. The gentlemen in private meetings which A.W. frequented,
played three, four and five parts all with viols, as treble-viol, tenor,
counter-tenor and bass, with either an organ or virginal or harpsichord
joined with them: and they esteemed a violin to be an instrument only
belonging to a common fiddler, and could not endure that it should
come among them for fear of making their meetings seem to be vain
and fiddling. But before the restoration of King Charles II and
especially after, viols began to be out of fashion, and only violins used,
as treble-violin, tenor and bass-violin; and the King according to the
French mode would have 24 violins playing before him; while he was at
meals, as being more airy and brisk than viols.

    Life and Times of Anthony Wood, Antiquary of Oxford, 1632–1695,
                                          Described by Himself

PUBLIC CONCERTS

The first of those was in a lane behind Pauls, where there was a
chamber organ that one Phillips played upon, and some shop-keepers,
and foremen came weekly to sing in consort, and to hear and enjoy ale
and tobacco . . . and their music was chiefly out of Playford's Catch
book. (Catch that catch can, or a choice Collection of Catches, Rounds,
and Canons, for 3 or 4 Voices.)
    The next essay was of the elder Banister . . . he procured a large room
in Whitefriars near the Temple back gate, and made a large raised box
for the musicians, whose modesty required curtains. The room was
rounded with seats and small tables, alehouse fashion. One shilling was
the price, and call for what you pleased; there was very good music, for
Banister found means to procure the best hands in town and some
voices to come and perform there, and there wanted no variety of
humour, for Banister himself did wonders upon a flageolet to a thro'

bass, and the several masters had their solos. This continued full one
winter, and more I remember not.

Roger North, *Memoirs of Musick*

VIOLINS IN THE CHURCHES
21 December 1662. One of his Majesty's Chaplains preached, after
which, instead of the ancient, grave and solemn wind music accom-
panying the organ, was introduced a concert of 24 violins between
every pause, after the French fantastical light way, better suiting a
tavern or playhouse than a church. This was the first time of change,
and now we no more heard the cornet which gave life to the organ, that
instrument quite left off in which the English were so skilful. I dined at
Mr Povey's, where I talked with Cromer, a great musician.

John Evelyn, *Diary*

VIRGINALS
2 September 1666. Good hopes there was of stopping [the Fire] at the
Three Cranes above, and at Buttolph's Wharf below bridge; but the
wind carries it into the City. . . . River full of lighters and boats taking in
goods, and only I observed that hardly one lighter or boat in three that
had the goods of a house in, but there was a pair of Virginals in it.

Samuel Pepys, *Diary*

WIND-MUSIC
27 February 1668. [At a performance of *The Virgin Martyr*] ... But that
which did please me beyond anything in the whole world was the
wind-music when the angel comes down, which is so sweet that it
ravished me, and indeed, in a word, did wrap up my soul so that it made
me really sick, just as I have formerly been when in love with my wife;
that neither then, nor all the evening going home, and at home, I was
able to think of any thing, but remained all night transported, so as I
could not believe that any music hath that real command over the soul
of man as this did upon me: and makes me resolve to practise
wind-music, and to make my wife do the same.

Samuel Pepys, *Diary*

PSALM-TUNES
Let the parish clerk be taught to pulse or strike the common psalm-
tunes for a trifle 20 *s*., 30 *s*., or 40 *s*. per year. This will lead to business
for the clerk, for he will be so doted on by all the pretty ingenuous
children and young men of the parish that they will beg a shilling from
their parents for a lesson on how to pulse the psalm-tune, which they
may learn in a week or fortnight's time very well, and so in a short time

the parish will swarm with organists, and no parent will grutch [grudge] the money so given.

Thomas Mace, *Musick's Monument*, 1676

SHELTER YOUR LUTE

. . . how to shelter your lute in the worst weathers (which is moist) you shall do well, ever when you lay it by in the day-time, to put it into a Bed, that is constantly used, between the rug and the blanket; but never between the sheets, because they may be moist with sweat, etc. . . . only to be excepted, that no person be so inconsiderate, as to tumble down upon the bed whilst the lute is there; for I have known several good lutes spoiled with such a trick.

Thomas Mace, *Musick's Monument*, 1676

CHAMBER MUSIC

We had for our grave music, fancies of 3,4,5 and 6 parts to the organ; interposed (now and then) with some pavins, allmaines, solemn, and sweet delightful airs; all which were (as it were) so many pathetic stories, rhetorical, and sublime discourses; subtle, and acute argumentations; so suitable, and agreeing to the inward, secret and intellectual faculties of the soul and mind; that to set them forth according to their true praise, there are no words, sufficient in language; yet what I can best speak of them, shall be only to say, that they have been to my self (and many others) as divine raptures, powerfully captivating all our unruly faculties, and affections (for the time) and disposing us to solidity, gravity, and a good temper; making as capable of heavenly, and divine influences. . . .

And these things were performed, upon so many equal, and truly-sized viols; and so exactly strung, tuned and played upon, as no one part was any impediment to the other.

Thomas Mace, *Musick's Monument*, 1676

SINGING OF PSALMS

I shall not need to blazon it abroad in print, how miserably the prophet David's Psalms are (as I may say) tortured or tormented, and the Service of God dishonoured, made coarse, or ridiculous thereby: seeing the general outcries of most parochial churches in the nation are more than sufficient to declare and make manifest the same, so often as they make any attempt to sing at those Psalms. . . .

'Tis sad to hear what whining, yelling or screeching there is in many country congregations, as if the people were affrighted, or distracted.

Thomas Mace, *Musick's Monument*, 1676

HENRY PURCELL AND *AMPHITRYON*

What has been wanting on my part [in *Amphitryon*] has been abundantly supplied by the excellent composition of Mr Purcell; in whose person we have at length found an Englishman, equal with the best abroad. At least my opinion of him has been such, since his happy judicious performances in the late opera [*Dioclesian*]; and the experience I have had of him, in the setting my three songs for this *Amphitryon*.

John Dryden, in a letter prefixed to the published text of
Amphitryon, 1690

HENRY PURCELL

There is nothing better, than what I intended, but the Music; which has since arrived to a greater perfection in England, than ever formerly; especially passing through the artful hands of Mr Purcell, who has composed it with so great a genius, that he has nothing to fear but an ignorant, ill-judging audience.

John Dryden, *Preface to 'King Arthur'*, 1691

SEEKING ITALIAN ELEGANCE

Music is yet but in its nonage, a forward child, which gives hope of what it may be hereafter in England, when the masters of it shall find more encouragement. 'Tis now learning Italian, which is its best master, and studying a little of French air, to give it something more of gaiety and fashion. Thus being farther from the sun, we are of later growth than our neighbour countries and must be content to shake off our barbarity by degrees.

Henry Purcell

MR CLINCH, THE IMITATOR

An entertainment by Mr Clinch of Barnet, who imitates the flute, double curtel [type of bassoon], the organ with 3 voices, the horn, huntsman and pack of hounds, the sham-doctor, the old woman, the drunken-man, the bells: all instruments are performed by his natural voice. To which is added an Essex song by Mr Clinch himself. To be seen this present evening at 7 a clock, at the Queen's Arms Tavern on Ludgate-Hill. Price 1s.

Daily Courant, 2 January 1714

PAINTING

Painting now meant portraiture, the capturing of the likenesses of the Cavendish, Wriothesley, Spencer, Bentinck families. The taste of the connoisseur in the immediate circle of Charles I stirred interest in the arts of the Renaissance. The Grand Tour, that extension of a

gentleman's education, brought experience of European civilization.
The arrival of Anthony van Dyck in London in 1632 was the turning-
point in the development of the English portrait. The greatest of the
pupils of Rubens, van Dyck became a court painter of Charles I, and
some of his work ranks him with Titian and Velazquez. He was the new
phenomenon in English society. Soon he was followed by other
renowned painters – John Hoskins, William Dobson, John Greenhill,
Michael Wright. Samuel Cooper with vivid directness sets before us the
men and women and this lively age. Peter Lely, the leading fashionable
painter in the reign of Charles II, did not confine himself to one circle
of society. To him succeeded Godfrey Kneller, German-born, trained
in Holland and Italy. His style is swifter and leaner than Lely's, and his
men appear in close-fitting velvet coats.

The Dutchman Hendrick Danckerts is celebrated for his topographical prints and drawings. The Van de Veldes, father and son,
were the two most distinguished naval painters of the day, and did most
of their work in this country. Pride in possessions caused the move to
animal painting; Francis Barlow took delight in portraying wild and
domestic animals. William Faithorne was the first great master of line
engraving and raised it to its place in art in England. By 1700 engrav-
ings brought further knowledge of harmony, lights and shadows to a
widening number of people.

LIMNING, MINIATURE PAINTING
I wish it were so that none should meddle with limning but gentlemen
alone, for that it is a kind of gentle painting of less subjection than any
other; for one may leave when he will, his colours nor his work taketh
any harm by it. Moreover it is secret, a man may use it and scarcely be
perceived of his own folk; it is sweet and cleanly to use, and it is a thing
apart from all other painting or drawing, and tendeth not to common
men's use, either for furnishing of houses or any patterns for tap-
estries, or building, or any other work whatsoever, and yet it excelleth
all other painting whatsoever in sundry points, in giving the true lustre
to pearl and precious stone, and worketh the metals gold or silver with
themselves, which so enricheth and ennobleth the work that it seemeth
to be the thing itself.
    Nicholas Hilliard, *A Treatise Concerning the Arte of Limning,* 1624

A LETTER FROM RUBENS ON ENGLAND
If I were allowed to dispose of my affairs according to my wishes and to
arrange my occupation as I like, I should have come to you long ago, or
I should be with you now, but I do not know what spirit, whether good
or bad, is always disturbing my projects and drawing me in opposite

directions. My only pleasure is to see, during my pilgrimages, so many various countries, so many peoples following different customs. I am far from finding in this island the barbarous ways which its climate might warrant, since it is so different from gracious Italy, I must even confess that, from the point of view of painting, I have never seen such a quantity of pictures by great masters as in the Palace of the King of England and in the gallery of the late Duke of Buckingham. The Earl of Arundel possesses an enormous number of antique statues and of Greek and Latin inscriptions, which you have seen since they have been published by John Selden, with the learned commentaries which one might have expected from that talented and cultivated author. You have no doubt seen his treatise *De Diis Syris,* which has just been reprinted in a revised and enlarged edition. But I wish that he would confine himself to the bounds of science without mixing in political disorders, which have made him lose his liberty, with several other members of Parliament, who are accused of offending the King during the last session.

There are also here the 'Cavalier' Cotton, a great antiquarian, very remarkable for the variety of his knowledge, and the secret Boswell, and other people whom you must know perfectly and with whom you are no doubt in correspondence, as you are with all the distinguished men of the world.   Rubens to Peiresc, 1629

DEDICATED HIS BOOK TO LORD ARUNDEL

. . . to whose liberal charges and magnificence this corner of the world owed the first sight of Greek and Roman statues with whose admired presence he began to honour the gardens and galleries of Arundel House about twenty years ago (1614) and hath hitherto continued to transplant old Greece to England.

Henry Peacham, *Perfect Gentleman,* 1634

DOROTHY OSBORNE TO SIR WILLIAM TEMPLE
October 1653
. . . thinking of sending you my picture till I could come myself, but a picture is but dull company and that you need not; besides I cannot tell whether it be very like me or not, though 'tis the best I have ever had drawn for me, and Mr Lely will have it that he never took more pains to make a good one in his life, and that it was I think that spoiled it: he was condemned for making the first he drew for me a little worse than I, and in making this better he has made it unlike as the other. . . .

June 1654
I would have had [a picture] drawn since I came, and consulted my

glass every morning when to begin, and to speak freely to you that are my friend, I could never find my face in a condition to admit on it, and when I was not satisfied with it myself I had no reason to hope that any body else should; but I'm afraid as you say that time will not mend it and therefore you shall have it as it is, as soon as Mr Cooper will vouchsafe to take the pains to draw it for you.

COUNTESS OF SUSSEX RECEIVES THE PICTURE AT GORHAMBURY

Sweet Mr Verney, the picture came very well, many hearty thanks to you for it. The frame is a little hurt, the gilt being rubbed off. The picture is very ill favoured, makes me quite out of love with myself, the face is so big and so fat that it pleases me not at all. It looks like one of the winds puffing – but truly I think it is like the original. If ever I come to London before Sir Vandyck go, I will get him to mend my picture, for though I be ill favoured I think that makes me worse than I am.

F. P. Verney, *Memoirs of the Verney Family, c.* 1639

OLIVER CROMWELL

Mr Lilly, I desire you would use all your skill to paint my picture truly like me and not flatter me at all but [pointing to his own face] remark all these roughnesses, pimples, warts and everything as you see me; otherwise I will never pay a farthing for it.

Cromwell's own instructions to his painter; George Vertue, *Notebooks, c.* 1720

ART OF GRINLING GIBBONS

I went to Windsor, dining by the way at Chiswick, at Sir Stephen Fox's, where I found . . . Signor Verrio, who brought his draught and designs for the painting of the stair-case of Sir Stephen's new house. That which was new at Windsor since I was last there was the incomparable fresco in St George's Hall representing the legend of St George and Triumph of the Black Prince . . . I liked the contrivance of the unseen organ behind the altar, nor less the stupendous and beyond all description the incomparable carving of our Gibbons, who is, without controversy the greatest master, both for invention and rareness of work that the world ever had in any age.   John Evelyn, 16 June 1683

PICTURE OF AN OX

Owners of country estates now wanted portraits of their animals as well as of themselves. Francis Barlow is the earliest English animal painter, followed by John Wootton. Celia Fiennes drinking beer at Newby saw a huge canvas on the pantry wall.

... a fine place of Sir Edward Blackets [Newby Hall], it looks finely in the approach in the midst of a good park ... there are good stables and coach-house and all the offices are very convenient, very good cellars all arched and there I drank small beer four years old – not too stale very clear good beer well brewed. In the pantry hangs a picture of the dimensions of a large ox that was fed in these grounds with the account of its weight ... this gentleman breeds and feeds much cattle in his grounds and has one of the largest beeves in England.

Celia Fiennes, *Journeys,* 1697

ADVERTISEMENT, 1713

At the Eagle and Child in Bedford Street, Covent Garden, will be continued the Sale by Auction of a collection of Paintings, Drawings, and Prints, by the most famous Italian, and other great masters. The Drawings are of the most celebrated masters of the several Schools of Italy. A great number of them in frames and glasses. The Prints are in great perfection, a great many etched by the masters themselves, others graved by the most eminent gravers. There are a great many extraordinary rare Wood Cuts, they have been collecting these 30 years with great industry and expense, most out of the chiefest auctions in England, and others bought in Holland and France, by Mr William Gibson, Limner.

Sports and Pastimes

Sir Roger de Coverley, though benevolent, felt that he must speak of a man upon the road before him, 'he is a Yeoman of about an hundred Pounds a Year: He is just within the Game-Act, and qualified to kill an Hare or a Pheasant. . . . He would be a good Neighbour if he did not destroy so many partridges.' Sir Roger is hinting at the growing power of the squire in late Stuart times – who could now shoot, on his own land, game that wandered over it. The Game Law of 1671 prevented yeomen of under a hundred pounds a year from killing game at all. This preservation of game for the benefit of the wealthy came from the adoption of the shotgun. Hawking, once 'a most princely and serious delight', was giving way to shooting, and birds were more rapidly destroyed – especially as they were often targets on the ground.

Dogs were trained to point wild birds hidden in the grass, which were then netted. It was a trade in the fens to lure wild duck into a decoy upon the edge of the water. Grouse and blackcock were listed as game, bred for the shotgun.

Hunting with hounds was a favourite sport from early times. Stag hunting was the king of sports, but agricultural claims caused cries of indignation. William Harrison declaimed: 'Is hee a Christian that liveth to the hurte of his neighbour in treadinge and breaking downe his hedges, in casting open his gates, in tramplinge of his corne, and otherwise annoying him, as hunters doo?'

James I is believed to have hunted boars in Windsor Forest in 1617, and showed keen interest in 'three maner of courses with Greyhounds – at the Deare, at the Hare, and at the Foxe'. Of these, hare-coursing was always the most favoured form of the sport. It was only after the Restoration that foxhunting really became a serious rival. Robert Jennings in 1669 describes a hunt starting in Windsor Forest, 'ran the fox six miles, earthed him, dug him out, set him down in the middle of the Forest; he ran two hours and a half'. Izaak Walton speaks in gentle praise of angling: 'have the luck to hit also where there is store of Trouts, a dark day and a right wind, he will catch such store of them'.

120

Athletic sports were widely popular. Young men were trained to ride, hunt, shoot, fence, hawk. Activities included leaping, running, pitching bars, tossing the pike, quarter-staff, riding at the quintain, tossing the hammer. Wrestling flourished in Cornwall and Cumberland. Richard Carew wrote in 1602: 'You will hardly find an assembly of boys in Devon or Cornwall where the most untowardly among them will not as readily give you a muster (or tryal) of this exercise as you are prone to require it.' Which bears out what J. Misson says in his *Travels*: 'Anything that looks like fighting is delicious to an Englishman.' Pepys describes a foot-race, 'run this day on Banstead Downes between Lee, the Duke of Richmond's footman, and a tyler, a famous runner. And Lee hath beat him; though the King and Duke of York and all men almost did bet three or four to one upon the tyler's head'. Stretches of ice provided opportunity for sliding or skating on bone skates. Evelyn records 'the strange and wonderful dexterity of the sliders on the new canal in St James's Park, performed before their Majesties'.

'Beastely fury and extreme violence' were found in bear-baiting, bull-running, and cock-fighting. Football, though not so violent, was played roughly, without rules, in the open street. James I, in *Basilicon Doron*, said it was 'meeter for lameing than making able the users thereof'. Perhaps he was happier to think that he had brought south with him the Scottish game of golf.

It was the Stuart kings who established horse-racing in this country. James I built stables at Newmarket. His son increased the importance of public races, and in 1640 the first race-meeting was held at Newmarket. Charles II had his own course on Datchet Meads, near Windsor, and rode, successfully, in races himself. Pepys tells us, on 27 May 1663: 'This day there is a great throng to Banstead Downs upon a great horse-race and foot-race.' Queen Anne, the last of the Stuarts, founded the Ascot meeting.

GREAT GOLDEN PLAY

17 January 1603. The world hath not been altogether so dull and dead this Christmas as was suspected, but rather the Court hath flourished more than ordinary, whether it be that the new Comptroller, Sir Edward Wotton, hath put new life into it by his example (being always freshly attired and for the most part all in white, *cap à pied*), or that the humours of themselves grow more gallant: for besides much dancing, bear-baiting, and many plays, there hath been great golden play, wherein Master Secretary, Sir Robert Cecil, lost better than £800 in one night and as much more at other times, the greatest part whereof came to Edward Stanley's and Sir John Lee's share.

John Chamberlain, *Letters, 1597–1626*

DANCES IN JOHN PLAYFORD'S *ENGLISH DANCING MASTER* INCLUDE:

An Old Man is a Bed full of Bones, Cheerily and Merrily, Friar and the Nun, Petticoat Wag, Whirligig, Lady Carey's Dompe, Flaunting Two, Mopsy's Tune, the Bishop of Chester's Jig, Farnaby's Woodycock, Dusty My Dear.

Scottish Dances:
All Christien Men Dance, Long Flat Foot of Garioch, The Lamb's Wind, Shake-a-Trot, The Alman Hey, Rank at the Root.

DUELLING

It is reputed so great a shame to be accounted a liar, that any other injury is cancelled by giving the lie; and he that receiveth it standeth so charged in his honour and reputation, that he cannot disburden himself of that imputation, but by striking of him that hath so given it, or by challenging him the combat.

Lodowick Bryskett, *A Discourse of Civill Life,* 1606

DUEL BETWEEN SIR GEORGE WHARTON AND SIR JAMES STEWART, COURTIERS AND FAVOURITES OF JAMES I, 1609

These two men hated each other, and 'reproachful words passed betwixt them'. Wharton was ready to fight and Stewart replied to the challenge:

Sir: Your message either being ill-delivered, or else not accepted, you have since, though ill-advised, retracted, and have repented it; for your messenger willed me from you, that either of us should make choice of a friend to debate the matter. To which I confess I did but lightly hearken, since I knew some odds which no breath could make even. And now you have to acknowledge no other speeches than you charged me with, which is, that I said you durst not meet me in the field to fight. True it is, your barbarous and uncivil insolence in such a place, and before such a company (for whose respect I am only sorry for what I then did or said), made me do and say that which I now will make good. Wherein, since you find yourself behind, I am ready to do you all the right you can expect. And to that end have I sent you the length of my rapier, which I will use with a dagger, and so meet you at the farther end of Islington (as I understand nearer you than me) at three of the clock in the afternoon; which things I scorn to take as advantages, but as my due, and which I have made indifferent. And in respect I cannot send any of my friends without great hazard of discovery, I have sent my servant, herewith who is only acquainted with this business.

James Stuarte [*sic*].

John Nichols describes the duel in his History of Canonbury:
> Seven thrusts in turn these gallants had
> Before one drop of blood was drawn,
> The Scottish Knight then valiant spoke –
> 'Stout Wharton, still thou hold'st thy own.'
> With the next thrust that Wharton thrust
> He ran him through the shoulder-bone.
> The next was through the thick o' thigh.
> They made a deadly desperate close,
> And both fell dead upon the ground.
> Our English Knight was the first that fell –
> The Scotch Knight fell immediately,
> Who cried out both to Jesus Christ,
> 'Receive our Souls, Oh Lord, we die!
> God bless our noble King and Queen,
> And all the noble progeny!'

THE CRY OF HOUNDS

If you would have your kennel for depth of mouth, then you shall compound it of the largest dogs, which have the greatest mouths and deepest flews, such as your west-country Cheshire and Lancashire dogs are, and to five or six couple of bass mouths you shall not add above two couple of counter-tenors, as many means, and not above one couple roarers, which being heard but now and then, as at the opening or hitting of a scent, will give much sweetness to the solemnness and graveness of the cry, and the music thereof will be much more delightful to the ears of every beholder.

Gervase Markham, *Countrey Contentments,* 1611

DUEL BETWEEN THE EARL OF DORSET AND LORD BRUCE

They 'departed the realm in order to fight', and met at Bergen-op-Zoom, near Antwerp, in 1613.

The Earl of Dorset describes the duel:

I made a thrust at my enemy, but was short, and in drawing back my arm I received a great wound thereon, which I interpreted as a reward for my short shooting; but in revenge, I pressed into him, though I then missed him also; and then received a wound in my right pap, which passed level through my body and almost to my back. And there we wrestled for the two greatest and dearest prizes we could ever expect trial for – honour and life; in which struggling, my hand, having but an ordinary glove on it, lost one of her servants, though the meanest, which hung by a skin, and to sight yet remaineth as before, and I am put in hope one day to recover the use of it again. But at last breathless, yet keeping our holds, there past on both sides propositions of quitting each other's swords; but when amity was dead, confidence could not live, and who should quit first was the question, which on neither part either would perform; and restriving afresh, with a kick and a wrench together I freed my long-captive weapon, which incontinently levying at his throat, being master still of his, I demanded if he would ask his life or yield his sword? Both which, though in that imminent danger, he bravely denied to do. Myself being wounded, and feeling loss of blood, having three conduits running on me, began to make me faint, and he courageously persisting not to accord to either of my propositions, remembrance of his former bloody desire, and feeling of my present estate, I struck at his heart, but with his avoiding, missed my aim, yet passed through his body, and drawing back my sword, repassed through again, through another place, when he cried: 'Oh! I am slain,' seconding his speech with all the force he had to cast me: but being too weak, after I had defended his assault, I easily became master of him, laying him on his back, when, being upon him, I redemanded if he would request his life? But it seems he prized it not at so dear a rate to be beholding for it, bravely replying he scorned it, which answer of his was so noble and worthy, as I protest, I could not find in my heart to offer him any more violence, only keeping him down; till at length, his surgeon, afar off, cried out he would immediately die if his wounds were not stopped: whereupon I asked if he desired his surgeon should come? which he accepted of; and so, being drawn away, I never offered to take his sword, accounting it inhumane to rob a dead man, for so I held him to be. This thus ended, I retired to my surgeon, in whose arms after I had remained awhile, for want of blood I lost my sight, and withal, as I then thought, my life also; but strong water and his diligence, quickly recovered me; when I escaped a great danger, for my Lord's surgeon, when nobody dreamt of it, came full at me with my Lord's sword; and had not mine, with my sword, interposed himself, I had been slain by those base hands, although my Lord Bruce, weltering in his blood, and past all expectation of life, conformable to all his former carriage, which was undoubtedly noble, cried out: 'Rascal, hold thy hand!'

POINT OF PLEASURES

It is a singularity in the nature of the English, that they are strangely addicted to all kinds of pleasure above all other nations. This of old was justly attributed to idleness, when the multitude of monasteries and the great trains and large house-keepings of lords and gentlemen were nurseries of thieves and idle persons, so as we were served for the most part by strangers in all manual trades. But since the putting down of monasteries and of those great trains and large house-keepings – howsoever I cannot deny that, out of this natural addiction to pleasure (or idleness if you will so call it) and out of natural boldness less to fear death than want, more persons are executed in England for stealing and robberies by the highway, than in many vast kingdoms abroad – yet do not these offences so much abound as in those former times, and for manual trades, we are now almost altogether served by natives, who for necessity to eat their own bread, are in good measure grown industrious artisans. But for the point of pleasures, the English, from the lords to very husbandmen, have generally more fair and more large gardens and orchards than any other nation. All cities, towns, and villages swarm with companies of musicians and fiddlers, which are rare in other kingdoms. The city of London alone hath four or five companies of players with their peculiar theatres capable of many thousands, wherein they play every day in the week but Sunday, with most strange concourse of people, besides many strange toys and fancies exposed by signs to be seen in private houses, to which and to many musterings and other frequent spectacles, the people flock in great numbers. . . . As there be, in my opinion, more plays in London than in all the parts of the world I have seen, so do these players or comedians excel all other in the world. . . . Not to speak of frequent spectacles in London exhibited to the people by fencers, by walkers on ropes, and like men of activity, nor of frequent companies of archers shooting in all the fields, nor of Saints' days, which the people not keeping (at least most of them, or with any devotion) for church service, yet keep for recreation of walking and gaming.

What shall I say of dancing with curious and rural music, frequently used by the better sort, and upon all holidays, by country people dancing about the maypoles with bagpipes or other fiddlers, besides the jollities of certain seasons of the year, of setting up maypoles, dancing the Morris with hobby horses, bringing home the lady of the harvest, and like plebeian sports, in all which vanities no nation cometh anything near the English. What shall I say of playing at cards and dice, frequently used by all sorts, rather as a trade than as recreation, for which all strangers much blame us.

As the English are by nature amorous, so do they above other nations assert and follow the pleasant study of poetry, and therein have in good measure attained excellency.

To conclude with hawking and hunting. No nation so frequently useth these sports as the English. No nation of greater compass, alloweth such great proportions of lands for parks to impale fallow and red deer. And as England hath plenty of red deer, so I will boldly say that it, perhaps one shire of it, hath more fallow deer than all the continent of the world that I have seen. . . .

No nation followeth these pastimes and exercises on horseback and on foot, so frequently and painfully in any measure of comparison. England yields excellent sparrow hawks, and Ireland hawks of divers kinds; but especially goshawks, and gentlemen with great charge procure plenty of the best hawks from foreign parts.

Not only gentlemen, but yeomen frequently hunt the hare, not only with greyhounds, but hounds in keeping whereof for that purpose divers yeomen join together. . . .

And for all these sports and other uses, England hath without comparison greater number and better dogs than any other nation, as mastiffs for keeping the house, rough water dogs for the duck, greyhounds for the hare, divers kinds of hounds for all huntings and spaniels for hawking, and bloodhounds to track stolen deer or other things, and little dogs for women's pleasure, and all these beautiful and good, and some most rare.   Fynes Moryson, *Itinerary,* 1617

CLASHING OF SWORDS

Englishmen, especially being young and unexperienced, are apt to take all things in snuff [to take offence]. Of old, when they were fenced with bucklers, as with a rampier [rampart], nothing was more common with them, than to fight about taking the right or left hand, or the wall, or upon any unpleasing countenance. Clashing of swords was then daily music in every street, and they did not only fight combats, but cared not to set upon their enemy upon advantages and unequal terms. But at this day when no nation labours more than the English (as well by travelling into foreign kingdoms, as by the study of good letters, and by other means) to enrich their minds with all virtues, I say in these days, they scorn such men, and esteem them of an idle brain who for ridiculous or trifling causes run the trial of single fight, and howsoever they behave themselves stoutly therein, yet they repute them to have lost as much opinion of wisdom, as they gained of daring. Much more do they despise them who quarrel and fight in the streets publicly, and do not rather make private trial of their difference, as also those who make quarrels with men of base condition, yea they think them infamous who with disparity of number do many assail one man, and for this beastly quality, comparing them to hogs, whereof, when one grunts, all the herd comes to help him, they think them worthy of any punishment: besides that upon killing any man mercy is seldom or never shewed them, howsoever in other fair combats the prince's mercy hath many times given life to the man-slayer. And the cause why single fights are more rare in England in these times is the dangerous fight at single rapier, together with the confiscation of man-slayer's goods. So as I am of opinion, contrary to the vulgar, and think them worthy of praise who invented dangerous weapons, as rapiers, pistols, guns, and gunpowder, since the invention whereof much smaller number of men hath perished by single fights or open war than in former times. . . .

I return to the purpose, and do freely profess, that in case of single fights in England, the magistrate doth favour a wronged stranger more than one of the same nation, howsoever the law favours neither, and that a stranger, so fighting, need fear no treason by any disparity or otherwise. But in the mean time, here and in all places happy are the peaceable. Let me add one thing of corrupt custom in England, that those who are not grown men, never have the opinion of valour, till in their youth they have gained it with some single fight, which done, they shall after live more free from quarrels: but it were to be wished that a better way were found to preserve reputation than this of single fights, as well contrary to the law of God, as a capital crime by the laws of men.

Fynes Moryson, Itinerary, 1617

A FOOTRACE

10 April 1618. On Wednesday a race of two footmen from St Albans to Clerkenwell, the one an Englishman belonging lately to the Countess of Bedford but now to the King, the other an Irish youth, who lost the day and I know not how much money laid on his head. The sums no doubt were very great, when the Lord of Buckingham for his part went away with £3000, and it is said for certain there was more than twice as much won and lost that day. The Irish youth serves a younger son of the Lord Treasurer, and the general opinion is that if the race had been shorter and the weather and the ways not so extreme foul, our man had been put to the worse, though he had made good proof of himself heretofore and is a very lusty, able fellow, but carried it now by main strength, so that the other gives over twixt this and Highgate when he was not twice his length behind him. . . . All the Court in a manner, Lords and Ladies (some further off, some nearer), went to see this race, and the King himself almost as far as Barnet. It is verily thought there was as many people as at the King's first coming to London. And for the courtiers on horseback, they were so pitifully berayed and bedaubed all over that they could scant be known one from another.

John Chamberlain, Letters, 1597–1626

AT A SOLEMN DANCING

The Court of England has much altered. At a Solemn dancing, first you have the grave measures, then the corantos and the galliards, and all this is kept up with ceremony, at length they fall to trenchmore, and so to the cushion dance, lord and groom, lady and kitchen maid, no distinction: so in our Court. In Queen Elizabeth's time, gravity and state were kept up. In King James time things were pretty well. But in King Charles time there has been nothing but trenchmore and the cushion dance, Omnium gatherum, tolly polly, hoyte come toyte.

John Selden, *Table Talk*, 1634–1654

A COCK-FIGHT

At Stanwick, my son had going with his hens a young cock of a stout and large breed, with very large jollops hanging down on either side of his beak. And a friend of his giving him afterwards a cock and a hen of the game, as they call them (cockscomb and jollops being finely cut off, close to the head, for the advantage of fighting) it fell out that the two cocks, meeting in the yard together, fell close to their fight; where the younger cock fought stoutly a good while, till the old cock, taking advantage of his large jollops hanging so low, took hold thereof, for raising himself to wound the young cock at every blow: which being observed by the spectators, they parted the fray for the present, and caused the young cock's pendant jollops to be cut off, and his head trimmed for the fight, as the old cock's was, who had at first so beaten the young cock, that he durst not stay within his view. But after the sores of the jollops' cut were healed, the young cock coming abroad again, the old cock ran presently upon him to have made him run away as he was wont to do before. But the young cock turning again, and they falling to a new fight, very sharp and eager on both sides, at last the old cock finding his old hold of the young cock's jollops taken away from him, was fain to cry creak, and to run away as fast from the young cock, as the young cock did from him before; and ever after the young cock was master of the field.

R. Willis, *Mount Tabor*, 1639

HORSE RACING

1639. My Lord Carlisle's white nag hath beaten Dandy, and Sprat won the cup, and Cricket the plate; and which you will most wonder at the Weaver hath beaten the Shepherd shamefully, and offers to run the same number of miles for £500 with the Shepherd, and be tied to hop the last 12 score yards. My Lord of Salisbury's horse Cricket was matched with Banister's bold horse for £1000 a horse and £200 forfeiture – they are to run the four miles at Newmarket – they would never run for so much money unless they certainly know Banister's horse to be sound.

Ralph Verney to his brother Henry at the Hague

ANGLING AN ART
O Sir, doubt not but that angling is an art. Is it not an art to deceive a trout with an artificial fly? a trout that is more sharp-sighted than any hawk you have named, and more watchful and timorous than your high-mettled merlin is bold! and yet I doubt not to catch a brace or two tomorrow for a friend's breakfast. Doubt not, therefore, sir, but that angling is an art, and an art worth learning; the question is rather, whether you be capable of learning it? for angling is somewhat like poetry, men are to be born so – I mean with inclination to it, though both may be heightened by discourse and practice; but he that hopes to be a good angler must not only bring an inquiring, searching, observing wit, but he must bring a large measure of hope and patience, and a love and propensity to the art itself; but having once got and practised it, then doubt not but angling will prove to be so pleasant that it will prove to be like virtue, a reward to itself.

Izaak Walton, *The Compleat Angler*, 1653

MAY DAY OBSERVED
Hyde Park, May 1st, 1654. – This day there was a hurling of a great ball by fifty Cornish gentlemen of one side, and fifty on the other; one party played in red caps, and the other in white. There was present his highness the lord-protector, many of his privy council, and divers eminent gentlemen, to whose view was presented great agility of body, and most neat and exquisite wrestling, at every meeting of one with the other, which was ordered with such dexterity, that it was to show more the strength, vigour, and nimbleness of their bodies than to endanger their persons. The ball they played withal was silver, and designed for that party which did win the goal.

   Monday, 1st May. – This day was more observed by people going a-maying than for divers years past; and, indeed, much sin committed by wicked meetings with fiddlers, drunkenness, ribaldry, and the like; great resort came to Hyde Park, many hundreds of coaches, and gallants in attire, but most shameful powdered-hair men, and painted and spotted women. Some men played with a silver ball, and some took other recreation. But his highness the lord-protector went not thither, nor any of the lords of the Commonwealth, but were busy about the great affairs of the Commonwealth.   *Moderate Intelligencer*

TURK, THE ROPE-DANCER
15 September 1657. – We stept in to see a famous rope-dancer, called the *Turk*. I saw even to astonishment the agility with which he performed. He walked barefooted, taking hold by his toes only of a rope almost perpendicular, and without so much as touching it with his

hands. He danced blindfold on the high rope, and with a boy of twelve years old tied to one of his feet about twenty feet beneath him, dangling as he danced, yet he moved as nimbly as if it had been but a feather. Lastly, he stood on his head, on the top of a very high mast, danced on a small rope that was very slack, and finally flew down the perpendicular, on his breast, his head foremost, his legs and arms extended, with divers other activities.   John Evelyn, *Diary*

HOW TO CATCH A PARTRIDGE
Partridge love deer exceedingly and are cozened by their skin. Thus, if a man put on a deer's skin, and the horns upon his head, and come closely to them, they supposing it is a deer indeed, will entertain him and draw near to him and will not fly away, and embrace him as much as one would do a friend come from a long journey; but by this great friendliness they get nothing but nets and snares.
                J. B. Porta, *The Fifteenth Book of Natural Magic*, 1658

THE YACHT COMES TO ENGLAND
1 October 1661. I sailed this morning with his Majesty in one of his yachts (or pleasure boats), vessels not known among us till the Dutch East India Company presented that curious piece to the King.
                                   John Evelyn, *Diary*

GAMES AND AMUSEMENTS
1. *Tennis*
   1664, January 4. – To the Tennis Court, and there saw the King play at Tennis and others: but to see how the King's play was extolled, without any cause at all, was a loathsome sight, though sometimes, indeed, he did play very well, and deserved to be commended; but such open flattery is beastly.

2. *Cock-Fighting*
   1663, December 21. – To Shoe Lane to see a cock-fighting at a new pit there, a spot I was never at in my life: but, Lord! to see the strange variety of people, from Parliament man, by name Wildes, that was Deputy Governor of the Tower when Robinson was Lord Mayor, to the poorest 'prentices, bakers, brewers, butchers, draymen, and what not; and all these fellows one with another cursing and betting. I soon had enough of it. It is strange to see how people of this poor rank, that look as if they had not bread to put in their mouths, shall bet three or four pounds at a time and lose it, and yet bet as much the next battle; so that one of them will lose 10 or 20 pounds at a meeting.

3. Fencing

1663, June 1. – I with Sir J. Minnes to the Strand May-pole; and there light out of his coach, and walked to the New Theatre, which, since the King's players are gone to the Royal one, is this day begun to be employed by the fencers to play prizes at. And here I come and saw the first prize I ever saw in my life: and it was between one Mathews, who did beat at all weapons, and one Westwicke, who was soundly cut several times both in the head and legs, that he was all over blood: and other deadly blows they did give and take in very good earnest, till Westwicke was in a sad pickle. They fought at eight weapons, three bouts at each weapon. This being upon a private quarrel, they did it in good earnest; and I felt one of their swords, and found it to be very little, if at all, blunter on the edge than the common swords are. Strange to see what a deal of money is flung to them both upon stage between every bout. Samuel Pepys, *Diary*

RACING AT NEWMARKET

1671, *October* 9. – I went, after evening-service, to London, in order to a journey of refreshment with Mr Treasurer, to Newmarket, where the King then was, in his coach with 6 brave horses, which we changed thrice, first, at Bishop Stortford and last, at Chesterford; so, by night, we got to Newmarket, where Mr Henry Jermain (nephew to the Earl St Alban's) lodged me very civilly. We proceeded immediately to Court, the King and all the English gallants being there at their autumnal sports. Supped at the Lord Chamberlain's; and, the next day, after dinner, I was on the heath, where I saw the great match run between Woodcock and Flatfoot, belonging to the King, and to Mr Eliot of the Bedchamber, many thousands being spectators; a more signal race had not been run for many years.

October 16*th*. – Came all the great men from Newmarket. . . . In the morning, we went hunting and hawking; in the afternoon, till almost morning, to cards and dice, yet I must say without noise, swearing, quarrel, or confusion of any sort. I, who was no gamester, had often discourse with The French Ambassador, Colbert, and went sometimes abroad on horseback with the ladies to take the air, and now and then to hunting. John Evelyn, *Diary*

RICHARDSON, THE FIRE-EATER

8 October 1672. – I took leave of my Lady Sunderland, who was going to Paris to my Lord, now Ambassador there. She made me stay dinner at Leicester House, and afterwards sent for Richardson the famous Fire-eater. He devoured brimstone on glowing coals before us,

chewing and swallowing them. He melted a beerglass and eat it quite up. Then taking a live coal on his tongue, he put on it a raw oyster, the coal was blown on with bellows till it flamed and sparkled in his mouth, and so remained till the oyster gaped and was quite boiled. Then he melted pitch and wax with sulphur, which he drank down as it flamed, I saw it flaming in his mouth a good while. He also took up a thick piece of iron, such as laundresses use to put in their smoothing-boxes, when it was fiery hot, held it between his teeth, then in his hand, and threw it about like a stone. But this I observed he cared not to hold very long. Then he stood on a small pot, and bending his body took a glowing iron with his mouth from between his feet, without touching the pot or ground with his hands.   John Evelyn, *Diary*

ALL MANNER OF GAMES
The Compleate Gamster, *published in 1674, gives:*
Instructions How to play at Billiards, Trucks, Bowls, and Chess. Together with all manner of usual and most gentile games either on cards or dice. To which is added The Arts and Mysteries of Riding, Racing, Archery, and Cock-Fighting.

Billiards from Spain at first derived its name,
Both an ingenious, and a cleanly game.
One gamester leads (the table green as grass)
And each like warriors strive to gain the pass.

Next here are Hazzards played the other way,
By box and dice; tis Hazzard in the play.

Not t' Irish, or Back-Gammoners we come,
Who wish their money, with their men safe home;
By topping, knapping, and foul play some win;
But those are losers, who so gain by sin.

After these three the Cock-pit claims a name;
A sport gentile, and called a Royal Game.
Now see the gallants crowd about the pit,
And most are stocked with money more than wit;
Else sure they would not, with so great a stir,
Lay ten to one on a cock's faithless spur.

Lastly, observe the women with what grace
They sit, and look their partners in the face.
The women knew their game, then cried, enough,
Let's leave off Whist, and go to Putt, or Ruff.

Ruff and Honours (alias Slamm) and Whist are games so commonly known in England in all parts thereof, that every child of almost eight years old hath a competent knowledge in that recreation.

And Putt is the ordinary rooking [cheating] game of every place, and seems by the few cards that are dealt to have no great difficulty in the play, but I am sure there is much craft and cunning in it.

Charles Cotton, *The Compleate Gamster*, 1674

SPORTS AND RECREATIONS

For variety of divertisements, sports and recreations no nation doth excel the English⸗ [After mentioning the hunting, hawking, horse-racing, bowls, tennis and many other recreations of the nobility.] . . . The citizens and peasants have hard-ball, football, skittles or nine-pins, shovel-board, stowball, goffe, trol-madam, cudgels, bear-baiting, bull-baiting, bow and arrow, throwing at cocks, shuttle-cock, bowling, quoits, leaping, wrestling, pitching the bar, and ringing the bells, a recreation used in no other country of the world.

Edward Chamberlayne, *Angliae Notitia, or The Present State of England,* 1676

HURLING

There are two kinds of hurling, the in-hurling and the out-hurling. In the first there are chosen 20 or 25 of a side, and two goals are set up; then comes one with a small hard leather ball in his hand; and tosses it up in the midst between both parties; he that catches it endeavours to run with it to the furthermost goal; if he be stopped by one of the opposite side, he either saith I will stand, and wrestles with him, letting fall the ball by him (which one of the opposite side must not take up, but one of his own) or else throws away the ball to one of his own side (if any of them can catch it). He that is stopped may chose whether he may wrestle, or throw away the ball; but it is more generous to wrestle. He that stops must answer, and wrestle it out. When any one wrestles, one of his side takes up the ball, and runs with it towards the goal, till he be stopped, and then, as before, he either wrestles or throws away the ball, so that there are commonly many pairs wrestling. An out-hurling is played by one parish against another, or eastern men against western, or Devonshire men against Cornish; the manner they enter upon it is as follows:— Any one that can get leave of a justice, etc., goes into a market town, with a little wooden ball in his hand, plated over with silver, and there proclaims the hurling, and mentions the time and place. They play in the same manner as in the other, only they make the churches their goals, that party which can cast the ball into, or upon a church, wins.

John Ray, *Itineraries, c.* 1700

ROPE-DANCERS UNPARALLIZED

At the Great Booth over against the *Hospital* Gate in *Bartholomew* Fair, will be seen the Famous Company of Rope-Dancers, they being the greatest performers of Man, Women and Children that can be found beyond the Seas, so that the World cannot parallize them for dancing on the Low-Rope, Vaulting on the High-Rope, and for walking on the slack, and Sloping Ropes, out-doing all others to that Degree, that it has highly recommended them, both in *Bartholomew* Fair and *May* Fair last, to all the best persons of Quality in *England*. And by all are owned to be the only amazing Wonders of the World, in every thing they do: 'tis there you will see the *Italian* Scarramouch dancing on the Rope, with a Wheel-Barrow before him, with two Children and a Dog in it, and with a Duck on his Head; who sings to the Company and causes much Laughter. The whole Entertainment will be so extremely Fine and Diverting, as never was done by any but this Company alone.

Daily Courant, 21 August 1702

TRULY ENGLISH SPORT

June 23, 1710: Towards evening we drove to see the bull-baiting, which is held here nearly every Monday in two places. On the morning of the day the bull, or any other creature that is to be baited, is led round. It takes place in a large open space or courtyard, on two sides of which high benches have been made for the spectators. First a young ox or bull was led in and fastened by a long rope to an iron ring in the middle of the yard; then about thirty dogs, two or three at a time, were let loose on him, but he made short work of them, goring them and tossing them high in the air above the height of the first storey. Then amid shouts and yells the butchers to whom the dogs belonged sprang forward and caught their beasts right side up to break their fall. They had to keep fast hold of the dogs to hinder them from returning to the attack without barking. Several had such a grip of the bull's throat or ear that their mouths had to be forced open with poles. When the bull had stood it tolerably long, they brought out a small bear and tied him up in the same fashion. As soon as the dogs had at him, he stood up on his hind legs and gave some terrific buffets; but if one of them got at his skin, he rolled about in such a fashion that the dogs thought themselves lucky if they came out safe from beneath him. But the most diverting and worst of all was a common little ass, who was brought out saddled with an ape on his back. As soon as a couple of dogs had been let loose on him, he broke into a prodigious gallop—for he was free, not having been tied up like the other beasts—and he stamped and bit all round himself. The ape began to scream most terribly for fear of falling off. If the dogs came too near him, he seized them with his mouth and twirled them round, shaking them so much that they howled prodigiously. Finally another bull appeared, on whom several crackers had been hung: when these were lit and several dogs let loose on him on a sudden, there was a monstrous hurly-burly. And thus was concluded this truly English sport, which vastly delights this nation but to me seemed nothing very special.   Zacharius von Uffenbach

DUEL BETWEEN LORD MOHUN AND THE DUKE OF HAMILTON IN 1712

Jonathan Swift describes the encounter the same day in a letter to Mrs Dingley.
Before this comes to your hands, you will have heard of the most terrible accident that hath almost ever happened. This morning, at eight, my man brought me word that Duke Hamilton had fought with Lord Mohun, and had killed him, and was brought home wounded. I immediately sent him to the Duke's house to know if it was so, but the porter could hardly answer his inquiries, and a great rabble was about the house. In short, they fought at seven this morning. The dog Mohun was killed on the spot, but while the Duke was over him, Mohun shortened his sword, and stabbed him in the shoulder to the heart. The Duke was helped towards the lake-house, by the ring, in Hyde Park (where they fought), and died on the grass, before he could reach his house, and was brought home in his coach by eight, while the poor Duchess was asleep. Maccartney and one Hamilton were the seconds, who fought likewise, and both are fled. I am told that a footman of Lord Mohun's stabbed Duke Hamilton, and some say Maccartney did too. Mohun gave the affront, and yet sent the challenge. I am infinitely concerned for the poor Duke, who was a frank, honest, and good natured man, They carried the poor Duchess to a lodging in the neighbourhood where I have been with her two hours, and am just come away. I never saw so melancholy a scene, for indeed all reasons for real grief belong to her; nor is it possible for anyone to be a greater loser in all regards – she has moved my very soul. The lodging was inconvenient, and they would have moved her to another, but I would not suffer it, because it had no room backwards, and she must have been tortured with the noise of the Grub Street screamers dinging her husband's murder in her ears.

Health

William Harvey expounded his theory of the circulation of the blood to the College of Physicians in 1616. He was a Fellow of the Royal College of Physicians, and became Physician-Extraordinary to James I in 1618. Physician to Charles I, he was with him at the battle of Edgehill, 1642. The Royal College of Physicians had many activities, and one of these was the harrying of Quacks. What John Halle, a practising surgeon in Maidstone, wrote in 1565, applied to the seventeenth century:

> Whereas there is one Surgeon that was apprenticed to his Art, and one Physician that has travelled in the time study and exercise of Physic, there are ten that are presumptuous smearers, smatterers and abusers of the same; yea, smiths, cutlers, carters, cobblers, coopers, carriers of leather, carpenters, and a great rabble of women. . . . Alas, there are goodly orders taken, and profitable laws made, for making cloth, tanning of leather, making shoes and other external things, but not for making Surgeons.

Many Apprentices could only 'poule or shave, draw a tooth or dress a broken pate'.

The Great Plague was not the only bad one of the seventeenth century. Insanitary houses and streets spread disease. This gave quack doctors their opportunity. An anonymous publication, *The Anatomies of the True Physician and Counterfeit Mountebank*, 1605, vividly portrays the Quacks:

> Runagate Jews, the cut-throats and robbers of Christians, slow-bellied monks who had made their escape from their cloisters, Simoniacal and perjured shavelings, busy St John-lack-Latins, thrasonical and unlettered chemists, shifting and outcast pettifoggers, light-headed and trivial druggers and apothecaries, sun-shunning night-birds and corner creepers, dull-pated and base mechanics, stage players, jugglers, pedlars, prittle-prattling barbers, filthy graziers, curious bath-keepers, common shifters and cogging cavaliers, bragging soldiers, lazy clowns, one-eyed and lamed fencers, toothless and tattling old wives, chattering charwomen and nurse-keepers, 'scape-Tyburns, dog-leeches and suchlike baggage. In the next rank, to second this goodly troupe, fellow poisoners, enchanters, wizards, fortune tellers, magicians, witches and hags.

136

Hannah Woolley at this time had a remedy for the 'Gravel': 'well-powdered roe of a red herring beaten to powder and taken in a glass of Rhine wine'. Another quack, calling herself Agnodice, had an office at the 'Hand and Urinal' producing a Handbill – 'if Venus should misfortunately be wounded with Scorponious poison by tampering with fiery Mars . . . it is then she brings comfort and by her antidotes expels the poison Jovelike'. Agnodice also offered an Italian wash for skin blemishes, and a Spanish Roll for concealing pock marks. Lady Anne Clifford treated her child for convulsions with 'a salt powder to put in her beer'. Charles II in his last hours had to undergo bleeding and cupping. The current prescriptions – 'snail water, the hiera picra, the mithridates, orbiculi, Bezoartis' – would have been of no avail.

THE FOUR HUMOURS

The four humours of the body – blood, phlegm, choler, and melancholy – kept in perfect balance, meant good health. Poynter and Bishop in A Seventeenth Century Doctor *said:*
To draw off the 'superfluous humours' before they could give rise to overt disease was a logical extension of the accepted doctrine, and it was this idea which lay at the back of therapeutic measures like blood-letting.

THE PLAGUE
The purple whip of vengeance, the plague, having beaten many thousands of men, women, and children to death, and still marking the people of this city every week by hundreds for the grave, is the only cause that all her inhabitants walk up and down like mourners at some great solemn funeral, the City herself being the chief mourners. The poison of this lingering infection strikes so deep into all men's hearts that their cheeks, like cowardly soldiers, have lost their colours; their eyes, as if they were in debt and durst not long abroad, do scarce peep out of their heads; and their tongues, like physicians ill-paid, give but cold comfort. By the power of their pestilent charms all merry meetings are cut off, all frolic assemblies dissolved, and in their circles are raised up the black, sullen, and dogged spirits of sadness, of melancholy, and so, consequently, of mischief. Mirth is departed and lies dead and buried in men's bosoms; laughter dares not look a man in the face; jests are, like music to the deaf, not regarded; pleasure itself finds now no pleasure but in sighing and bewailing the miseries of the time. For, alack! What string is there now to be played upon whose touch can make us merry? Playhouses stand like taverns that have cast out their masters, the doors locked up, the flags, like their bushes [ivy-bush outside a tavern], taken down – or rather like houses lately infected,

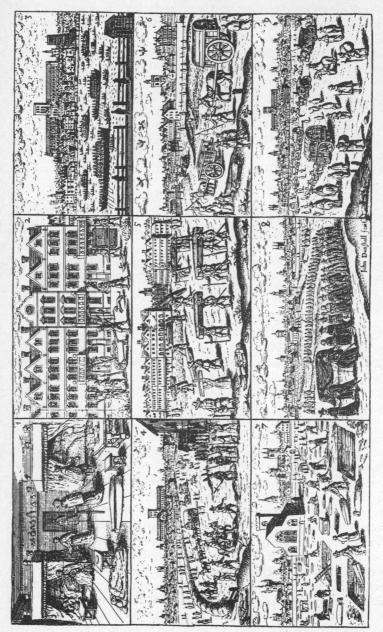

42. A contemporary pictorial broadside showing some of the scenes of the Great Plague, which broke out in London in May 1665. In six months, over 31,000 people died. The scenes depict: 1. Plague illness in a home; 2. Removing the dead and marking houses with a red cross where folk have the plague; 3. and 4. People leaving the city by the Thames and by road; 5. and 6. Carrying the dead by hand and in carts; 7. Burial in large pits; 8. A funeral procession; 9. The Londoners returning to their homes.

from whence the affrighted dwellers are fled, in hope to live better in
the country.   Thomas Dekker, *Work for Armourers*, 1609

TREATMENT FOR THE PLAGUE

To preserve your body from the infection of the plague, you shall take
a quart of old ale, and after it hath risen upon the fire and hath been
scummed, you shall put thereinto of.aristolochia longa, of angelica and
of celandine of each half an handful, and boil them well therein; then
strain the drink through a clean cloth, and dissolve therein a drachm of
the best mithridate, as much ivory finely powdered and searced, and
six spoonful of dragon-water, then put it up in a close glass; and every
morning fasting take five spoonful thereof, and after bite and chew in
your mouth the dried root of angelica, or smell, as on a nosegay, to the
tasselled end of a ship rope, and they will surely preserve you from
infection.

But if you be infected with the plague, and feel the assured signs
thereof, as pain in the head, drought, burning, weakness of stomach
and such like: then you shall take a drachm of the best mithridate, and
dissolve it in three or four spoonful of dragon-water, and immediately
drink it off, and then with hot cloths or bricks, made extreme hot and
laid to the soles of your feet, after you have been wrapt in woollen
cloths, compel the sick party to sweat, which if he do, keep him
moderately therein till the sore begin to rise; then to the same apply a
live pigeon cut in two parts, or else a plaster made of the yolk of an egg,
honey, herb of grace chopped exceeding small, and wheat flour, which
in very short space will not only ripen, but also break the same without
any other incision; then after it hath run a day or two, you shall apply a
plaster of melilot unto it until it be whole.

Gervase Markham, *The English Hus-wife*, 1615.

SIGNS OF THE SCURVY

*Any prolonged sea voyage caused the disease in epidemic form among ships'
crews due to a shortage of vitamin C in their diet.*
Of the scurvy. The signs of the scurvy are many, as namely a general
laziness and evil disposition of all the faculties and parts of the body.

A discolouring of the skin as if it were fouler than ordinary, with
spots darker coloured than the rest, and sometimes also darkish blue
spots.

Also itching or aching of the limbs are signs of the grief . . . and
stinking of the breath . . . shortness and difficulty of breathing especially when they move themselves. Their eyes of a leady colour, or
like dark violets. Great swelling in the face, legs, and over all the
body . . . swellings of the gums, rottenness of the same, with the issuings

of much filthy blood and other stinking corruption thence, looseness of
the teeth.   John Woodall, a ship's surgeon, 1617

HANDBILL OF SEVENTEENTH-CENTURY BEAUTY SPECIALIST
THE FAMOUS WATER OF TALK AND PEARL

Being the Clearest of all Waters, and is of that Excellent Quality for
Beautifying the Face, that in a short time it will turn the Brownest
Complexion to a Lovely White; It takes away Freckles, Scurf and
Morphew, makes the Skin smooth and soft, Illustrates Beauty to
Admiration.

If any Persons Faces are Wrinkled, or damaged by using poisonous
Powders, this Water will not only bring them to their former Complexion, but create Beauty.

Also an Excellent Oyntment, that takes away the Redness of the Face,
if it were Rubies or never so bad, in ten times using.

Also a Water that fastens Hair that is falling, and makes it grow very
thick.

And an Excellent Oyntment that takes away the Hair from any part,
that it shall never grow again.

Also a Water that will turn the Reddest Hair to a perfect Dark
Brown.

Likewise you may have White and Red, or any other things to adorn
the Face, as Talk finely prepared, which is a rare thing for the Skin.

A Salve for the Lips, that gives them a good Colour, and makes them
smooth, rare Pomatoms and Fore-headpieces, Powders for the Teeth,
with several other things for the adorning of Beauty, never the like
prepared in England.

Are to be had at the Blew Ball in Blew-Ball-Court in the
Square in Salisbury-Court, Fleetstreet.

MOST EXCELLENT DENTIFRICE

Most excellent and approved DENTIFRICE to scour and cleanse the teeth,
making them white as ivory, preserves from the tooth-ache; so that,
being constantly used, the parties using it are never troubled with the
tooth-ache; it fastens the teeth, sweetens the breath, and preserves the
gums and mouth from cankers and impostumes [abscess]. Made by
Robert Turner, Gentleman; and the right are only to be had at Thomas
Rookes, Stationer, at the Holy Lamb at the east end of St Paul's Church,
near the School, in sealed papers at 12d the paper.

If a gentleman had lost his teeth, there were dentists who advertised
their willingness to insert in his gums teeth pulled from the jaws of
impoverished youths.   *Mercurius Politicus*, 20 December 1660

THE KING'S EVIL

Whitehall, 14 May 1664. His Sacred Majesty, having declared it his Royal will and purpose to continue the healing of his people for the Evil during the month of May and then to give over till Michaelmas next, I am commanded to give notice thereof that the people may not come up to Town in the Interim and lose their labour.

Public Intelligencer, 1664

THE PLAGUE

I was much troubled this day to learn at Westminster, how the officers do bury the dead in open Tuttlefields. It was so dark before I could get home and so land at Churchyard Stairs, where to my great trouble, I met a dead corpse of the Plague in the narrow alley.... After church to my inn, and eat and drink, and so about seven o'clock by water, and got between nine and ten to Queenhithe, very dark: and I could get my waterman to go elsewhere for fear of Plague. Thence with lanthorn, in great fear of meeting dead corpses. To Mr Calvill the goldsmiths: having not for some days been in the streets: but now how few people I see, and those looking like people that have taken leave of the world. To the Exchange and there was not fifty people upon it ... a complaint brought against a man in the town for taking a child from an infected house. It was the child of a very able citizen in Gracious Street, a saddler, who had buried all the rest of his children of the Plague, and himself and wife now being shut up in despair of escaping, did desire to save the life of this little child: and so prevailed to have it received stark naked into the arms of a friend, who brought it, having put it into new, fresh clothes, to Greenwich.

Samuel Pepys, *Diary*, 1665

BLOOD TRANSFUSION

First, take up the Carotid Artery of the Dog or other animal, whose blood is to be transfused into another of the same or a different kind, and separate it from the nerve . . . and lay it bare a half an inch. Then make a strong ligature on the upper part of the Artery, not to be untied again: but an inch below, toward the Heart, make another ligature of a running knot, which may be loosened or fastened as there shall be occasion. Having made these two knots, draw two threads under the artery, between the two ligatures: then open the Artery and put in a Quill, and tie the Artery upon the Quill very fast by those two threads, and stop the Quill with a stick. After this, make bare the Jugular vein in the other Dog about an inch and a half long: and at each end make a ligature . . . then make an incision in the vein and put in two Quills, one in the descendant part of the vein to receive the blood from the other

Dog . . . the other into the other part of the Jugular vein which comes from the head into the other point of the Jugular vein.

All things being thus prepared, tie the Dogs on their sides towards one another so conveniently that the Quills may go into each other. . . .

Philosophical Transactions, Monday 16 December 1666

QUACK DOCTOR

When people acquaint him with their griefs and their ills, though he knows not what ails them no more than a horse, he tells them it is a scorbutick humor caused by a defluxion from the os-scarum, afflicting the diaphiaragma and circoary-thenordal muscles! with which the poor souls are abundantly satisfied, and wonder that he should hit on their distemper so exactly. He undertakes to spy out diseases, whilst they are yet lurking in their remotest causes! and has an excellent talent for persuading well people that they are sick, and by giving them his trash soon verifies the prediction. He especially succeeds in preying upon women, for he says 'I never yet knew a female mind but ailed something when she came in presence of a doctor.'

Pamphlet *c.* 1670

PLAGUE WATER

Take rosemary, red balm, burrage, angelica, carduus, celandine, aragon, feathfew, wormwood, pennyroyal, elecampane roots, mugwort, bural, tormentil, egrimony, sage, sorrel, of each of these one handful, weighed weight for weight, put all these in an earthen pot, with four quarts of white wine, cover them close, and let them stand eight or nine days in a cool cellar, then distil it in a glass still.

Hannah Woolley, *The Queen-like Closet,* 1684

HOSPITAL, PLYMOUTH, 1672

The following winter I had the hospital full of men, at times above 200, for the most part sick, and that of malignant diseases, so that between Christmas and the end of March I fell sick 3 times of malignant spotted fevers, the last of which had well nigh killed me. My wife and both servants lay sick of the same disease by me, and during my lying-in this last time, my wife's sister, Elizabeth Cramporn (a good-natured ingenuous girl, 22 years old) by watching and attendance among us got the disease and died, as did also Dr Jennins (who was . . . infected by but one visit). Mr Avent, my mate at the same time, lay down 8 weeks, and the chief nurse after 5 weeks died. Such a sad contagion was there among us; blessed be God all my family escaped.

James Yonge, Plymouth surgeon, *Journal,* 1672

QUACK-DOCTOR AND BEAUTY SPECIALIST
Described in 1678.

[His dress comprised] a decent black suit, and if credit will stretch so far as Long Lane, a plush jacket; not a pin the worse though it be threadbare as a tailor's cloak, as it shows the more reverend antiquity. Like Mercury, you must always carry a caduceus or conjuring japan [wand] in your hand, capped with a civet-box [cassolette], with which you must walk with Spanish gravity. A convenient lodging, not forgetting a hatch at the door; a chamber hung with Dutch pictures or looking-glasses, belittered [littered] with empty bottles, gallipots [glazed pots], and vials, filled with tar-drippings of fair-water coloured with saunders [sandalwood]. Any sexton will furnish you with a skull, in hope of your custom, over which hang up the skeleton of a monkey to proclaim your skill in anatomy. Let your table never be without some old musty Greek or Arabic author and the Fourth Book of Cornelius Agrippa's 'Occult Philosophy', wide open to amuse spectators, also half a dozen of gilt shillings, as being so many 'guineas' received that morning for fees.

TO CURE THE BITING OF MAD DOGS
Sir Hans Sloane to Mr Ray

London, 21 June 1687

Sir,

I send you here enclosed the specimen of a plant growing on Newmarket Heath, and in Surrey, known by the name of *Star of the Earth* in those parts. It is particularly taken notice of on the account of its extraordinary and admirable virtue in curing the bitings of mad dogs, either in beasts or men. One of his Majesty's huntsmen having proved it a great many times, gave the King his way of using it, which was an infusion in wine with treacle, and one or two more simples. His Majesty was pleased to communicate it to Gresham College, to the Royal Society; and nobody knowing the plant by that name, some there present confirming its use in that disease in some places of England, and procuring the herb itself, it is as little known here as if it had come from the Indies. I told the Society I would let you have this best specimen of it, which I question not but 'tis known to you. If you please to give your sentiments about it, you'll extremely oblige, etc.

Mr Ray's answer

Sir,

I received your letter with the specimen enclosed, which seems to me to be the Sesamoides Salamanticum magnum of Clusius, or Lychnis viscosa flore muscoso of C.B. which I have observed to grow plentifully upon Newmarket Heath, that part I mean that is in Suffolk; for on Cambridgeshire side I have not found it. I wonder it should have such a virtue as you mention; but it seems it is well attested. Dr Hulse writes to me he finds it in Gray's *Farrier*.

A CURIOUS SCHEME
1. A certain time shall be agreed upon for the cure of the diseases before they are undertaken.
2. The sick shall know first what the medicines will cost that are necessary for their cure, tho' they shall pay for them only as they use them.
3. Whatever is received for medicines of them shall be faithfully return'd, if the case be not perfected within the time prefixt.
4. That they may be sure of either having their money or their health restored: they or their friends for them, shall have a note, if they desire it, under my hand and seal, for the performance of these proposals.

I will visit them in any part of the City of London in the daytime for two shillings and sixpence, and will ride to visit patients in the City of Westminster or in Southwark or the Suburbs, for two and sixpence a mile: the messenger that comes for me, leaving the said fee at my house, and the name of the person that sends for me and of the place of his or her abode.

Dr John Pechey, who practised in 1687 at the Golden Angel and Crown in King Street, Cheapside, London

THE SPA AT HARROGATE
After Queen Catherine of Braganza began to visit Tunbridge or Bath, taking the waters as a cure for her sterility, the fashion of spas became widespread. Celia Fiennes tells us of her visit to one near Harrogate, c. 1690.

From thence we went over to Harrogate which is just by the spa, two mile further over a common that belongs to Knarsborough. It's all marshy and wet and here in the compass of 2 miles is 4 very different springs of water: there is the sulphur or stinking spa, not improperly termed for the smell being so very strong and offensive that I could not force my horse near the well; there are two wells together with basins in them that the spring rises up in . . . it comes from brimstone mines for taste and smell is much of sulphur . . . I drank a quart in a morning for two days and hold them to be a good sort of purge, if you can hold your breath so as to drink them down. Within a quarter of a mile is the sweet spa or chalybeate, a spring which rises off iron and steel like Astrop or Tunbridge and like the German spa.

FEVER AND SMALL-POX

From my correspondent in Devonshire, I have this following account: viz, we have a terrible fever. It began about Michaelmas last, at the east end of a valley that borders on Somerset, and reached westward beyond Crediton; in which are these towns: Samford-Perenel, Halberton, Collumpton, Bradninch, Silverton, Tharverton, Crediton-Bow. So far I hear the fever is gone westward; but it moves like a great shower, having some droppings before and behind it, but its main body is violent. For about two months it has been very terrible in Collumpton, where now it abates, and is most terrible in Silverton and Tharverton, though several have been sick of it, and some died there all this Spring.

Since this hot weather, 'tis got into Exeter, where several are dead that I knew to be strong healthy men. Before this hot weather they would lie 10 or 14 days before they died; but now many lie not above 3 or 4 days.

Some have spots, some have none; such as have spots, are observed not to relapse; such as have none have been taken a second some a third time after they have been very well, as they thought.

It appears to be very infectious; so that now the sick have few visitors but those that have been so.

Most of them are taken with an extraordinary deafness, that a trumpet or hunting-horn does not affect them. These, at first, were thought to be dying when this deafness seized them, people not knowing their defect of hearing and so let them lie looking for their departure; but now they present things to their sight, which the sick do accept or refuse; and this way they come to take in some refreshment.

The small-pox goes with it, but not mortal, but where the fever and that meets in one.   Houghton's *Collection*, 5 July 1695

SIR KENELM DIGBY'S INCOMPARABLE APOPLECTIC POWDER OR SNUFF

Which at once, or at the most three times using of it (with God's blessing) absolutely cures the apoplexy and lethargy, also vapours, drowsiness, impostumes, dizziness, and heaviness of the head; and by its reviving flavour (being no perfume) highly strengthens the animal spirits and faculties. This remedy being compounded of noble cephalic subjects, wholly differs from any other of this kind, as is manifest by its colour, smell, and virtue; which will not decay in some years, and may be used in any season with the greatest safety and advantage.

Price 1s.6d. per paper, with printed directions, each sealed up with this seal, (*viz.*) two twins and a mullet for the crest. Sold at Mr Brook's, Stationer, upon London-Bridge; Mr Crouch, Bookseller, at the Bell in

the Poultrey; Mr Cristien, Drugster, at the Star against Somerset-
House in the Strand; Mr Dawson, Grocer, against the Green Dragon,
Pallmall; and at the Surgeon's Sign in Buckeridge-street, near St
Giles-Church.   *English Post*, 27–30 March 1702

CURES FOR TOOTHACHE
The only famous remedy for the tooth-ache
'Tis a liquid to be held a little while in the mouth, and wholly free from
the poisonous quality of Aqua-Fortis and Red Mercury in powder, too
commonly used in this distemper. Whereas this incomparable remedy,
being as safe as a drop of cordial water, immediately allays all pains of
the teeth or gums, and with God's blessing infallibly cures it, without
danger of return, whether it proceeds from rheum, decayed teeth,
worms in 'em, or stumps [malformation]. It also preserves them, and
absolutely clears 'em from the scurvy. Price 1s. Each bottle with printed
directions, each sealed up with a Lion-Rampant Gardant, the Crest a
Griffin Passant.   *English Post*, 9–11 March 1702

BARTLET'S STEEL TRUSSES
Bartlet's Inventions of steel trusses and instruments, medicines and
methods to make the weak strong, and the crooked straight; which
might be prevented by the timely and frequent use of my Elixir
Mirabile, 1s.6d. the bottle, dose from 1 drop to 3 or 4 to a child; and so
to 20, 40, or 60 in extreme pains in men and women, etc. as gripes,
cholics, etc. – pleurisies it helps in a minute, without bleeding, gives
natural rest, and cures thrush, redgum, fits, coughs, ruptures, green-
sickness, vapours, jaundice, and without fail cures agues, and kills all
kind of worms, and gives great relief in the consumption, hectic or
malignant fevers, and after small-pox. Take it in any liquor fasting, or 2
hours before meat; it's safe and seldom purges. My Royal Cephalic
Snuff 6d the paper, a powerful yet gentle and safe purger of the head
by the nose, excellent for the headache, coughs and fits, and other
diseases caused by the foulness of the head. At my house at Bethnal-
Green for the cure of mad people, where I am at night; and at my
house at the Golden Ball in Chamber-street in Goodmans-fields,
London: where I am the forenoons till Change-time, and then on the
Eastland walk till 3, or at Hamlins Coffee-house in Swethin's-Alley,
except on the day called Saturday, which he thinks is the real Christian
Sabbath.   *English Post*, 19–22 June 1702

KIRLEUS CURES ALL
These are to give notice,
That John Kirleus, son of Dr Tho. Kirleus, who was a Sworn Physician

43. This signboard, dated 1623, shows the doctor helping his patients. On the left he bleeds a woman, amputates a leg, and extracts a tooth. Above his head, he examines a patient's urine; on the right he treats a dislocation, deals with a tumour of the breast, and sees a patient out.

The Latin says, 'The highest created medicine from the earth of which a sensible man will not be afraid.'

in Ordinary to King Charles II many years since, till his death, but first a Collegiate Physical of London, with the same Drink and Pill (hindering no business) cures all ulcers, sores, scabs, itch, scurfs, scurvies, leprosies, and venereal or French disease, and all such like malignities, be the same never so great, at all times of the year, in all bodies (as his father did) without sweating, smoking, fluxing, or any mercurial medicines, which are known to be dangerous, and often deadly.... Therefore take heed when you trust to these cures, for there are but few that can cure any of these distempers without the use of mercury. He deals with all persons according to their abilities. The Drink at three shillings the Quart; the Pill one shilling the Box, with directions. He gives his Opinion for nothing, to all that write or come to him, and as well to those afar off, as if they were present. He lives at the Glass-Lanthorn, in Plough-Yard, in Grays-Inn Lane.

Flying Post, 19–22 December 1702

DR READ, OCULIST

A particular account of some people lately couched [removed a cataract] and brought to perfect sight in London 1703 by Dr William Read the approved occulist. Mrs Mary Benning at the Wheat-Sheaf in High Holborn aged 80, Madam Blows over against my Lord Craven in Drury-lane aged 76, Mr John Blows near the Coach and Horses in Carnaby-street near Golden-square aged 70, Mr Scott, shoe-maker in Chancery-Lane aged 70, Ellen Jones in Black-Friars, Mrs Joanna Campion at the Crooked Billet in Monmouth-street, Mrs Payn, a goldsmith's wife, at the New Exchange in the Strand. And several hundreds more, not only of cataracts but other distempers relating to the eyes. He likewise couched Mrs Katharine and Alice Newson, sisters, at Cocklie near Haisworth in Suffolk notwithstanding they were both born blind, yet brought them to perfect sight, which continues. The said Dr Read is to be advised with constantly at his house at the Black-a-moor's Head in Shandois street Covent-Garden, London, where he has cured above a hundred poor people *gratis* within this 18 months, some of cataracts, albrigos [eye disease, opaque spot forms on the cornea] and defluxion of humours. And has cured several of wens, hare lips and wry necks, without any deformity.

Daily Courant, 17 January 1704

BIRTHS AND DEATHS

London. By the General Bill of Christenings and Burials, from the 14th of December 1703 to the 19th of December 1704 it appears that there were christened in this city during that time: Males 8153, Females

7742, in all 15895. Buried 11401, Females 12283, in all 23684. Increased in the Burials 1664. . . .

The principal diseases and casualties were: Aged 1799. Childbed 236. Cholic 125. Consumption 3013. Convulsion 5987. Dropsy 918. Fever 3243. Griping in the Guts 1134. Rickets 421. Rising of the Lights 107. Small Pox 1501. Pthysick 295. Worms 25. Abortive 102. Drowned 52. Executed 9. Found dead in the streets 25. Hanged and made away themselves 25. Killed by several accidents 63. Overlaid [suffocated] 71. Stillborn 486.   *Flying Post*, 23–26 December 1704

RECIPE FOR FORGETFULNESS

Take rue, red mint, oil olive, and very strong vinegar, and let your nostrils be held over the smoke of it. Also burn your own hair and mingle it with a little vinegar and pitch, and apply it to your nostrils, for it wonderfully stirs and quickens the person diseased with forgetfulness. Also, the lights of a hog held to your head, shaven, is very good.

From a collection of books sold by the Earl of Powys, said to have been owned by Margaret, second Duchess of Portland

PURGING SUGAR-PLUMS FOR CHILDREN

Purging sugar-plums for children, and others of nice palates, nothing differing in taste, colour, etc. from sugar-plums at the confectioners, having been experienced by thousands to sweeten and purify the blood to admiration, kill worms, cure the green-sickness in maids, pale looks in children, rickets, stomach pains, King's-Evil, scurvies, rheumatisms, dropsies, scabs, itch, tetters [skin disease] etc., good in all cases, where purging is necessary, doing all that is possible to be done by a purging medicine, being the cheapest, safest, and pleasantest purge in the world, fit for persons of all ranks, ages and sexes. Price 1s. the box, to be had only at Mr Spooner's at the Golden Half-Moon in Buckle-Street in Goodmans-fields near White-Chapel, with directions.

Flying Post, 1–3 January 1705

COUGH DROPS FROM THE GOLDEN HALF-MOON

Pleasant drops for the chin-cough, and the whooping cough in children, which, to the astonishment of all that use them, certainly cures in two or three days time, and oftentimes in one day, even when the fits of coughing have been so violent, as to render the children black in the face, their breath almost spent, and ready to drop dead; and for all other coughs and in old or young, is a most excellent and approved remedy. Price 3s.6d. the bottle, to be had only at Mr Spooner's, at the Golden Half-Moon in Buckle-street in Goodman's-Fields near White-Chapel, with directions.   *Daily Courant*, 20 December 1706

FOR KING'S EVIL (SCROFULA)

An infallible cure for the KING'S-EVIL, in all its most direful circumstances; by an excellent Electuary [medicinal powder], particularly adapted for that end, and largely experienced; the surprising effects of which, in quickly accomplishing the cure, are admired by all learned and ingenious physicians, and the medicine itself by them recommended, as the only specific remedy to be depended on for the cure of that distemper. For, it not only disposes ulcers in the legs, or other parts of the body, to heal presently, but also makes any kernels or hard swellings in the neck, throat, or other parts, vanish as it were by a charm. In a word, let the patient be never so bad, or the King's-Evil seated in what part soever, as the eyes, etc. This most noble medicine infallibly performs a cure, completing it without trouble of confinement, so soon, that one would really conclude it was done by a miracle. It also clears and strengthens the stomach, promotes digestion, rectifies the blood and juices, cleanses the whole body from all manner of impurities; and most certainly cures all stubborn scrofulous humours, inveterate tetters, scabs, itch, or breakings out, beyond any other medicine in the world, as numbers to their inexpressible joy and satisfaction have found. Price 3s. a pot, with directions. Sold only at Mr Spooner's at the Golden Half-Moon in Buckle-Street in Goodman's-Fields near White-Chapel. . *Generous Advertiser*, 14–18 March 1707

CHARLES LILLY, BEAUFORT BUILDINGS, STRAND

His amber, orange-flower, musk, and civet-violet, put only into a handkerchief, shall have the same effect towards an honourable lover's wishes as if he had been wrapped in his mother's smock. Wash-balls perfumed, camphired and plain, shall restore complexions to that degree, that a country fox-hunter who uses them shall, in a week's time, look with a courtly and affable paleness.

Richard Steele, *The Tatler*, 1710

HANDBILL TO DRAW GREAT SHOALS OF SPECTATORS, 1710

God, the Author of all things, to make man in love with his wife in her state of innocency, he made her smooth, soft, delicate and fair to entice him; I therefore, that woman might be pleasing to their husbands, and that they might not be offended by their deformities and turn to others, do commend unto you the Virtue of an eminent and highly approved 'Balsamick Essence', with several other Incomparable Cosmeticks, faithfully prepared without Mercury.

The 'Balsamick Essence' takes away the broadest freckles be they never so long standing, wrinkles, morphew, tan, sunburn, or yellowness in Thirty Days, and renders the skin plump, soft, fair, bright, smooth, and of a lovely colour. 'Tis of that mighty Influence, that the like was never found out to Beautify the Face, and there is nothing of paint relating to it.

The aged it makes appear fair and young, and preserves beauty to their lives' end. 'Tis a most delicate thing to anoint the Face with when the smallpox begins to dry, for it certainly prevents all scars and pits. Price One Shilling each bottle of the Noble Balsamick Essence.

At the Surgeon's sign, just at the corner of Coventry-court in the Haymarket, near Pickadilly.

Work and Wages

No agricultural, social or industrial change of any great importance took place during the forty years when this country was moving towards the Civil War.

Four-fifths of the population were working on the land. The desire was now to drain, clear, and improve many wide acres. Woods were trimmed, waste expanses were cultivated. Vermuyden and other Dutch engineers cut canals in the Fens. Land there was reclaimed for farming, reed-growing, fishing, and fowling.

Throughout the country sturdy, self-reliant peasants were attached to the soil. They enjoyed the beauty of the landscape, the established ways of rural life, the ale-house, folk songs. Craftsmen lived in every village and market town; as traditional artists – blacksmiths, wheel-wrights, masons, saddlers, carpenters, thatchers, tanners, weavers, straw-plaiters and the like – they were proud of their work in an all-important inter-dependent community.

In 1688 the 'able publicist' Gregory King calculated the probable numbers in various classes of the population. The two largest classes were cottagers and paupers (who were living off the common), and labouring people and out-servants (who were wage-earners). The latter had small gardens or holdings, though they had not yet gained the rank of yeoman. As G. M. Trevelyan says: 'On the stony heights around Halifax each clothworker had "a cow or two" in a field walled off on the steep hillside whereon his cottage stood. On the other hand there were very large numbers of employees both in agriculture and industry who had no rights in land and no means of subsistence but their wages.'

It was now the day of small businesses, which were growing in number. A man could open a shop, set up a manufacturing business, employing apprentices, journeymen; buying horses, carts, pack-saddles. Defoe writes: 'New discoveries in metals, mines and minerals, new undertakings in trade, engines, manufactures, in a nation pushing and improving as we are; these things open new scenes every day, and make England especially shew a new and differing face in many places, on every occasion of surveying it.'

Celia Fiennes at the end of the century tells us how tin was mined in Cornwall; fine flowered silks were woven in Canterbury; yarn, crapes, callimanco, damasks were made in Norwich; serges in Exeter; stockings in Nottingham and Leicester; paper in Kent; bayes [baize] in Colchester; lace in Honiton. She reports the 'makeing of fine tea-potts in Staffordshire', linsiwoolseys in Kendall, kersey and the famous Yorkshire Cloth in Leeds. Stony Stratford was famous for bonelace, Stourbridge for glass, Derby for gloves, Manchester and Salford for 'linnen, cotten tickings and incles [linen tape]'. There was much copperace [green vitriol] at Brownsea, 'cleare like sugar-candy'. Somerset and Wiltshire were renowned for fine woollen cloths, 'this prodigy of trade'. Coal was being produced on a large scale in Northumberland, Durham and Cumberland. Iron founderies were still flourishing in the Weald, and Sheffield was the source of cutlery. Writing of another journey, Celia Fiennes praised Kentish hops and cherries, and a wealth of corn and orchards in Herefordshire and the Vale of Evesham.

In 1694 the Bank of England was founded, and two years later Isaac Newton was made Warden of the King's Mints and Exchanges. He soon set a new standard in the Mint.

Gregory King's estimate calculated for the year 1688 gives a fair idea of families and incomes. Yearly incomes: noblemen, £2,800; bishops, £1,300; knights, £650; gentlemen, £280; merchants and traders by sea, £400; merchants and traders by land, £200; clergymen, £60; farmers, £44; naval officers, £80; military officers, £60.

The wages of farm labourers and artisans were fixed by magistrates.

In 1610, the Rutland magistrates met at Oakham and made their assessment. The day wages of a mower were 10d.; of a reaper, 8d., if a man, if a woman 6d. Artisans were to have from 10d. to 9d. in the summer, 8d. in the winter. Master artisans, with skill as draughtsmen, were to receive 1s. a day in summer, 10d. in winter. These rates were maintained till at least 1634.

In 1651, the Essex magistrates met at Chelmsford, and fixed the wages for the county. The day wages of a mower were 1s. 6d., reaping at 1s. 10d. Women in the harvest field had 1s. 2d.; in the hay-field, 10d. Artisans had from 1s. 5d. a day in summer and 1s. 2d. in winter to 1s. 6d. and 1s. 4d.

In 1682, the Suffolk magistrates at Bury St Edmund's fixed the day wages of haymakers – men at 10d., women at 6d.; of male reapers in harvest at 1s. 8d., of women at 1s. The wages of artisans were from 1s. 6d., to 1s. 4d.

In 1684, the magistrates of Warwick made their assessment. Artisans' wages 1s. a day; free mason 1s. 4d.; plasterer 8d.; common labourers (except harvest) 8d.; mower of grass and corn 1s.; reaper 1s.; woman 8d.; haymaker 8d., woman 4d. These were summer wages; winter pay, a penny a day less.

Hours of labour as defined between March and September were from 5 in the morning till between 7 and 8 at night. Of this time, 2½ hours were allowed for meals – ½ hour for breakfast; 1 hour for dinner; 1 hour for 'drinkings'. And between the middle of May and the middle of August ½ hour for sleep.

From the middle of September till the middle of March the labourer was to work from daybreak till night, and to forfeit a penny an hour for absence.

At the turn of the century into the Stuart Age wheat cost 22s. 6d. per quarter, malt 20s., oatmeal 38s., beef 2d. a pound, leg of mutton 1s. 6d., butter 6d. a pound, sugar 20s. a pound, eggs 100 for 2s., asses' milk 3s. 6d. a quart, salt 3 bushels for 6d. Other prices of the time were: potatoes 2s. a pound, carrots 2d. a bunch, onions 2d. a rope, cherries 3d. a pound, pears 1s. a peck, olives 1s. a pint, oranges seven for 2d., artichokes 8 for 10d., Naples biscuits 2s. 6d. a pound, sack two gallons 5s. 8d., tobacco 5s. an ounce.

The staple diet was bread, beer, and usually meat. Gregory King tells us that half the population ate meat daily, the rest ate it at least twice a week. Defoe tells us: 'English labouring people eat and drink, especially the latter, three times as much in value as any sort of foreigners of the same dimensions in the world.'

HIRE-PURCHASE IN 1604
Penelope Whorehound in Dekker's The Honest Whore *says:*
God is my judge, sir, I am in for no debts; I paid my tailor for this gown the last five shillings a-week that was behind, yesterday.

A SHEPHERD
I cannot well resolve you whether his sheep or he be more innocent. Give him fat lambs and fair weather, and he knows no happiness beyond them. He shows, most fitly among all professions, that nature is contented with a little. For the sweet fountain is his fairest alehouse: the sunny bank his best chamber. Adam had never less need of neighbours' friendship; nor was at any time troubled with neighbours' envy less than he: the next grove or thicket will defend him from a shower: and if they be not so favourable, his homely palace is not far distant. He proves quietness to be best contentment, and that there is no quietness like a certain rest. His flock affords him his whole raiment, his little

garden yields hemp enough to make his lockram shirts: which do preserve his body sweetened against court-itch and poxes, as a sear-cloth sweetens carcases. . . . His daily life is a delightful work, what-soever the work be; whether to mend his garments, cure a diseased sheep, instruct his dog, or change pastures: and these be pleasant actions, because voluntary, patient, not interrupted. He comprehends the true pattern of a moderate wise man: for as a shepherd, so a moderate man hath the supremacy over his thoughts and passions, neither hath he any affection of so wild a nature, but he can bring it into good order, with an easy whistle. The worst temptation of his idleness teaches him no further mischief, than to love entirely some nut-brown milk-maid, or hunt the squirrel, or make his cosset [pet lamb] wanton. He may turn many rare esteemed physicians into shame and blushing: for whereas they, with infinite compounds and fair promises, do carry men to death the furthest way about; he with a few simples preserves

44. Cast-iron fireback, 1636, from the foundry of Richard Lenard at Brede in Sussex. In the bottom left corner is the earliest known portrayal of the blast furnace in England. It was fed with charcoal, and produced molten metal run from the bottom into moulds.

himself and family to the most lengthened sufferance of nature. Tar
and honey be his mithridates and syrups; the which, together with a
Christmas carol, defend his desolate life from cares and melancholy.

John Stephens, *Essays and Characters*, 1615

LADY ANNE BERKELEY
Country huswifry seemed to be an essential part of this lady's constitution; a lady that . . . would betimes in winter and summer mornings

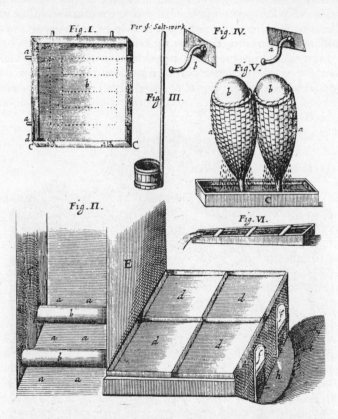

45.   This engraving shows methods used in the seventeenth century for evaporating
brine from inland springs at Nantwich, Cheshire. Brine was delivered in large cisterns,
then ladled by using the long-handled bucket (*Fig. III*) into the iron salt-pans (*Fig. II, d,
d, d, d*) under which were furnaces (*f, f*). Smoke and flames from these passed through
pipes (*b, b*) to the chimney (*C*) and heated a 'hot-house' (*a, a*) where salt was dried. A
further stage was to use skimmers (*Fig. IV*) to collect the salt and pack it into conical
baskets (*Fig. V*) to drain for final drying. Salt was then taken to market by packhorse to all
parts of England. Royal Society, *Philosophical Transactions*, 1669.

make her walks to visit her stable, barns, day-house, poultry, swine-troughs and the like; which huswifry her daughter-in-law . . . seeming to decline, and to betake herself to the delights of youth and greatness, she would sometimes to those about her swear, By God's blessed sacrament, this gay girl will beggar my son Henry.

John Smyth, Berkeley Manuscripts

COUNTRY-FOLK

You ask me how I pass my time here. . . . The heat of the day is spent in reading and working, and about six or seven o'clock I walk out into a common that lies hard by the house where a great many young wenches keep sheep and cows and sit in the shade singing of ballads. I talk to them and find they want nothing to make them the happiest people in the world, but the knowledge that they are so. Most commonly when we are in the midst of our discourse, one looks about her and spies her cows going into the corn, and then away they all run as if they had wings at their heels.

Dorothy Osborne in a letter to Sir William Temple, June 1653

DRAINING-ENGINES
Evelyn wrote in 1670:
Being arrived at some meres, we found Lord Wotton, and Sir John Kiviet about their draining-engines, having, it seems, undertaken to do wonders on a vast piece of marsh-ground they had hired of Sir Thomas Chicheley. They much pleased themselves with the hopes of a rich harvest of hemp and coleseed, which was the crop expected.

Here we visited the engines and mills, both for wind and water, draining it through two rivers, or graffs, cut by hand, which went thwart one the other, discharging the water into the sea.

THE FARMER'S LOT
It is much easier with the handicraft labourer that hath a good trade. A joiner or a turner can work in the dry house with tolerable and pleasant work and knoweth his price and wages. A weaver, a shoemaker or a tailor can work without the wetting or the tiring of his body and can think and talk of the concerns of his soul without impediment to his labour. . . . And though the labour of a smith be hard, it is in a dry house, and but by short fits, and little, in comparison of threshing and reaping, but as nothing in comparison to the mowing which constantly pulls forth a man's whole strength. . . . The carrier's work is toilsome and done in all weathers but he knoweth his work and wages and is free from the abundance of his toils and cares.

46. In the seventeenth century, the ribbon-weaving loom, known as the Dutch or inkle loom, was introduced into England. Many of these looms were established in Spitalfields, Coventry and parts of Lancashire. The complicated mechanism is shown in this engraving. We see the sturdy framework, the numerous treadles and cords designed to produce many ribbons at the same time. *Universal Magazine,* 1747.

The nailors, and spurryers [spurmakers] and sithsmiths [scythe-smiths] and swordmakers and all the rest about Dudley and Stour-bridge and Brummicham [Birmingham] and Walsall and Wedgbury [Wednesbury] and Wolverhampton and all that country. They live in poverty, but not in the husbandman's case: they know their work and wages and have little further care.

Richard Baxter, *The Poor Husbandman's Advocate to Rich,*
Racking Landlords, c. 1680

47. A machine for boring wooden pipes to be used in supplying water to towns. The undershot water-wheel drives the boring bar by means of gears made of wood. The workman is pushing a movable support, holding the tree-trunk, up to the boring tool, some of which are lying in the front of the engraving. John Evelyn, *Sylva, or A Discourse of Forest-Trees*, 1670.

GREGORY KING'S TABLES, 1688

Number of Families	Ranks, Degrees, Titles and Qualifications	Heads per Family	Number of Persons	Yearly Income per Family
160	Temporal lords	40	6,400	£3,200
26	Spiritual lords	20	520	1,300
800	Baronets	16	12,800	880
600	Knights	13	7,800	650
3,000	Esquires	10	30,000	450
12,000	Gentlemen	8	96,000	280
5,000	Persons in greater offices and places	8	40,000	240
5,000	Persons in lesser offices and places	6	30,000	120
2,000	Eminent merchants and traders by sea	8	16,000	400
8,000	Lesser merchants and traders by sea	6	48,000	198
10,000	Persons in law	7	70,000	154
2,000	Eminent clergymen	6	12,000	72
8,000	Lesser clergymen	5	40,000	50
40,000	Freeholders of the better sort	7	280,000	91
120,000	Freeholders of the lesser sort	5½	660,000	55
150,000	Farmers	5	750,000	42 10s.
15,000	Persons in liberal arts and sciences	5	75,000	60
50,000	Shopkeepers and tradesmen	4½	225,000	45
60,000	Artisans and handicrafts	4	240,000	38
5,000	Naval officers	4	20,000	80
4,000	Military officers	4	16,000	60
50,000	Common seamen	3	150,000	20
364,000	Labouring people and out-servants	3½	1,275,000	15
400,000	Cottagers and paupers	3¼	1,300,000	6 10s.
35,000	Common soldiers	2	70,000	14
	Vagrants, as gipsies, thieves, beggars, etc.		30,000	
	Total		5,500,520	

(Printed in *Charles Davenant's Works* (1771), Vol. II, p.184, with further figures.)

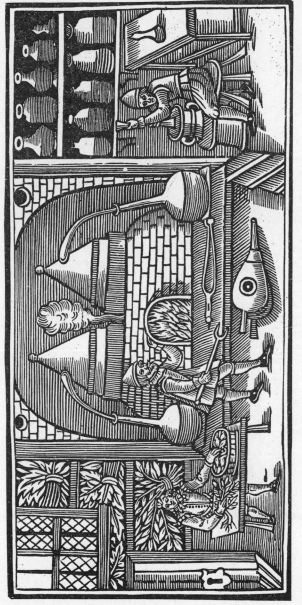

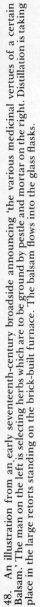

48. An illustration from an early seventeenth-century broadside announcing 'the various medicinal vertues of a certain Balsam. The man on the left is selecting herbs which are to be ground by pestle and mortar on the right. Distillation is taking place in the large retorts standing on the brick-built furnace. The balsam flows into the glass flasks.

Coal

ESTIMATED ANNUAL PRODUCTION IN TONS

	1551–1560	1681–1690
Durham and Northumberland	65,000	1,225,000
Scotland	40,000	475,000
Wales	20,000	200,000
Midlands	65,000	850,000
Cumberland	6,000	100,000
Kingswood Chase and Somerset	10,000	100,000
Forest of Dean	3,000	25,000
Devon and Ireland	1,000	7,000

Approximate increase: 14 fold

49.   A water-wheel pumping engine, late seventeenth century, which drained Sir Roger Mostyn's coal mine in Flintshire. The water-wheel on the right worked the chain-pump on the left of the drawing, by means of a shaft, crown-wheel and pinion. *The Account of the Official Progress of . . . Henry the First Duke of Beaufort through Wales in 1684*, by T. Dinely.

50. Coopers at work, mid seventeenth century. Here two coopers are binding the timber staves of the barrel with hazel hoops. On the right is the bench on which the hazel rods were cut and shaved. The coopers also made wash-tubs, scuttles and buckets, shown in the engraving. J. A. Comenius, *Orbis Sensualium Pictus,* translated by C. Hoole, 1672.

THE FOREST OF ARDEN DISAPPEARS

For the ironworks in the counties round destroyed such prodigious quantities of wood that they quickly lay the country a little open, and by degrees made room for the plough. Whereupon the inhabitants, partly by their own industry, and partly by the assistance of marl have turned so much of wood and heath-land into tillage and pasture that they produce corn, cattle, cheese and butter enough not only for their own use but also to furnish other counties.

Edmund Gibson, Britannia, 1695

POVERTY AND POOR-RELIEF

In 1697, John Locke drew up a report for the Board of Trade on poverty and poor-relief.

The children of labouring people are an ordinary burthen to the Parish. . . . A great number of children giving a poor man a title to an allowance from the parish, this allowance is given once a week, or once a month, to the father in money, which he not infrequently spends at the alehouse, whilst his children are left to suffer or perish from the want of necessaries. . . . What they can have at home from their parents is seldom more than bread and water, and that very scantily too.

WORKING IN MINES

Here we entered Derbyshire and went to Chesterfield 6 mile, and came by the coal mines where they were digging; they make their mines at the entrance like a well and so till they come to the coal, then they dig all the ground about where there is coal and set pillars to support it and so bring it to the well, where by a basket like a hand-barrow by cords they pull it up, so they let down and up the miners with a cord. . . .

Thence to Buxton, 9 miles over those craggy hills whose bowels are full of mines of all kinds of black and white and veined marbles, and some have mines of copper, others tin and leaden mines in which is a great deal of silver . . . they dig down their mines like a well, for one man to be let down with a rope and pulley and so when they find ore they keep digging under ground to follow the ore, which lies amongst the

51.   Late seventeenth-century engraving shows a tailor cutting out cloth with shears, his assistant sewing on the platform on which is a pressing iron. J. A. Comenius, *Orbis Sensualium Pictus*, translated by C. Hoole, 1672.

52. Paper-making by hand in the late seventeenth century. The pulping of linen rags was done by water-powered hammers. The engraving shows the paper-maker scooping the pulp from the vat with a wire-mesh. This then went to the 'coucher' who put it on a piece of felt. Layers were built up, then water squeezed out by a press. Sheets of paper were then smoothed out, dried, and glazed. J. A. Comenius, *Orbis Sensualium Pictus*, translated by C. Hoole, 1672.

stone . . . they generally look very pale and yellow that work under-ground, they are forced to keep lights with them and sometimes are forced to use gunpowder to break the stones, and that is sometimes hazardous to the people and destroys them at the work.

The Journeys of Celia Fiennes, 1697

FULLING IN EXETER

The carriers I met . . . with their loaded horses, they bring them all just from the loam and so they are put into the fulling mills, but first they will clean and scour their rooms with them – which by the way gives no pleasing perfume to a room, the oil and grease, and I should think it would rather foul a room than cleanse it because of the oil – but I perceive it's otherwise esteemed by them, which will send to their acquaintances that are tuckers [fullers] the days the serges come in for a roll to clean their house, this I was an eye witness of; then they lay them in soak in urine then they soap them and so put them into the fulling-mills and so work them in the mills dry till they are thick enough; then they turn water into them and so scour them; the mill does draw out and gather in the serges, it's a pretty diversion to see it, a sort of huge notched timbers like great teeth, one would think it should injure the serges but it does not, the mills draw in with such a great violence that if one stands near it, and it catch a bit of your garments it be ready to draw in the person even in a trice.

The Journeys of Celia Fiennes, 1698

DEARNESS OF WAGES

How well some of them do live who are good husbands and regard
their families, who only by their handy labour as journeymen can earn
from fifteen shillings to fifty shillings per week wages as thousands of
artisans in England can. . . . 'Tis plain the dearness of wages forms our
people into more classes than other nations can show. These men live
better in England than the masters and employers in foreign countries
can, and you have a class of your topping workmen in England, who,
being only journeymen under manufacturers, are yet very substantial
fellows, maintain their families very well.

Daniel Defoe, *Review*, 14 April 1705

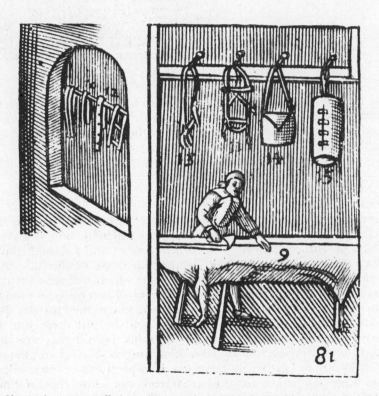

53.   Shoemakers were called 'cordwainers' as workers in Cordovan leather. This mid
seventeenth-century engraving shows how cordwainers were producing a variety of
leather goods from straps to pouches. The man here is cutting pieces from a large hide.
J. A. Comenius, *Orbis Sensualium Pictus,* translated by C. Hoole, 1672.

54. An engraving of a shoemaker's shop, mid seventeenth century. The shoemaker is
sewing with lingel or waxed thread. Several lasts hang at the top of the wall. J. A.
Comenius, *Orbis Sensualium Pictus*, translated by C. Hoole, 1672.

WORKING TRADES

Take the fourth sort [working trades] for a medium . . . suppose a
carpenter, a smith, a weaver or any such workman . . . that is industrious works hard and feels no want, let him live in the country or city. . . .
If the gentleman eats more puddings, this mans eats more bread, if the
rich man drinks more wine, this drinks more ale or strong beer, for it is
the support of his labour and strength. If the rich man eats more veal
and lamb, fowl and fish, this man eats more beef and bacon, and add to
it it has a better stomach. As to the milk, if the rich man eats more
butter, more cream, more white meats . . . our workman eats more hard
cheese and salt butter than all the other put together.

Daniel Defoe, *Review*, 1709

Trade and Money

In the country the regulation of wages and prices was much the same as in the day of Elizabeth. Changes in the economic and social life came slowly. But new influences from outside were just beginning to be felt. European commerce and finance were no longer directed from Paris, but as Peter Laslett says, 'from Amsterdam, Rotterdam and other large cities of the United Provinces of Holland. The British Isles were set much of the century in a Dutch seascape, and a strong sea-breeze from Holland blew through the huge city of London and over the whole English commercial and industrial community.'

Out of this rivalry our interest in trade began to expand. Traders like the East India Company wanted to borrow money to improve business. Lending money on acceptable terms had been made legal by an Act of Parliament. This stimulated borrowing. John Selden, the eminent lawyer, said: ''Tis a vain thing to say money begets no money, for that no doubt it does.' Thomas Mun, a member of the committee of the East India Company, wrote: 'How many merchants and shopkeepers have begun with little or nothing of their own, and yet are grown very rich by trading with other men's money.'

Goldsmiths had undertaken the function of bankers. They had to take every safeguard in their trade, and make use of strong-boxes. They now took charge of their clients' money or valuables. The receipts they gave were passed on as bonds from hand to hand, becoming a kind of paper currency.

The Civil War complicated coinage. Several districts issued their own, often clipped from silver ware and stamped, or moulded from melted plate. After the Restoration the holding and lending of money passed more and more into the hands of goldsmiths, who were glad to become 'the merchants' cash-keepers'. The goldsmiths even paid interest to encourage more deposits, and made Lombard Street a financial centre of the City.

USURY

The chief cause of poverty is usury, which doth too much enrich some few, and doth impoverish too much a great many. So that men cannot live contentedly and proportionably in their vocation, according to their profession, taking away the chiefest comfort of the poor, which is the quietness of their minds, and giving ability to the rich to do all the mischief that can be devised.

G. Malynes, *St. George For England*, 1601

FREE TRADE

The general remote cause of our want of money is the great excess of this kingdom, in consuming the commodities of foreign countries, which prove to us discommodities, in hindering us of so much treasure which otherwise would be brought in, in lieu of these toys. . . . And by this means we draw unto us, and consume amongst us, that great abundance of the wines of Spain, of France, of the Rhine, of the Levant, and of the Islands: the raisins of Spain, the currants of the Levants, the lawns and cambrics of Hannault and the Netherlands, the silks of Italy, the sugars and tobacco of the West Indies, the spices of the East Indies: all of which are of no necessity unto us, and yet are bought with ready money, which otherwise would be brought over in treasure if these were not.

E. Misselden, *Free Trade, or The Means to Make Trade Flourish*, 1622

VOYAGES FROM BRISTOL TO VIRGINIA

Certain of the Chief Merchants of the City of Bristol induced thereto by the inducements of Master Richard Hakluyt, resolve to set forth a voyage for the further discovery of the northern parts of Virginia. . . . They prepared a small ship called the *Speedwell*, of about 50 tons, manned with thirty men and boys, and a bark called the *Discoverer* of 26 tons with thirteen men and a boy, victualled for eight months, and furnished with certain merchandise to trade with the people of the country; as hats of divers colours, apparel of coarse kersey and canvas ready-made, stockings, shoes, saws, pickaxes, hooks, knives, scissors, bells, beads, looking-glasses, thimbles, needles, thread and suchlike. They set sail from Milford Haven on the 10th April.

Purchas His Pilgrims, 1625

PAYMENTS MADE IN 1647

11 August 1647. This morn I went with Edward Mitchell to Barnsley, and called at Joseph Shirt's by the way where I had my hair cut, and paid for nails 12*d.*; to Woodcock, for meat, which we had three weeks ago, 6*s.* 6*d.*; for tobacco for my wife, 10*d.*; for thread 2*d.*; and spent 1*s.* 6*d.*; and came by Coyts home with Joseph Ellisson. This morn I gave my wife 10*s.*; who at night kept the gates shut, and said she would be

master of the night for that night. This day's travels was 15 miles, and disbursements 20s. Yesterday's news was confirmed, and I sent to Wakefield a letter to Joseph Jackson, to send to How's, by the post, for our augmentation order, which he promised to send ere now.

Captain Adam Eyre, *Diary*

LOTTERY
A lottery is a tax upon unfortunate, self-conceited fools. . . . Because the world abounds with this kind of fool, it is not fit that every man that will may cheat every man that would be cheated, but it is ordained that the Sovereign should have the guardianship of these fools, or that some favourite should beg the Sovereign's right of taking advantage of such men's folly.

Sir William Petty, *Treatise of Taxes and Contributions*, 1667

EXPENSES IN THE RESTORATION PERIOD
I am debtor to your last kind letter, and to the best of my remembrance you formerly gave for a bed, so if you please to show this letter to my brother William, I question not but he will pay you what I owe for balance of account as it shall be stated at close of my letter. . . .

	£	s	d
For a silk vest	0	17	0
For a hat, a silver galloon			
[narrow braid] and hat-case		13	6
A porter			6
A child's coat		13	6
Marriage-a-la Mode		1	0
Combs and brushes		1	10
Box and porter		1	4

. . . Here is an excellent new-fashioned fringe with brave things to put on top of your bed. . . . It may be bought for £3 15 . . . they cannot be bought at the shops under £6.   R. Sitwell to his sister, 6 April 1675

THE FARM DESCRIBED
First cast your eye upon a rustic seat,
Built strong and plain, yet well contrived and neat,
And situated on a healthy soil,
Yielding much wealth with little cost or toil.
Near by it stand the barns framed to contain
Enriching stores of hay, pulse, corn and grain;
With bartons large, and places where to feed
Your oxen, cows, swine, poultry, with their breed.

On the other side hard by the house, you see
The apiary for the industrious bee.
Walk on a little farther, and behold
A pleasant garden from high winds and bold
Defended (by a spreading fruitful wall
With rows of lime, and fir-trees straight and tall),
Full fraught with necessary flowers and fruits,
And nature's choicest sorts of plants and roots.
Beyond the same are crops of beans and pease,
Saffron, and liquorice, or such as these.
Then orchards so enriched with fruitful store,
Nature could give (nor they receive) no more,
Each tree stands bending with the weight it bears
Of cherries some, of apples, plums and pears.
Not far from thence see other walks and rows
Of cider fruits, near unto which there flows
A gliding stream; the next place you discover
Is where St Foyn, La Lucern, hops and clover
Are propagated. Near unto those fields,
Stands a large wood, mast, fuel, timber yields.
In yonder vale hard by the river stands
A water-engine, which the wind commands
To fertilize the meads, on the other side
A Persian wheel is placed both large and wide
To the same intent. Then do the fields appear
Clothed with corn, and grain, for the ensuing year.
The pastures stocked with beasts, the downs with sheep,
The cart, the plough, and all, good order keep.
Plenty unto the husbandman, and gains
Are his rewards for's industry and pains.

J. Worlidge, *Systema Agriculturae*, 1668

SALE CATALOGUE FROM JOSEPH MOXON'S SHOP, LUDGATE HILL, 1679

Globes 26" in diameter, £20 the pair. A large map of the world, 10' long 7' deep, pasted on cloth and coloured, £2. A map of the English Empire in America, describing all places inhabited there by the English nation, 15s. Sea Plates for Sailing – to all parts of the world, price 6d. the sheet. Playing-cards 6d.; Astronomical, 6d. Geographical cards, describing all the Kingdoms of the Earth, very cheap, and (a very serious subject) – cards representing modes of carving at the dinner-table.

A PENNY IN TWOPENCE

Esther St Michel to Pepys, her brother, 24 September 1681.

Although I am in the country all things are as dear here as at London, and some dearer. . . . As for butcher's meat, bread, beer, and roots, as turnips, carrots, onions, in fine all gardinage [produce from the garden] is dearer here a penny in twopence. Then for soap, starch, oatmeal, salt, pepper, candles, thread, tape etc. stockings, gloves, cloth, mending tabes, and a great many more things too many to trouble you with.

TRADE RIVALRY

In spite of strong Dutch rivalry, we were able to keep for ourselves some trade in the seventeenth century.

The Trades we yet retain are:

1st. For Fish, the Trade of Red Herrings from Yarmouth, Pilchards in the West-Country, and Codfish in Newfound-Land, and New-England.

2dly. A good part of the Turky, Italian, Spanish, and Portugal Trades.

Our Trades to and from our own Plantations, viz. Virginia, Barbadoes, New-England, Jamaica, and the Leward Islands.

If any here shall ask me, how it comes to pass that the Dutch . . . hath not cashiered (*turned*) us out of these Trades, as well as the former? I shall answer . . .

Particularly the Red-Herring Trade we retain, by reason of two natural Advantages, one is, the Fish for that purpose must be brought fresh on Shore, and that the Dutch cannot do with theirs, because the Herrings swim on our Coast, and consequently at too great a distance from theirs.

The other is, those Herrings must be smoked with Wood, which cannot be done on any reasonable terms, but in a Wood Country, such as England is, and Holland is not. . . .

The Newfound-Land Fishing is managed by West-Countrymen, whose Ports are properly situated for that Country, and the Country itself is his Majesties; so the Dutch can have no footing there. . . .

Sir Josiah Child, *A New Discourse of Trade*, 1694

THE EXCHANGE

The Exchange is the Land's Epitome, or you might call it the little Isle of Great Britain did the waters encompass it. It is more, 'tis the whole world's map which you may here discern in its perfectest motion, justling and turning. 'Tis a vast heap of stones, and the confusion of languages makes it resemble Babel. The noise in it is like that of bees; a strange humming or buzzing, of walking tongues and feet; it is a kind of a still roaring, or loud whisper. It is the great Exchange of all discourses, and no business whatsoever but is here on foot. All things are sold here, and honesty by inch of candle; but woe be to the purchaser, for it will never thrive with him. *Hickelty Pickelty, c.* 1700

TRADE WITH VIRGINIA

This is part of a letter from a man in England to his brother in Virginia, and shows what good openings for trade the colonies provided.

If I have not answered expectation in providing this cargo exactly to your orders, or made any mistake in the accounts of the goods I send, I hope you will ascribe it to the haste I have been in and not to want of my endeavours.... I send you two hats of different rates, the prices set out on each hat. One thin wig the lightest I could find, for now bobs are made so extremely full that it is very hard to light upon a thin one, especially of a light colour. Being you writ for knives, I send you one with a marble shaft and also a plush saddle, and cravat with gold fringe which I suppose you may sell to advantage, being they look fine and are really good; though I have set them of a price in the list of particulars, yet sell them as you please, for being you are bound out from trading for others, I will not expect any advantage from my things but make the best of them to your profit. Two pair black stockings, one fine and short, other rollers and coarser, the price the same. Two muslin cravats rowed at the ends as they are now worn. Six pair of gloves, the best Mr Moorecroft gives you. Liverpool and all Chester Fair would not afford such kaps as you desired, nor could Mr Moorecroft find six fit to send you, so has only bought you four. I have sent you I think good soap. My father has disposed of his dictionary, so that I have none to spare, nor could I light on a second-hand one either at Warrington or Liverpool, so I have bought you a new one.... I have sent all the ink Mr Moss could spare; I know you like his best so would not buy elsewhere; an old trunk of my own but have set a new lock to it; lace paper and ribanding is to be bought at Chester Fair by Harrop of Warrington. Knives, razors, hones and tobacco tongs to be bought at Chester by John Stuard.... If I send any clocks to you it must be by the next vessel for now I have not time to procure them before this is bound out. I have agreed for a good watch but have not yet received it. I have sent you three dozen of strong October [ale brewed in that month] in your own bottles; one hogshead of mugs, one cask of Prescott Ware ... being told they are like to be a good commodity.... My mother has sent you a worked comb-case, a cravat with one row of gold through each end, an apron and nightrail which she presents you with for your own trade.

Blundell's Diary and Letter Book, 1702–1728

INCREASE OF TRADE

First let him [any man] reckon up all the houses that are now let and are actually shut up, and then let him set aside all the pastry cooks, coffee houses, perriwig makers, cane chair men, looking glass shops and the like whose places of trade used to be found only in back streets, lanes and alleys and are fittest for such places. . . . We find the most noble shops in the city taken up with the valuable utensils of the tea table. . . . Two thousand pounds reckoned a small stock in copper pots and lacker'd kettles, and the very fitting up one of these brazen people's shops [braziers] with fine sashes [sash-windows], &c., costs above £500 sterling, which is more by half than the best draper's or mercer's shop in London requires. This certainly shows the increase of our trade, brass locks for our doors, chambers and parlours, brass knockers for our doors and the like, add to the lustre of our shops . . . and the same sash works and shop windows, only finer and larger, are now used to range your brass and copper, that the goldsmiths had always to set out their less valuable silver and gold plate. . . . How do pastry cooks and perriwig makers, brandy shops and toy shops succeed linen drapers, mercers, upholsterers and the like, a hundred pound rent for a house to sell jellies and apple pies, two hundred to set up a brandy shop and afterwards not a hundred pound stock to put into it . . . view the famous Churchyard of St Paul's! . . . What takes up the whole row there and supplies the place of eighteen or nineteen topping drapers? Who can but observe it! Cane chair makers, gilders of leather, looking glass shops – and pedlars or toy shops [selling trinkets].

Daniel Defoe, Review, 1713

Religion

A stern struggle arose in the seventeenth century. It called for endurance on the part of those whose faith differed from that which had been established by law. Now Anglicanism was more rigorous; guided by William Laud, supported by the Stuart monarchy. Now was the time of the 'divine right' of king and bishop. There was little encouragement to toleration. Laud resisted the claim of Papacy to infallibility, and equally resisted the claims of Puritanism. Catholics suffered all the early part of the century. The Pilgrim Fathers sailed in *The Mayflower* from Southampton in 1620 to Cape Cod, Massachusetts, to practise their religion there in peace.

When Charles I and the Anglicans were involved in hostilities with Scotland, Presbyterian hopes rose, especially when the Scottish army joined Parliament. But the Covenanters' intentions were not fulfilled. Under Cromwell the Puritans had their way. The use of the Anglican Prayer Book was forbidden, church government by prelates abolished. The form of religion in the country was ill-defined. All but the extremists were tolerated.

In this period of conflict a great part of the English people were 'intoxicated with the poetry of the Bible and with the hope for a heaven on earth'. . . . The Authorised Version, the most important of all, was published in 1611. It became the daily reading of the country. Milton was aware that the Protestant should allow no appeal from the Scripture: 'Let them chant while they will of prerogatives, we shall tell them of Scripture; of custom; we of Scripture; of Acts and Statutes, still of Scripture, till the quick and piercing word enter to the dividing of their souls, and the mighty weakness of the Gospel throw down the weak mightiness of man's reasoning'.

At the restoration of Charles II, the Church of England was also restored. The Prayer Book was revised, the Anglican position clearly stated. The gulf between the Church and Nonconformists widened. The Catholicism of James II brought religious parties together for a short time and this alliance led to the famous Toleration Act of William

175

O   P

 By His Highneſs:

A PROCLAMATION
PROHIBITING

HORSE-RACES
FOR
SIX MONETHS.

Hereas notwithſtanding the many Eminent Teſtimonies the Lord in his Providence hath given againſt the Secret and Miſchievous Plots, which have been laid and contrived by perſons diſ-affected to the Peace and Welfare of this Commonwealth, in the timely Diſcovery of them, whereby the ſame have been hitherto hindered from being brought to effect; yet foraſmuch as due Care ought to be taken for preventing whatſoever may miniſter an Opportunity to give any Diſturbance to the Publique Peace, His Highneſs the Lord Protector being informed that ſeveral Horſe-Races are appointed in divers parts of this Common-wealth, and conſidering how great a Concourſe of People do uſually frequent ſuch Meetings, and the evil Uſe made thereof by ſuch ill-diſpoſed Perſons as watch for opportunities to raiſe New Troubles; For the better preventing of the Evils which may ariſe thereby to the People of this Commonwealth, His Highneſs by the advice of His Council, Doth hereby prohibit and forbid all Horſe-races, and all meetings of any perſons whatſoever upon pretence or colour of any Horſe-races, in any Place within England or Wales, for the ſpace of ſix Moneths, from the ſix and twentieth day of February, one thouſand ſix hundred fifty and four. And doth hereby ſtraightly charge and command, That no Perſon or Perſons whatſoever, during the ſpace of the ſaid ſix Moneths, from the ſaid ſix and twentieth day of February, do appoint any Horſe-race, or do aſſemble or meet together upon, or by colour of any appointment of any Horſe-race, or be preſent at ſuch Horſe-race, as they would avoid being guilty of the Danger that may enſue thereupon, and as they tender the Peace and Security of this Nation. And His Highneſs doth likewiſe charge and enjoin all Mayors, Sheriffs, Juſtices of the Peace, Bayliffs, Conſtables, and all other Miniſters of Juſtice, to uſe their utmoſt diligence and care, That all meetings upon Pretence or colour of any Horſe-race or Horſe-races, during the time aforeſaid, be prevented and hindred, as they will anſwer the contrary at their perils. And all Officers and Soldiers of the Army, quartered or lying in or neer ſuch Place and Places, are hereby authoriſed and required, upon notice, to be aiding and aſſiſting to the ſaid Mayors, Sheriffs, Juſtices, Bayliffs, Conſtables, and other Miniſters of Juſtice herein.

Given at *White-Hall* the 24. day of *February* 1654.

London, Printed by *Henry Hills* and *John Field*, Printers to His Highneſs,
MDCLIV.

55.   Proclamation prohibiting horse-races for six months, 1654.

III. Many years had to pass before this limited toleration became religious equality.

THE DECLARATION OF SPORTS, 1618

The report of this growing amendment amongst them made us the more sorry, when with our own ears we heard the general complaint of our people, that they were barred from all lawful recreations and exercise upon the Sunday's afternoon, after the ending of all divine service, which cannot but produce two evils: the one the hindering of the conversion of many, whom their priests will take occasion hereby to vex, persuading them that no honest mirth or recreation is lawful or tolerable in our religion, which cannot but breed a great discontentment in our people's hearts, especially of such as are peradventure upon the point of turning: the other inconvenience is, that this prohibition barreth the common and meaner sort of people from using such exercises as may make their bodies more able for war, when his Majesty or his successors shall have occasion to use them; and in place thereof sets up filthy tippling and drunkenness, and breeds a number of idle and discontented speeches in their ale-houses. For when shall the common people have leave to exercise, if not upon the Sundays and Holy-days, seeing they must apply their labour and win their living in all working days! . . .

And as for our good people's lawful recreation, our pleasure likewise is, that after the end of divine service our good people be not disturbed, letted or discouraged from any lawful recreation, such as dancing, either men or women; archery for men, leaping, vaulting, or any other such harmless recreation, nor from having of May-games, Whitsun-ales, and Morris-dances; and the setting up of May-poles and other sports therewith used: so as the same be had in due and convenient time, without impediment or neglect of divine service and that women shall have leave to carry rushes to the church for the decorating of it, according to their old custom; but withal we do here account still as prohibited all unlawful games to be used upon Sundays only, as bear and bull-baitings, interludes, and at all times in the meaner sort of people by law prohibited, bowling. . . .

Our pleasure likewise is, that they to whom it belongeth in office, shall present and sharply punish all such as, in abuse of this our liberty, will use these exercises before the end of all divine services for that day: and we likewise straitly command that every person shall resort to his own parish church to hear divine service, and each parish by itself to use the said recreation after divine service: prohibiting likewise any offensive weapons to be carried or used in the said times of recreation.

Harleian Miscellany

PURITAN VIEW OF ROMAN CATHOLICISM
Parliament's Petition of 3 December 1621 to James I
Most gracious and dread Sovereign: We, your Majesty's most humble and loyal subjects, the knights, citizens and burgesses now assembled in Parliament . . . finding how ill your Majesty's goodness hath been requited by princes of different religion, who even in time of treaty have taken opportunities to advance their own ends, tending to the subversion of religion, and disadvantage of your affairs and the estate of your children; by reason whereof your ill-affected subjects at home, the popish recusants, have taken too much encouragement, and are dangerously increased in their number and in their insolencies, we cannot but be sensible thereof. . . .

We humbly offer to your Majesty that we foresee and fear there will necessarily follow very dangerous effects both to church and state. For, 1. The popish religion is incompatible with ours, in respect of their positions. 2. It draweth with it an unavoidable dependency on foreign princes. 3. It openeth too wide a gap for popularity to any who shall draw too great a party. 4. It hath a restless spirit, and will strive by these gradations; if it once get but a connivance, it will press for a toleration; if that should be obtained, they must have an equality; from thence they will aspire to superiority, and will never rest till they get a subversion of the true religion.

OF PURITANS
I find many that are called Puritans, yet few, or none that will own the name. Whereof the reason sure is this, that 'tis for the most part held a name of infamy; and is so new, that it hath scarcely yet obtained a definition: nor is it an appellation derived from one man's name, whose tenets we may find digested into a volume: whereby we do much err in the application. It imports a kind of excellency above another, which man (being conscious of his own frail bendings) is ashamed to assume to himself. So that I believe there are men which would be Puritans; but indeed not any that *are*. One will have him one that lives religiously, and will not revel it in a shoreless [boundless] excess. Another, him that separates from our divine assemblies. Another, him that in some tenets only is peculiar. Another, him that will not swear. Absolutely to define him is a work, I think, of difficulty. Some I know that rejoice in the name, but sure they be such as least understand it. As he is more generally in these times taken, I suppose we may call him a Church-rebel, or one that would exclude order that his brain might rule. To decline offences, to be careful and conscionable in our several actions is a purity that every man ought to labour for, which we may well do without a sullen segregation from all society.

If there be any privileges, they are surely granted to the children of the King, which are those that are the children of heaven. If mirth and recreations be lawful, sure such a one may lawfully use it. If wine were given to cheer the heart, why should I fear to use it for that end? Surely, the merry soul is freer from intended mischief than the thoughtful man. . . . I know we read of Christ's weeping, not of his laughter, yet we see he graceth a feast with his first miracle, and that a feast of joy. And we think that such a meeting could pass without the noise of laughter? Change anger into mirth, and the precept will hold good still: be merry, sin not. As there be many, that in their life assume too great a liberty, so I believe there are some that abridge themselves of what they might lawfully use.

Behold then what I have seen good! That it is comely to eat, and to drink, and to take pleasure in all his labour wherein he travaileth under the Sun, the whole number of the days of his life, which God giveth him. For this is his portion. Nay, there is no profit to Man, but that he eat, and drink, and delight his soul with the profit of his labour. For he that saw other things but vanity saw this also, that it was the hand of God. Methinks that the reading of *Ecclesiastes* should make a Puritan undress his brain, and lay off all those fanatic toys that jingle about his understanding. For my own part, I think the world has not better men than some that suffer under that name; nor withal more villains. For when they are once elated with that pride, they so contemn others that they infringe the laws of all humane society.

Owen Felltham, *Resolves: Divine, Moral, Political, c.* 1623 ——

VERY LONG SERMONS
With a long extempory prayer before and another very long prayer after them many of which sermons and prayers have been ended so late in the evening that some of the parishioners have called for candle and lantern to go home by and the young people and others of the said parish church have been thereby debarred of their lawful recreations graciously allowed them by his Majesty and of sufficient and convenient for fothering [feeding] of their cattle and doing of other business of necessity.

Villager in evidence before the archdeacon's Court against the rector of Shawell, 1637

THE WICKED CAT
>   To Banbury came I, O profane one,
>   Where I saw a Puritáne one
>   Hanging of his cat on Monday,
>   For killing of a mouse on Sunday.
Richard Brathwaite, *Drunken Barnaby's Four Journeys*, 1638

56. A broadsheet of 1647 portraying different religious sects.

ILL-TREATMENT OF A QUAKER, 1640

So of a sudden all the people in the steeplehouse were in an outrage and an uproar: that they fell upon me in the steeplehouse before his face and knocked me down, and kicked me, and trampled upon me before his face: and people tumbled over their seats for fear: and at last he came and took me from amongst the people again: and led me out of the steeplehouse, and put me into the hands of the constables and other officers' hands, and bid them whip me and put me out of the town, and then they led me about a quarter of a mile, some taking hold by my collar and some by the arms and shoulders, and shook and dragged me, and some got hedgestakes: and holme bushes and other staffs: and many friendly people that was come to the market: and some came into the steeplehouse to hear me: many of them they knocked down, and broke their heads also (and the blood ran down several people so as I never saw the like in my life: as I looked at them when they was dragging me along).

And Judge Fell's son running after to see what they would do with me: they threw him into a ditch of water, and cried, 'Knock out the teeth of his head!'

And when they had led me to the common (moss), and a multitude of people following: there they fell upon me with their staffs and hedgestakes, and the constables and officers gave me some blows over my back with their willow rods, and so thrust me amongst the rude multitude: and they then fell upon me as aforesaid with their stakes and clubs, and beat me on my head and arms and shoulders, till they had mazed me, and at last I fell down upon the wet common; and when I recovered my self again and saw my self lying on a watery common, and all the people standing about me, I lay a little still, and the power of the Lord sprang through me, and the eternal refreshings refreshed me, that I stood up again in the eternal power of God, and stretched out my arms amongst them all, and said again with a loud voice: 'Strike again! here is my arms, my head, and my cheeks!'

Journal of George Fox, 1694

THE PURITANS

Among other affected habits, few of the puritans, what degree soever they were of, wore their hair long enough to cover their ears, and the ministers and many others cut it close round their heads, with so many little peaks, as was something ridiculous to behold; whereupon Cleaveland in his Hue and Cry after them, begins,

'With hayre in Characters and Luggs in Text,' &c. From this custom of wearing their hair, that name of round-head became the scornful term given to the whole parliament party, whose army indeed marched out as if they had been only sent out till their hair was grown. Two or three years after any stranger that had seen them, would have inquired the reason of that name. It was very ill applied to Mr Hutchinson, who having naturally a very fine thickset head of hair, kept it clean and handsome, so that it was a great ornament to him; although the godly of those days, when he embraced their party, would not allow him to be religious because his hair was not in their cut, nor his words in their phrase, nor such little formalities altogether fitted to their humour; who were, many of them, so weak as to esteem such insignificant circumstances, rather than solid wisdom, piety, and courage, which brought real aid and honour to their party.

Memoirs of Colonel Hutchinson, 1642

PURITAN ICONOCLASTS

There was not care and moderation used in reforming the cathedral church bordering upon my palace. It is no other than tragical to relate the carnage of that furious sacrilege, whereof our eyes and ears were the sad witnesses, under the authority and presence of Linsey, Tofts the sheriff, and Greenwood. Lord, what work was here, what clattering of glasses, what beating down of walls, what tearing up of monuments, what pulling down of seats, what wrestling out of irons and brass from the windows and graves, what defacing of arms, what demolishing of curious stone work, that had not any representation in the world, but only the cost of the founder, the skill of the mason, what toting and piping upon the destroyed organ pipes, and what a hideous triumph on the market day before all the country, when in a kind of sacrilegious and profane profession, all the organ pipes, vestments, both copes and surplices, together with the leaden cross, which had been newly sawn down from over the green yard pulpit, and the service books and singing books that could be had were carried to the fire in the public market-place; a lewd wretch walking before the train, in his cope, trailing in the dirt, with a service book in his hand, imitating, in an impious scorn, the tune, and usurping the words of the Litany, used formerly in the church; near the public cross all these monuments of idolatry must be sacrificed to the fire, not without much ostentation of a zealous joy in discharging ordnance to the cost of some now who professed how much they had longed to see that day. Neither was it any news, upon this Guild day, to have the cathedral now open on all sides to be filled with musketeers, waiting for the major's return, drinking and tobaccoing as freely as if it had turned ale-house.

Joseph Hall, *Hard Measure*, 1647

ACT FOR THE BETTER OBSERVATION OF THE LORD'S DAY

Be it enacted that whatsoever person or persons within this Commonwealth shall be found guilty according to this Act, of committing the offences hereinafter mentioned upon the said Lord's Day shall be adjudged to be guilty of profaning the Lord's Day; that is to say every inn-keeper, victualler or alehouse-keeper, who shall lodge and entertain any waggoner, carrier, butcher, higler, drover, or their servants, coming and travelling; any person using or employing any boat, wherry, lighter, barge, horse, coach or sedan, or travelling or labouring with any of them upon the day aforesaid (except it be to and from some place for the service of God, or except in case of necessity to be allowed by a Justice of the Peace). Every person being in any tavern, tobacco-house, cellar or shop, or sending for any wine, ale or beer, tobacco or strongwater, and to tipple within any other house or shop; every person dancing or profanely singing or playing upon musical instruments, every persons working in the washing, whiting or drying of clothes; and every butcher, costermonger, poulterer, herb-seller, cord-wainer, shocmaker, or other persons selling, exposing, or offering to sell any their wares or commodities, upon the day aforesaid; All tailors fitting or going to fit any wearing apparel; and barbers trimming upon the day aforesaid; and all persons vainly and profanely walking on the day aforesaid, and it is enacted that every person being of the age of fourteen years and upwards, offending and being convicted thereof shall for every such offence forfeit the sum of ten shillings.

Provided that nothing in this Act contained shall extend to the prohibiting the dressing of meat in private families, or the dressing or sale of victuals in a moderate way in inns, for to the crying or selling of milk before nine of the clock in the morning or after four of the clock in the afternoon from the tenth of September till the tenth of March; or before eight of the clock in the morning or after five of the clock in the afternoon, from the tenth of March till the tenth of September yearly, not to hinder any other works of piety, necessity or mercy to be allowed by a Justice of the Peace. . . .

And to the end that no profane, licentious person may in the least measure receive encouragement to neglect the performance of religious and holy duties on the said day. Be it enacted that all and every person shall (having no reasonable excuse for their absence) upon every Lord's Day diligently resort to some church or chapel where the true worship and service of God is exercised upon pain that all and every such person so offending shall forfeit the sum of two shillings and six pence.

Acts and Ordinances of the Interregnum, 1642–1660

THE CORPORATION ACT, 1661

IV. And be it further enacted that all persons who upon the four and
twentieth day of December, one thousand six hundred and sixty
and one, shall be mayors, aldermen, recorders, bailiffs, town clerks,
common council-men, and other persons then bearing any office
or offices of magistracy, or places, or trusts, or other employment
relating to or concerning the government of the said respective

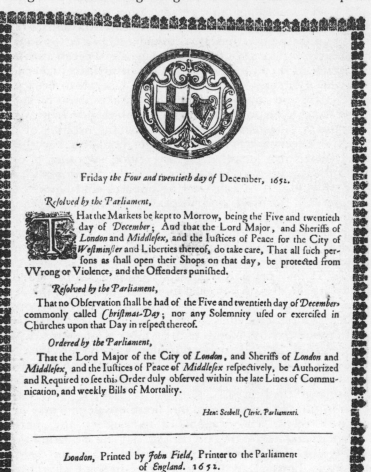

Friday *the Four and twentieth day of* December, 1652.

Resolved by the Parliament,

THat the Markets be kept to Morrow, being the Five and twentieth
day of *December*; And that the Lord Major, and Sheriffs of
London and *Middlesex*, and the Iustices of Peace for the City of
Westminster and Liberties thereof, do take care, That all such per-
sons as shall open their Shops on that day, be protected from
VVrong or Violence, and the Offenders punished.

Resolved by the Parliament,

That no Observation shall be had of the Five and twentieth day of *December,*
commonly called *Christmas-Day*; nor any Solemnity used or exercised in
Churches upon that Day in respect thereof.

Ordered by the Parliament,

That the Lord Major of the City of *London*, and Sheriffs of *London* and
Middlesex, and the Iustices of Peace of *Middlesex* respectively, be Authorized
and Required to see this Order duly observed within the late Lines of Commu-
nication, and weekly Bills of Mortality.

Hen: Scobell, Cleric. Parliamenti.

London, Printed by *John Field,* Printer to the Parliament
of *England.* 1652.

57. Resolution to end observation of Christmas Day, 1652.

The Vindication of

CHRISTMAS,

OR,

His Twelve Yeares Obſervations upon the
Times, concerning the lamentable Game called Sweep-
ſtake ; acted by General *Plunder*, and Major General *Tax*;
With his Exhortation to the people ; a deſcription of that
oppreſſing Ringworm called *Excize* ; and the manner how
our high and mighty Chriſtmas-Ale that formerly would
knock down *Hercules*, & trip up the heels of a Giant, ſtrook
into a deep Conſumption with a blow from *Weſtminſter*.

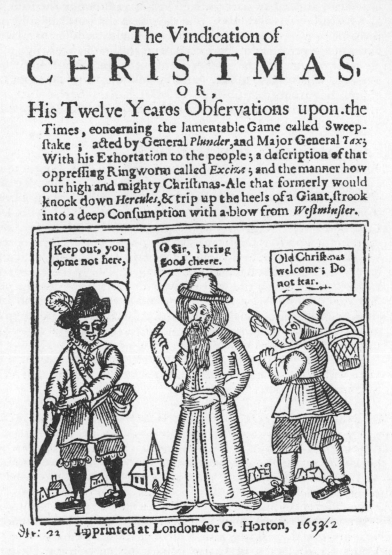

Þr: 22   Imprinted at London for G. Horton, 1653.2

58.   The title-page of a pamphlet published in 1653. It is a vindication of Christmas,
and a complaint against taxation.

cities, corporations, and boroughs, and cinque ports, and their members, and other port towns, shall at any time before the five and twentieth day of March, one thousand six hundred sixty and three be required by the said respective commissioners to take the oaths of allegiance and supremacy, and this oath following:

V. 'I, A.B. do declare and believe, that it is not lawful, upon any pretence whatsoever, to take arms against the King; and that I do abhor that traitorous position of taking arms by his authority against his person, or against those that are commissioned by him: So help me God.'

THE ACT OF UNIFORMITY, 1662

I. Be it enacted that all and singular ministers shall be bound to say and use the Morning Prayer, Evening Prayer, celebration and administration of both the sacraments, and all other public and common prayer and in the said book entitled, The Book of Common Prayer according to the use of the Church of England.

III. And to the end that Uniformity in the public worship of God may be speedily effected, be it further enacted every parson, vicar shall before the feast of St Bartholomew which shall be in the year of our Lord God one thousand six hundred and sixty two, openly, publicly, and solemnly read the Morning and Evening Prayer and after such reading thereof shall openly and publicly before the congregation there assembled, declare his unfeigned assent and consent to the use of all things in the said book contained.

V. That all and every person, who shall neglect or refuse to do the same within the time aforesaid shall *ipso facto* be deprived of all his Spiritual promotions.

THE DECLARATION OF INDULGENCE OF CHARLES II, 1672

Our care and endeavours for the preservation of the rights and interests of the Church have been sufficiently manifested to the world by the whole course of our government, since our happy restoration, and by the many and frequent ways of coercion that we have used for reducing all erring or dissenting persons, and for composing the unhappy differences in matters of religion, which we found among our subjects upon our return. But it being evident by the said experience of twelve years, that there is very little fruit of all those forcible courses, we think ourselves obliged to make use of that supreme power in ecclesiastical matters, which is not only inherent in us but hath been declared and recognized to be so by several statutes and Acts of Parliament. And therefore we do now accordingly issue out this our royal declaration, as well for the quieting the minds of our good subjects in these points, for inviting strangers in this conjuncture to come and live under us, and for the better encouragement of all to a cheerful following of their trades and callings, from whence we hope, by the blessing God, to have many good and happy advantages to our government; as also for preventing for the future the danger that might otherwise arise from private meetings and seditious conventicles. And in the first place, we declare our express resolution, meaning and intention to be, that the Church of England be preserved, and remain entire in its doctrine, discipline, and government, as it now stands established by law: and that this be taken to be, as it is, the basis, rule and standard of the general and public worship of God, and the orthodox conformable clergy do receive and enjoy the revenues belonging thereunto; and that no person, though of different opinion or persuasion, shall be exempt from paying his tithes, or other dues whatsoever. And further, we declare that no person shall be capable of holding any benefice, living, or ecclesiastical dignity or preferment of any kind in this kingdom of England, who is not exactly conformable. We do in the next place declare our will and pleasure to be, that the execution of all and all manner of penal laws in matters ecclesiastical, against whatsoever sort of non-conformists, or recusants, be immediately suspended, and they are hereby suspended.

His Majesties Declaration to all his loving subjects,
15 March 1672

THE TEST ACT, 1673
Parliament strengthens the Protestants with this Act.

I. That all and every person or persons that shall bear any office or shall receive any pay, salary, fee or wages, by reason of any patent or grant from his Majesty, or shall have command or place of trust from or under his Majesty take the several oaths of supremacy and allegiance and the said respective officers aforesaid shall also receive the Sacrament of the Lord's Supper, according to the usage of the Church of England, at or before the first day of August in the year of our Lord one thousand six hundred and seventy-three, in some parish church, upon some Lord's day, commonly called Sunday.

III. And every of the said persons shall first deliver a certificate of such his receiving the said sacrament as aforesaid, under the hands of the respective minister and churchwarden.

IX. That at the same time when the persons concerned in this act shall take the aforesaid oaths of supremacy and allegiance, they shall likewise make and subscribe this declaration following,

'I, A.B. do declare, that I do believe that there is not any transubstantiation in the sacrament of the Lord's Supper, or in the elements of Bread and Wine, at or after the consecration thereof by any person whatsoever.'

Statutes of the Realm

THE TOLERATION ACT, 1689

IV. And be it further enacted that all persons that shall take the said oaths, and make and subscribe the declaration aforesaid, shall not be liable to any pains, penalties, or forfeitures mentioned in an Act made in the five and thirtieth year of the reign of the late Queen Elizabeth nor an Act made in the two and twentieth year of the reign of the late King Charles the Second nor shall any of the said persons be prosecuted in any ecclesiastical court, for or by reason of their nonconforming to the Church of England.

V. Provided always that if any assembly of persons dissenting from the Church of England shall be had in place for religious worship with the doors locked, barred, or bolted, during any time of such meeting together, all and every person or persons, which shall come to and be at such meeting, shall not receive any benefit from this law, but be liable to all the pain and penalties of all the aforesaid laws recited in this Act, for such their meeting notwithstanding his taking the oaths, and making and subscribing the declaration aforesaid.

QUAKERS

The town [Scarborough] has abundance of Quakers in it, most of their best lodgings were in Quaker hands, they entertain all people so in private houses in the town, by way of ordinary, so much a meal, and their ale every one finds themselves, there are a few inns for horses only. I was at a Quakers' Meeting in the town where 4 men and 2 women spoke, one after another had done but it seemed such a confusion and so incoherent that it very much moved my compassion and pity to see their delusion and ignorance, and no less excited my thankfulness for the Grace of God that upheld others from such errors; I observed their prayers were all made on the first person and single, though before the body of people, it seems they allow not of one being the mouth of the rest in prayer to God though it be in the public meetings.... *Journeys of Celia Fiennes*, in 1697 and 1698

DISSENTERS

[Cullompton] . . . here was a large meeting of near 4 or 500 people, they have a very good minister but a young man, I was glad to see so many though they were but of the meaner sort, for indeed it's the poor receive the Gospel, and there are in most of the market towns in the West very good meetings; this little place was one continued long street, but few houses that struck out of the street.

Ashburton is a poor little town, bad was the best inn; it's a market town and here are a great many dissenters and those of the most considerable persons in the town, there was a Presbyterian and Anabaptist and Quaker meeting.

The Journeys of Celia Fiennes, in 1697 and 1698

POPERY LINGERS

[Durham] . . . In the vestry I saw several fine embroidered copes, 3 or 4, I saw one above the rest was so richly embroidered with the whole description of Christ's Nativity Life Death and Ascension; this is put on the Dean's shoulders at the administration of the Lord's Supper, here is the only place that they use these things in England, and several more ceremonies and rites retained from the times of Popery; there are many papists in the town and popishly affected, and daily increase. . . .

The Journeys of Celia Fiennes, 1698

THE OCCASIONAL CONFORMITY ACT, 1711

I.   Be it enacted by the Queen's most excellent Majesty that if any person or persons who by the said recited acts are obliged to receive the sacrament of the Lord's Supper according to the rites and usage of the Church of England shall at any time after their admission into their respective officers knowingly or willingly resort to or be present at any conventicle, assembly or meeting for the exercise of religion in other manner than according to the liturgy and practice of the Church of England shall forfeit forty pounds to be recovered by him or them that shall sue for the same in any of her Majesty's Courts.

II.   And be it further enacted that every person convicted shall be disabled from henceforth to hold such office and shall be adjudged incapable to bear any office or employment whatsoever.

III. Provided always that if any person who shall have been convicted shall after such conviction conform to the Church of England for the space of one year without having been present at any conventicle, assembly or meeting and receive the sacraments of the Lord's Supper according to the rites and usage of the Church of England at least three times in the year every such person shall be capable of the grant of any of the offices or employments aforesaid.

Science

In the seventeenth century Francis Bacon, urging the need for experiment, 'rang the bell that called the wits toge her'. By basing his studies on a right interpretation of nature he replaced that of Aristotle, and science started on a newer course. At the same time English biological science was made famous by William Harvey. His experiments turned to vivisections, and he discovered the circulation of the blood. 'I began to think,' he said, 'whether there might not be a motion, as it were in a circle.' His treatise on the subject was not published till 1628. This epoch-making event made possible modern physiology. Robert Boyle and Robert Hooke followed Harvey's methods when they made discoveries in the chemistry and mechanics of breathing.

The formation of scientific academies at this time extended new experimental work. The Philosophical Society was founded in 1645 and its operations were interrupted by the Civil War. At the Restoration its meetings were resumed, and it received its charter as the Royal Society in 1662. This formed a centre for experiment, enquiry, and information. Among the chief fellows were Abraham Cowley and Robert Boyle, the chemist. In 1661 he published *The Sceptical Chymist*, and was later described as 'Father of Chemistry and Uncle of the Earl of Cork'.

In 1669 Isaac Newton became Professor of Mathematics at Cambridge. He tells us that before this he had 'began to think of gravity extending to ye orb of the Moon . . . and . . . compared the force requisite to keep the moon in her orb with the force of gravity at the Surface of the Earth, and found them answer pretty nearly.' By the suggestions of Halley the astronomer, Newton collected his researches in the *Principia*, the 'Mathematical Principles of Natural Philosophy', in 1687. In this, the greatest book in the history of science, Newton 'laid down the fundamental principles of dynamics, distinguished finally between mass and weight, and established mathematical astronomy', (W. C. Dampier). For many years Newton was President of the Royal Society, acknowledged head of English science, and Master of the Mint.

Of the group of biologists meeting at Cambridge, Nehemiah Grew and John Ray were the most distinguished. Ray wrote many books about animals, birds, reptiles and fishes, and has been called the Father of English natural history. He followed Newton and other English astronomers and physicists in the belief in one God as creator and ruler of the universe.

WILLIAM HARVEY AND THE CIRCULATION OF THE BLOOD

I have heard him say, that after his book of the Circulation of the Blood came out, that he fell mightily in his practice, and that 'twas believed by the vulgar that he was crack-brained; and all the physicians were against his opinion, and envied him; many wrote against him. . . . With much ado at last, in about 20 or 30 years time, it was received in all the universities in the world; and as Mr Hobbes says in his book *De Corpore,* he is the only man, perhaps, that ever lived to see his own doctrine established in his life-time.   John Aubrey, *Lives,* 1628

THE ROYAL SOCIETY

12 November 1662. Sir Robert Moray proposed Mr Hooke as a curator of experiments to the Society; who being unanimously accepted of, it was ordered, that Mr Boyle should have the thanks of the Society for dispensing with him for their use; and that Mr Hooke should come and sit amongst them, and both bring in every day of the meeting three or four experiments of his own, and take care of such others, as should be mentioned to him by the Society.

A VISIT TO OXFORD

We went in the evening to Oxford. . . . We were handsomely entertained two days. . . . I went to visit Mr Boyle whom I found with Dr Wallis, and Dr Christopher Wren in the tower of the Schools, with an inverted-tube or telescope observing the discus of the Sun for the passing of Mercury that day before it, but the latitude was so great that nothing appeared; so we went to see the rareties in the library. . . . Thence to the New Theatre, now building at an exceeding and royal expense by the Lord Archbishop of Canterbury [Sheldon], to keep the Acts in for the future. . . . The whole [had been] designed by that incomparable genius, my worthy friend, Dr Christopher Wren, who showed me the model, not disdaining my advice in some particulars. . . . Thence to Wadham and the Physic Garden, where were two large locust trees, and as many plane trees, and some rare plants under the direction of Old Bobart [First Keeper of the Physic Garden at Oxford].
                                         John Evelyn, 24 September 1664

CHARLES II's EXAMPLE IN PROMOTING EXPERIMENTS

The King . . . has provok'd them to unwearied activity in their experiments by the most effectual means of his Royal example. . . . They design the multiplying and beautifying of mechanic arts, and the noise of mechanic instruments is heard in Whitehall itself. . . . They purpose the trial of all manner of operations by fire, and the King has under his own roof found room for chemical operators. They resolve to restore, to enlarge, to examine physic; and the King has endowed the College of London with new privileges, and has planted a Physic Garden under his own eye. . . . They have begun an exact survey of the heavens, and Saint James's Park may witness, that Ptolemy and Alphonso were not the only monarchs who observed the motions and appearances of the stars.

Bishop Sprat, *The History of the Royal Society*, 1667

THE ART OF FLYING IN THE AIR: MECHANICS, HOOKE'S FIRST AND LAST MISTRESS

I contrived and made many trials about the art of flying in the air, and moving very swift on the land and water, of which I shewed several designs to Dr Wilkins then Warden of Wadham College, and at the same time made a model, which by the help of springs and wings, raised itself in the air; but finding by my own trials, and afterwards by calculation, that the muscles of a man's body were not sufficient to do anything considerable of that kind, I applied my mind to contrive a way to make artificial muscles; divers designs whereof I showed also at the same time to Dr Wilkins, but was in many of my trials frustrated of my expectations.

Robert Hooke, *Diary*, c. 1670

EXPERIMENTAL PHILOSOPHICAL CLUB

At these meetings, which were about the year 1655 (before which time I knew little of them) divers experiments were suggested, discoursed and tried with various successes, though no other account was taken of them but what particular persons perhaps did for the help of their own memories; so that many excellent things have been lost. Some few only by the kindness of the authors have since been made public; among these may be reckoned the Honourable Mr Boyle's *Pneumatick Engine and Experiments*, first printed in the year 1660, for in 1658, or 9, I contrived and perfected the air-pump for Mr Boyle, having first seen a contrivance for that purpose made for the same honourable person by Mr Gratorix, which was too gross to perform any great matter.

Robert Hooke, *Diary*, c. 1670

ROBERT HOOKE AND THOMAS TOMPION

Saturday, May 2nd 1674. . . . To Tompion in Water Lane. Much discourse with him about watches. Told him the way of making an engine for finishing wheels, and a way how to make a dividing plate; about the form of an arch; about another way of teeth work; about pocket watches and many other things. At Sir Ch. Wren's: at Olden-burgs. Borrowed Dr Wallis his letter to Hevelius, and Petit his book about the variation of latitude. At Sir W. Petty in the Piccadilly. He was trimming his new house. . . . With Sir J. Cutler and Dr Whistler at Garaways. Sir J. Cutler promised £1600 for Theatre. At Garaways with Burt. Sent for quadrant from Tompion. I was to send him 25 *sh*. To dine at Lord Brounkers tomorrow with Sir Chr: Wren.

Robert Hooke, *Diary*, 1674

THE WEATHER CLOCK, 1679

. . . The new weather clock which was set up in Mr Hunt's lodgings made to keep an account of the quantity and time of all changes that happen in the air, as to its heat and cold, its dryness and moisture, its gravity and levity; as also of the time and quantity of the rain, snow, and hail, that fall: all which it sets-down in a paper so as to be very legible and certain. Robert Hooke, *Diary*

HOOKE AND TOMPION'S WATCH

Saturday, May 17th, 1679. At Tompion's paid him £8 for the watch with seconds. He would have had more. Mr Davys there. He went with us to Lincolns Inn Fields. At Mr Montacue's directed pillars, stairs, rails, arch, etc. At Man's, Court of Request. I gave Sir Chr. Wren the watch I paid Tompion for today. Spake to Dr Bushby and Mr Smeth-wick about Church. With Sir Chr. Wren to Temple Bar. From Mr Young for view 10 *sh*. With Sir Chr. Wren at Child's, then showed him at home my cylinder and also weather clock, divider and several other things. Robert Hooke, *Diary*

BECOMING A FELLOW OF THE ROYAL SOCIETY

I dined . . . once at Pontack's with the Royal Society. My friend Mr Haughton, one of the fellows was ordered by Sir J. Hoskins, vice president, to bring me to their meeting, which is every Wednesday at 4 afternoon in Gresham College . . . Several philosophical things hapt to be discussed of, and when they broke up, which was about 6, the Secretary, Dr Hooke, and Dr Tyson, with Mr Haughton, told me I must be one of them. I told them it was an honour I could not pretend to, but without it would serve them what I could. Their president, observing what I said, told me it was a thing seldom offered, and seldomer refused. I said nothing more but what I said at first. Then he invited me to dine at Pontack's with them next Wednesday, and then give them my answer.

The next Wednesday I dined with them at Pontack's, when there were in all 16, several of them knights, doctors, &c. I observed that they made no ceremony; every man sat as he came, but the president placed me by him; the reckoning was 3s. 6d. each and he paid for me. We went thence to the meetings, and there I modestly accepted the fellowship they offered, and I was then minuted down against next day of court and election. This time I saw the famous Mr Evelyn among them.

Journal of James Yonge (1647–1721), Plymouth Surgeon

THE ORIGINAL PRESSURE COOKER

12 April 1682. I went this afternoon with several of the Royal Society to a supper which was all dressed, both fish and flesh, in Monsieur Papin's Digesters, by which the hardest bones of beef itself, and mutton, were made as soft as cheese, without water or other liquor, and with less than 8 ounces of coals, producing an incredible quantity of gravy; and for close of all a jelly made of the bones of beef, the best for clearness and good relish, and the most delicious that I had ever seen or tasted. We eat pike and other fish bones, and all without impediment; but nothing exceeded the pigeons, which tasted just as if baked by a pie, all these being stewed in their own juice, without any addition of water save what swam about the Digester, as *in balneo;* the natural juice of all these provisions acting on the grosser substances, reduced the hardest bones to tenderness; but it is best decanted with more particulars for extracting tinctures, preserving and stewing fruit, and saving fuel, in Dr Papin's book, published and dedicated to our Society, of which he is a member.   John Evelyn, *Diary*

THE ROYAL SOCIETY

The Royal Society then, since their first Institution, hath made a vast number of Experiments in almost all the Works of Nature; They have made particular Enquiries into very many things of the Heavens, as well as of the Earth, Eclipses, Comets, Meteors, Mines, Plants, Animals, Earthquakes, Fiery Eruptions, Inundations: of Lakes, Mountains, Damps, Subterraneous Fires: Of Tides, Currents, and Depths of the Sea, and many hundred other things: They have composed many excellent short Histories of Nature, of Arts, of Manufactures, and of Works, whereof some are extreme curious. In a word, the Discoveries and Inventions made, should we say, but by some few Persons of this Society, if well considered, seem to surpass the Works of many foregoing Ages. . . .

The Coat of Arms granted by His Majesty to the Royal Society, is a Scutcheon with three Lyons of England, in chief, intimating, That the Society is Royal; the Crest is an Eagle, and the supporters Hunting Hounds, Emblems of the quickest Sight and Smelling, to intimate the Sagacity, employed in Penetrating and searching after the Works of Nature.   E. Chamberlayne, *Angliae Notitia, or The Present State of England,* 1687

ANATOMY
I went to see the Barber Surgeons Hall (in Newcastle) . . . there I saw a room with a round table in it, railed round with seats or benches for the conveniency in their dissecting and anatomising a body and reading lectures on all parts; there were two bodies that had been anatomised, one the bones were fastened with wires the other had had the flesh boiled off and some of the ligaments remained and dried with it, and so the parts were held together by its own muscles and sinews that were dried with it. . . .   *The Journeys of Celia Fiennes,* 1698

Travel

When William Harrison inserted in his *Description of England* a list of 'the common ways' of England and Scotland in 1577, he had produced the first road-book. Charles Hughes tells us:

> Along all the main roads provision was made for travelling at the most rapid rate then known, by means of post-horses, relays of which stood ready for service at fixed stages. . . . The cost of hire of post-horses by those engaged on public business was fixed by authority at 2½ d. a mile, and private persons were charged 3 d. a mile, with 6 d. for a mounted postboy, who brought back the hired horse from stage to stage. Speed was encouraged, and ten miles an hour was the common rate when the roads were in good condition. From 70 to 150 miles could at need be accomplished in one day.

English gentlemen rode their own horses, and after twenty miles or so put up at an inn. Carts were replacing the pack-horses, and coaches, the 'new invention', made steady progress in the seventeenth century. It was cheaper travel than the horse and more fashionable. Coaches and caroches were both four-wheeled, rested solidly on the axles, and had no springs. Coach-making soon 'became a substantial trade'. John Taylor, the water-poet, called hackney-coaches the 'caterpillar swarm of hirelings'. Soon there were stage coaches, 'long covered wagons', and carriers' carts. The Swan with Two Necks in Lad Lane was the starting-place of many coaches.

All travellers were greatly dependent on the inns. Frequent halts came on long journeys to folk in coaches, horsemen, or those walking on foot. London was well supplied with inns, eating-houses, and beer shops. In 1619 the largest and most famous inn was the White Hart, Southwark (Jack Cade's headquarters in 1450). Henry Peacham says one could find a dinner for threepence in Black Horse Alley, and such places. Thomas Brockbank supped in St Martin's Lane from 'sack, mutton stakes and pigeons', for breakfast 'toast and ale', and for dinner 'pigeons, Westphalia ham, chicken, wine, beef and cabbage, and a pudding'. This was in 1695. At Salisbury he had two trout for one shilling. Inns throughout the country sought to give the best accommodation to travellers in well-furnished rooms with good food, and wine.

196

But without doubt, travellers were exposed to many risks. Roads were in a very bad state. Many, merely covered with gravel, after heavy rain became a quagmire. In some parts enclosure made roads so narrow that coaches and wagons could not pass. In 1653 Samuel Hartlib said: 'I have observed that all or most part of these lands . . . in England are not set out in any good form; too much of England being left as waste ground in commons, moors, heaths, fens, marshes and the like.'

Highwaymen and organized bands of robbers waited to plunder at many places – Hounslow Heath, Gadshill near Rochester, Shooter's Hill near Blackheath, Salisbury Plain. Gamaliel Ratsey was a notorious highwayman; masked and well-mounted, he terrorized roads east of London. He was betrayed, and hanged at Bedford in 1605.

If inns were common on the wayside so also were gallows. John Taylor reminds us of this when he writes in a 'premature epitaph' on Thomas Coryate:

Who now will take the height of every gallows?
And who'll describe the sign of every alehouse?

Coryate, 'the leg-stretcher of Odcombe', was a prodigious walker, and a keen observer of every object on the road. He travelled through France, Italy, Switzerland, Germany, and Holland. In 1612 he set out overland to India, and wrote of his 'ten months' travel between Aleppo and the Mogul's Court'. Taylor himself went on foot from London to Braemer, and wrote descriptions as vivid as those in *Coryats Crudities* and *Coryats Cramb*.

In spite of the use of the horse, the coach, and the wagon, for poor men of every kind, walking still remained the common means of travel.

TO GAIN THE TIMELY INN

In the inns men of inferior condition used to eat at the host's table, and pay some sixpence a meal: but gentlemen have their chambers, and eat alone, except perhaps they have consorts and friends in their company and of their acquaintance. If they be accompanied, perhaps their reckoning may commonly come to some two shillings a man, and one that eats alone in his chamber with one or two servants attending him, perhaps upon reckoning may spend some five or six shillings for supper 'and breakfast. But in the northern parts, when I passed towards Scotland, gentlemen themselves did not use to keep their chambers, but to eat at an ordinary table together, where they had great plenty of good meat and especially of choice kinds of fish, and each man paid no more than sixpence and sometimes but fourpence a meal.

One horse's meat will come to twelve pence, or eighteen pence the night for hay, oats and straw, and in summer time commonly they put the horses to grass, after the rate of threepence each horse, though some who ride long journeys will either keep them in the stable at hard meat as they do in winter, or else give them little oats in the morning when they are brought up from grass. English passengers taking any journey seldom dine, especially not in winter, and withal ride long journeys. But there is no place in the world where passengers may so freely command as in the English inns, and are attended for themselves and their horses as well as if they were at home, and perhaps better, each servant being ready at call, in hope of a small reward in the morning. Neither did I ever see inns so well furnished with household stuff.   Fynes Moryson, *Itinerary*, 1617

INNS

The World affoords not such Innes as England hath, either for good and cheape entertainment after the Guests owne pleasure, or for humble attendance on passengers; yea, even in very poor villages. . . . For as sone as a passenger comes to an Inne, the servants run to him, and one takes his horse, and walkes him till he be cold, then rubs him and gives him meate, yet I must say that they are not much to be trusted in this last point, without the eye of the Master or his servant to observe them. Another servant gives the passenger his private chamber, and kindles his fier; the third puls of his bootes, and makes them cleane. Then the Host or Hostesse visit him; and if he will eate with the Host, or at a common table with others, his meale will cost him sixe pence, or in some places but foure pence (yet this course is lesse honourable, and not used by Gentlemen); but if he will eate in his chamber, he commands what meate he will, according to his appetite, and as much as thinks fit for him and his company, yea the kitchin is open to him, to command the meat to be dressed as he best likes; and when he sits at Table, the Host or Hostesse will accompany him, or if they have many Guests, will at least visit him, taking it for curtesie to be bid sit downe; while he eates, if he have company especially, he shall be offered musicke, which he may freely take or refuse; and if he be solitary, the musitians will give him the good day with musicke in the morning.
Fynes Moryson, *Itinerary*, 1617

POST-HORSES

In England towards the south, and in the west parts, and from London to Berwick upon the confines of Scotland, post-horses are established at every ten miles or thereabouts, which they ride a false gallop after some ten miles an hour sometimes, and that makes their hire the greater: for with a commission from the chief post-master, or chief lords of the Council (given either upon public business, or at least pretence thereof) a passenger shall pay twopence halfpenny each mile for his horse, and as much for his guide's horse: but one guide will serve the whole company, though many ride together, who may easily bring back the horses, driving them before him, who know the way as well as a beggar knows his dish. They which have no such commission pay threepence for each mile. This extraordinary charge of horses' hire may well be recompensed with the speed of the journey, whereby greater expenses in the inns are avoided. All the difficulty is to have a body able to endure the toil. For these horses the passenger is at no charge to give them meat, only at the ten miles' end the boy that carries them back will expect some few pence in gift.

Some nobleman hath the office of chief post-master, being a place of such account as commonly he is one of the King's Council. And not only he, but other lords of the Council, according to the qualities of their offices, use to give the foresaid commissions signed with their hands jointly or severally: but their hands are less regarded than the post-master's, except they be favourites, and of the highest offices, or the business be important. Fynes Moryson, *Itinerary*, 1617

A POSTAL SERVICE

If a carrier of York hath a letter or goods to deliver at any town in his way thither, he serves the turn well enough; and there are carriers and messengers from York to carry such goods and letter as are to be passed any ways north, broad and wide as far or farther than Berwick. So he that sends to Lancaster may from hence have what he sends conveyed to Kendal or Cockermouth; and what a man sends to Hereford may from thence be passed to St Davids in Wales. The Worcester carriers can convey anything as far as Carmarthen; and those that go to Chester may send to Caernarvon. The carriers or posts that go to Exeter may send daily to Plymouth or to the Mount in Cornwall . . . so likewise all the towns and places are served which are betwixt London and Lincoln, or Boston, Yarmouth, Oxford, Cambridge, Walsingham, or any place of the King's dominions, with safe and true carriage. John Taylor, *The Pennyles Pilgrimage*, 1630

ALE-HOUSES

If these houses have a box-bush, or an old post, it is enough to show their profession. But if they be graced with a sign complete, it's a sign of good custom. In these houses you shall see the history of Judith, Susanna, Daniel in the lion's den, or Dives and Lazarus painted upon the wall. It may be reckoned a wonder to see or find the house empty, for either the parson, churchwarden, or clerk, or all are doing some church or court business usually in this place. They thrive best where there are fewest: it is the host's chiefest pride to be speaking of such a gentleman, or such a gallant that was here, and will be again ere long.

Hot weather and thunder, and want of company are the hostess's grief, for then her ale sours. Your drink usually is very young, two days old: her chiefest wealth is seen, if she can have one brewing under another: if either the hostess, or her daughter, or maid will kiss handsomely at parting, it is a good shoeing-horn or birdlime to draw the company thither again the sooner. She must be courteous to all, though not by nature, yet by her profession; for she must entertain all, good and bad, tag and rag, cut and long-tail. She suspects tinkers and poor soldiers most, not that they will not drink soundly, but that they will not pay lustily.

She must keep touch with three sorts of men; that is, the malt-man, the baker, and the justice's clerks. She is merry, and half mad, upon Shrove Tuesday, May days, feast days, and morris-dances: a good ring of bells in the parish helps her to many a tester; she prays the parson may not be a puritan: a bagpiper, and a puppet-play brings her in birds that are flush, she defies a wine tavern as an upstart outlandish fellow, and suspects the wine to be poisoned. Her ale, if new, looks like a misty morning, all thick; well, if her ale be strong, her reckoning right, her house clean, her fire good, her face fair, and the town great or rich, she shall seldom or never sit without chirping birds to bear her company, and at the next churching or christening, she is sure to be rid of two or three dozen of cakes and ale by gossiping neighbours.

Donald Lupton, *London and the Countrey Carbonadoed*, 1632

CHEAPER TRAVEL BY HACKNEY COACHES COMES TO LONDON IN 1639

I cannot omit to mention any new thing that comes up amongst us, though never so trivial. Here is one Captain Bailey; he hath been a sea captain, but now lives on the land, about this city, where he tries experiments. He hath erected, according to his ability, some four hackney coaches, put his men in a livery, and appointed them to stand at the Maypole in the Strand, giving them instructions at what rate to carry men into several parts of the town, where all day they may be had. Other hackney men seeing this way, they flocked to the same place, and performed their journeys at the same rate; so that sometimes there is twenty of them together, which disperse up and down, that they and others are to be had everywhere, as watermen are to be had by the water-side. Everybody is much pleased with it; for, whereas before coaches could not be had but at great rates, now a man may have one much cheaper.

Letter from Mr Garrard to Wentworth, Earl of Strafford, London, 1 April 1639

ODDITIES OF FOREIGN TRAVEL

This passage comes from a book which was a forerunner of guide-books, and James Howell, a scholar by training as well as by instinct, speaks most effectively about men and manners.

Foreign travel oftentimes makes many to wander from themselves as well as from their country, and to come back mere mimics; and so in going far to fare worse, and bring back less wit than they carried forth. They go out figures (according to the Italian proverb) and return ciphers. They retain the vice of a country, and will discourse learnedly thereon, but pass by and forget the good, their memories being herein like hair-sieves, that keep up the bran and let go the fine flour. They strive to degenerate as much as they can from Englishmen, and all their talk is still foreign, or at least will bring it to be so, though it be by head and shoulders, magnifying other nations, and derogating from their own. Nor can one hardly exchange three words with them at an ordinary [eating house] (or elsewhere) but presently they are th' other side of the sea, commending either the wines of France, the fruits of Italy, or the oil and salads of Spain.

Some also there are who by their countenance more than by their carriage, by their diseases more than by their discourses, discover themselves to have been abroad under hot climates.

Others have a custom to be always relating strange things and wonders (of the humour of Sir John Mandeville), and they usually present them to the hearers through multiplying glasses, and thereby cause the thing to appear far greater than it is in itself. They make mountains of mole-hills, like Charenton bridge echo [Charenton-le-pont on the Maine; has a famous bridge of ten arches], which doubles the sound nine times. Such a traveller was he, that reported the Indian fly to be as big as a fox, China birds to be as big as some horses, and their mice to be as big as monkeys. But they have the wit to fetch this far enough off, because the hearer may rather believe it than make a voyage so far to disprove it.

Everyone knows the tale of him who reported he had seen a cabbage under whose leaves a regiment of soldiers were sheltered from a shower of rain. Another who was no traveller (yet the wiser man) said, he had passed by a place where there were four hundred braziers making of a cauldron, two hundred within and two hundred without, beating the nails in. The traveller asking for what use that huge cauldron was, he told him, 'sir it was to boil your cabbage'.

Furthermore, there is amongst many others (which were too long to recite here) an odd kind of anglicism, wherein some do frequently express themselves, as to say 'Your boors of Holland, sir; your Jesuits of Spain, sir; your courtezans of Venice, sir'; whereunto one answered (not impertinently) 'My courtezans, sir? Pox on them all for me, they are none of my courtezans.'

Lastly, some kind of travellers there are, whom their gait and strutting, their bending in the hams and shoulders, and looking upon their legs, with frisking and singing do speak them travellers.

Others by a fantastic kind of ribanding themselves, by their modes of habit and clothing . . . do make themselves known to have breathed foreign air.   James Howell, *Instructions for Forreine Travell*, 1642

YORK, CHESTER, AND EXETER

From the George Inn without Aldersgate, Stage Coaches do continue to go and carry Passengers to the Cities of York, Chester, and Exeter, and to other Towns in the same Roads, every Monday, Wednesday, and Friday, at and for reasonable rates.

As also to Wakefield, Leeds, and Hallifax, every Friday for 40s.

TO {
Durham and Newcastle upon every Monday for 3l.
Edinburgh in Scotland, once every three weeks for 4l. 10s.
Dover and Canterbury, twice every week in two days for 15s.
Bath and Bristol every Monday and Thursday for 20s.
}

With good Coaches, and fresh Horses in the Roads
               Advertisement from *Mercurius Politicus*, 1658

THE POST-BOY

Behold this Post-boy, with what haste and speed
He travels on the Road; and there is need
That he so does, his Business call for haste.
For should he in his Journey now be cast,
His Life for that default might hap to go;
Yea, and the Kingdom come to ruin too.
   Stages are for him fixt, his hour is set,
He has a Horn to sound, that none may let
Him in his haste, or give him stop or stay.
Then Post-boy blow thy horn, and go thy way.
               John Bunyan, *Book for Boys and Girls*, 1686

THE PENNY-POST

. . . there is established another Post, call'd the Penny-Post, whereby for one Penny any Letter or Parcel, not exceeding one Pound weight, or Ten Pounds value, is most speedily and safely conveyed to, and from all parts within the Bills of Mortality, and to most Towns within Ten Miles round London, not conveniently served by the General Post. . . . And for the better carrying on this useful Design, there are Six General Offices kept at a convenient distance from one another, at all which, Officers do constantly attend from Morning until Night, every day, Sundays only excepted; and a very great number of Messengers are employ'd, who have all given Security for the collecting and delivering of Letters, &c. Also five or six hundred Receiving Houses in London, and the other Towns; a List of which Towns will be delivered to any Person gratis at the General Offices. . . .

E. Chamberlayne, Angliae Notitia, or The Present State of England, 1687

LONDON–NORWICH COACHES

Whereas the Stage-Coaches that are driven between *London* and *Norwich*, have for several Years last past, been so ill performed, that the Passengers travelling therein, have been very much *Incommoded*, and the Journeying by the said Coaches rendered very *Irksome* and *Burdensome*. And, notwithstanding great Complaints have been made thereof, to the Masters of the said Stage, yet have they refus'd and neglected to remedy the same. And Forasmuch as no single Person, or five or six in Company would venture to set up a *New Stage*; it was therefore thought reasonable and necessary, that a more considerable Number should joyn together, and by a *Joynt Stock* set up a new and more convenient Stage, for the better Accommodation of themselves and all others that have occasion to travel upon that Road; which accordingly is done by the Subscription of above 200 Persons. And it is by the Subscribers agreed, That what Profit shall be made of the Moneys employed in the said Stock, above 10 *l. per cent. per Annum* shall be applyed to Charitable uses. And several of the Subscribers have agreed to give the whole profit of their Shares to the Poor; and it is not doubted, but many more will follow their Examples. By which means not only all Persons Travelling, will be much better accommodated, but a considerable Summ of Money may be brought in for the Relief of the Necessitous. It is therefore hoped, That all Persons who have occasion to Travel upon that Road, will give all due Encouragement to so *Generous, Necessary,* and *Charitable* an Undertaking.

This New Stage sets out from the Four *Swans* in *Bishopsgate-Street* in *London*, and from the *King's Head* in the Market-Place in *Norwich*, upon *Mondays, Wednesdays* and *Fridays*.

I Hear there goes to, and comes from *Norwich*, a Coach every *Wednesday*; both which perform the Stage in One Day, which is above 90 Miles.

Rival advertisements for the London–Norwich coaching service at the end of the seventeenth century. From Houghton's 'Collection' of 21 June and 9 August 1695

BAD ROADS

In the time of King Charles the Second, *Sir John Robbinson* being Lieutenant of the *Tower*, used to go hunt often into *Epping-Forest*, but the Ways without *White-Chappell* were very bad and troublesome to him, upon which he was resolved to have them mended, either by Indictment or other way: Upon this (as I have been informed) were laid cross the Ways, Trees, Earth, and then Gravel, and Ditches were made, which made it good for the present; and to keep it for every year, in the middle is laid a high Row of large Gravel, which is forc'd in, and keeps that Part highest to throw off the Water, and the Dirt is press'd or cast into the Ditches, which are every Year cleansed, and thus it's likely to last for ever. Indeed by reason of it's being a *Flat*, in the Winter 'tis pochy, but it's generally without Holes and even.

Sir Christopher Wren, the King's Surveyor General told me, that when he came first into his Place, he found the Way by the Privy Garden, between the 2 Gates at *White-hall*, to be extreme bad, and it had baffled all his Predecessors by means of being an ill Earth; upon this he dug it down (I think) 2 Feet, and there pitch'd and ramm'd it well: upon that he threw what came out, and pitch'd it again substantially, and it remains firm to this Day, only must be mended what the Coaches wear out.

To add to my Proposal of mending the High-ways, and the History how some have been mended, I must tell you that one *Dr Harvey* (the Inventor of the *Harvey-Apple*, Master of *Trinity Hall* in *Cambridge*) about 60 Years since, left an Estate to mend the Roads *versus Londinum* (towards *London*) and 'tis as well mended as any in *England* to *Fulmer*, 6 Miles. *Vide Fuller's History of Cambridge*.

The badness of the roads in and near London at the end of the seventeenth century. From Houghton's 'Collection', 17 April 1696

A VERY GREAT FLOOD

18 May 1709. I visited Mr Young's child, at Somerton, where there was still a very great flood occasioned by a storm of rain with thunder and lightning very dreadful, that fell Monday last there, and all along by Masson, Sherborne and the places adjacent with that fierceness for about 6 hours time that the like had never been seen by any man; it so

overfilling the rivers that Kingsmoor was even this day (when I rode in sight of it) all over covered very deep with water; and many houses were beat down, 8 at Masson. Such a weight of water broke out of the river and ran into Sherborne Church that it beat down many seats, and broke up the pavement of the church all over and was reckoned to have done in that town 5000£ damage. There were hailstones that fell in immensurable quantities, said to be 6 inches in the circumference. Mr Shirley measured one of 3 inches and half. The thunder was incessant. I lodged at Charleton at my brother Farwel's. There fell on Monday no rain at Wells, and there was very little thunder heard.

Dr Claver Morris, *The Diary of a West Country Physician*, 1684–1726

Law and Crime

The Star Chamber was so called according to John Stow 'because the roof thereof is decked with the likeness of Stars gilt'. It was an apartment in the royal palace of Westminster and here the chancellor and other members of the King's Council sat to administer law. The Court of Star Chamber developed from this, and in the reigns of James I and Charles I it became 'a proverbial type of an arbitrary and oppressive tribunal'. Merchants were severely dealt with for fraud, enclosers of arable land were heavily fined, puritan pamphleteers like William Prynne, Henry Burton, John Bastwick, and John Lilburne were savagely punished. Archbishop Laud was a leading figure in the Star Chamber. As an eminent historian has told us, the Parliaments that opposed James and Charles I, instructed by Edward Coke, the greatest of English lawyers, endeavoured to uphold the supremacy of the Common Law, and in 1641 were able to enforce it by legislation; the Star Chamber, the Ecclesiastical Court of High Commission and the jurisdiction of the Councils of Wales and of the North were then abolished.

From the beginning of Elizabeth's reign to the end of the seventeenth century, high treason and all felonies, except petty larceny, were punishable with death, subject to 'benefit of clergy' where it applied. This wholesale execution moved Coke to write in his third Institute:

> What a lamentable case it is to see so many Christian men and women strangled on that cursed tree of the gallows; insomuch as if in a *large field* a man might see together all the Christians that, but in one year, throughout England, came to that untimely and ignominious death, if there were any spark of grace or charity in him, it would make his heart bleed for pity and compassion.

The punishments inflicted by the Star Chamber varied from fines to the pillory, ear-cropping, branding or whipping. The victory of the Common Law in 1641 involved also the abolition of torture in England long before other countries. As G. M. Trevelyan says:

> Above all, the victory of the Common Law of law, as a thing that could not be brushed aside for the convenience of government, and could only be altered

in full Parliament, not by the King alone. This great principle . . . was indeed violated during the revolutionary period of the Commonwealth. But it re-emerged at the Restoration, and was confirmed at the Revolution of 1688, which was effected against James II precisely to establish the principle that law was above the King.

In the early seventeenth century rogues and vagabonds were found in every corner of England. 'Worke is left at home undone,' wrote Samuel Rid in *Martin Mark-all* in 1610, 'and loyterers laze in the streete, lurke in the Ale-houses, and range in the high-wares.' Some were old soldiers, others were labourers, thrown out of work by the enclosures, some were serving-men. There was a mob of jugglers, tinkers, chapmen. In London a 'rowsey, ragged rabblement of rakehelles'. We are told of Priggers or Prancers, lurking in the highways; of Fresh-water Mariners, whose ships have sunk in Salisbury Plain; of Swadders, Morts, Doxies, and Dells – they 'levied a toll upon rich and poor . . . and lent excitement of uncertainty to the lives of the people'. Thievery was an art, and there were many artists in crime. Moll Cut-purse was one – a notorious thief, forger, and fortune-teller. She did penance in 1612 at St Paul's Cross, and is the heroine of Dekker's *The Roaring Girle*. In *Bartholomew Fair,* Nightingale cries out:

> Repent then, repent you, for better, for worse,
> And kiss not the gallows for cutting a purse.
> Youth, youth, thou hadst better been starv'd by thy nurse,
> Than live to be hanged for cutting a purse.

John Taylor in *Description of Tyburn* writes:

> And there's a waterish Tree at Wapping,
> Whereas sea-thieves or pirates are catch'd napping.

There were many prisons: the Tower, five in Southwark, the Comp-ter, the Clink, the Marshalsea, the White Lion, the King's Bench, Cripplegate, Ludgate, the Fleet, and Newgate.

Shakespeare says in *3 Henry VI* 'the thief doth fear each bush an officer'. At this time many officers were often less effective than a bush. The constable, the headborough, and the watch were ridiculed in the plays. (It was not till the eighteenth century that the tithingman became the unpaid, elected parish constable.) But when a malefactor was caught he quickly suffered punishment. Thomas Fuller said: 'London juries hang half and save half.' The seventeenth century, however, was not a time of sentimentality. The criminal – robber, highwayman, 'popish priest' – accepted with courage death by hanging before a huge, excited crowd.

LAST STAR CHAMBER DAY

28 February 1603. The last Star Chamber Day one Darling, a youth of
Merton College (that pretended heretofore to be dispossessed of a
devil by Darrel), was censured to be whipped and lose his ears, for
libelling against the Vice-Chancellor of Oxford and diverse of the
Council. He had part of his punishment the last week in Cheapside; the
rest is or shall be performed at Oxford.

John Chamberlain, *Letters,* 1597–1626

MOLL CUT-PURSE

12 February 1612. This last Sunday Moll Cut-purse, a notorious
baggage (that used to go in man's apparel and challenged the field of
diverse gallants) was brought to Paul's Cross, where she wept bitterly
and seemed very penitent, but it is since doubted she was maudlin
drunk, being discovered to have tippled off three quarts of sack before
she came to her penance. She had the daintiest preacher or ghostly
father that ever I saw in pulpit, one Ratcliffe of Brazenose in Oxford, a
likelier man to have led the revels in some Inn of Court than to be
where he was; but the best is he did extremely badly, and so wearied the
audience that the best part went away, and the rest tarried rather to
hear Moll Cut-purse than him.

John Chamberlain, *Letters,* 1597–1626

APPRENTICES WRECK THE QUEEN'S PLAYERS

8 March 1617. On the 4th of this present, being our Shrove Tuesday,
the prentices or rather the unruly people of the suburbs played their
parts in diverse places, as Finsbury fields, about Wapping by St
Katherin's, and in Lincoln's Inn fields, in which places being assembled
in great numbers they fell to great disorders in pulling down of houses
and beating the guards that were set to keep rule, specially at a new
playhouse (sometime a cockpit) in Drury Lane where the Queen's
players used to play. Though the fellows defended themselves as well
as they could and slew three of them with shot and hurt diverse, yet
they entered the house and defaced it, cutting the players' apparel in
pieces, and all other their furniture, and burned their playbooks and
did what other mischief they could. In Finsbury they brake the prison
and let out all the prisoners, spoiled the house by untiling and breaking
down the roof and all the windows, and at Wapping they pulled down
seven or eight houses and defaced five times as many, besides many
other outrages, as beating the Sheriff from his horse with stones and
doing much other hurt too long to write. There be diverse of them
taken since and clapt up, and I make no question but we shall see some
of them hanged this next week, as it is more than time they were.

John Chamberlain, *Letters,* 1579–1626

FROM 'A RECANTATION OF AN ILL-LEDDE LIFE', *c.* 1640

So being come together, there you lie
In some odd corner, whence you may descry
Such booties as shall pass, and then says he
That is the oldest thief – be ruled by me.
And mark what I shall say. Thus must you place
Your masks and chin-clothes; thus then you your face
May soon disguise, and what is he can swear
Directly and precisely who we were?
And that your words may yield a differing tone,
Put in your mouths each one a pebble stone.
Now must we choose a watch-word somewhat common
As (what's a clock) for fear lest we should summon
Their thoughts into suspicion; then be sure,
The word once named, each man to deal secure;
We that are strongest at the gripe will seize;
Then be assured for to observe me these –
With your left hand to catch the bridle fast,
And let the right upon the sword be cast.
The one prevents escaping, t'other then
Quells their resistance. Let our weaker men
That are not thus employed, cry boldly Stand,
And with their swords and pistols them command.

John Clavel, *Gent.* (A highwayman who wrote in the King's Bench
prison a full confession of his misdeeds.)

ROBBERY ON THE HIGHWAY

11 June 1652. The weather being hot, and having sent my man on
before, I rode negligently under favour of the shade, till, within three
miles of Bromley, at a place called the Procession Oak, two cut-throats
started out, and striking with long staves at the horse, and taking hold
of the reins, threw me down, took my sword, and hauled me into a deep
thicket, some quarter of a mile from the highway, where they might
securely rob me, as they soon did. What they got of money was not
considerable, but they took two rings, the one an emerald with
diamonds, the other an onyx, and a pair of buckles set with rubies and
diamonds, which were of value, and after all, bound my hands behind
me, and my feet – having before pulled off my boots. They then set me
up against an oak, with most bloody threats to cut my throat if I offered
to cry out or make any noise, for they should be within hearing, I not
being the person they looked for. I told them that if they had not basely
surprised me, they should not have had so easy a prize, and that it
would teach me never to ride near a hedge, since, had I been in the

mid-way, they durst not have adventured on me. At which, they cocked their guns, and told me they had long guns, too, and were fourteen companions. I begged for my onyx, and told them it being engraved with my arms would betray them; but nothing prevailed. My horse's bridle they slipped, and searched the saddle, which they pulled off, but let the horse graze, and then turning again bridled him and tied him to a tree, yet so as he might graze, and thus left me bound. My horse was perhaps not taken because he was well known on that road.

Left in this manner, grievously was I tormented with flies, ants and the sun, nor was my anxiety little how I should get loose in that solitary place, where I could neither hear nor see any creature but my poor horse and a few sheep straggling in the copse. After near two hours attempting, I got my hands to turn palm to palm, having been tied back to back, and then it was long before I could slip the cord over my wrists to my thumb, which at last I did, and then soon unbound my feet, and saddling my horse, and roaming about a while, I at last perceived dust to rise and soon after heard the rattling of a cart, towards which I made, and by help of two countrymen, I got back into the highway. I rode to Colonel Bount's, a great justiciary of the times, who sent out hue and cry immediately.

The next morning, sore as my wrists and arms were, I went to London, and got 500 tickets printed and dispersed by an officer of Goldsmith's Hall, and within two days had tidings of all I had lost, except my sword, which had a silver hilt, and some trifles. The rogues had pawned one of my rings for a trifle to a goldsmith's servant, before the tickets came to the shop, by which means they escaped; the other ring was bought by a victualler, who brought it to a goldsmith, but he having seen the ticket seized the man. I afterwards discharged him on his protestation of innocence. Thus did God deliver me from these villains, and not only so, but restored what they took.

John Evelyn, *Diary*

A PUBLIC EXECUTION

21 January 1664 – Up, and after sending my wife to my aunt Wight's to get a place to see Turner hanged, I to the 'Change; and seeing people flock in the City, I enquired and found that Turner was not yet hanged. And so I went among them to Leadenhall Street, at the end of Lyme Street, near where the robbery was done; and to St Mary Axe, where he lived. And there I got for a shilling to stand upon the wheel of a cart, in great pain, above an hour before the execution was done; he delaying the time by long discources and prayers, one after another, in hopes of a reprieve; but none come, and at last was flung off the ladder in his cloak. A comely-looked man he was, and kept his countenance to the

end: I was sorry to see him. It was believed there were at least 12 or 14,000 people in the street.   John Evelyn, *Diary*

DANGERFIELD THE ROBBER TELLS HIS OWN STORY OF PUBLIC MISDEMEANOURS
Fryday, *Dec.* 26, 1684

Adventures

I had the Taylor to make me a Suit of Cloaths, and after he had taken Measure of me, we went to the *Pheasant-Tavern,* and Drank two Bottles of Sack; after which I went home to the *Raven* to Dinner; then after I had Slept a little I went to the Coffee-house, where I found a deal of good Company, with whom I stay'd, and play'd at Back-Gammon and Hazzard untill two a Clock the Next Morning.

Receiv'd

Given to the Fidlers there,	3*s.*	0.	Expences
Spent with Mr *Gibbons* the Taylor,	2*s.*	0.	
Paid for 3 Yards and a half of Cloath,	49*s.*	0.	
Paid for 4 Yards of Black-Satten,	29*s.*	0.	
Lost at Hazzard at the Coffee-house,	15*s.*	0.	
	98*s.*	0.	

Saturday, *Dec.* 27, 1684

Adventures

The Taylor made me sit within all day for want of my Cloaths, so that that day nothing hap'ned more then his coming to me very Drunk, and so became very Troublesome, and that it was Commonly reported about *Shrewsbury,* that I was the *Duke of Monmouth.*

Receiv'd

Paid for a Pair of Gloves,	5*s.*	0.	Expences
Paid for the Exchange of my Hat,	4*s.*	0.	
Spent at my Inn,	15*s.*	0.	
	24*s.*	0.	

Tuesday, *Feb.* 3, 1685

Adventures

I went from *Middlttton* to divers Villages thereabouts, and about 12 a Clock we were over-taken at the End of a Narrow Lane by 7 Horsemen, one of them bid me Stand, and drew forth his sword; but a fair Heath offering in it's Prospect Better Tearms, Call'd to me to Whip and Ride for it; and accordingly we did, and by much out-Rode all the

Pursuers for the space of an hour Whip and Spur: By this time finding our Horses much Impaired, and perceiving no more than 4 of the 7 in sight that Chased us, we e'en resolved to Turn Back and give 'em Battel; which was accordingly done, and after a Smart dispute as ever I met with, which held about a quarter of an hour, My Self, My Horse, and *Mark*, being wounded, we having put all 4 of 'em to Flight, whipped forwards, afresh, and by the help of several favourable Turnings, we got well off to *Burton* upon *Trent,* 10 Miles from the place of dispute: From thence we rode to *Ashby* which is 10 Miles more, and there I was dressed by Mr *Arme* the Chyrurgion, and Lay all Night.

Of a Parsons Wife,	10*s.* 0.	Receits
Of a Farmers Wife,	12*s.* 0.	
Of a Farmer,	10*s.* 0.	
Of a Blacksmith,	10*s.* 0.	
Of a Doctors Wife,	12*s.* 0.	
Of a Farmers Widow,	12*s.* 0.	
and then disturb'd	66*s.* 0.	

Spent at *Ashby,* where I Lay all night,	10*s.* 0.	Expences
Given to Mr *Arm* the Chirurgeon that drest me,	10*s.* 0.	
Paid for two Sword-Scabbards,	5*s.* 0.	
Given to Mr *Arm's* Man,	1*s.* 0.	
	26*s.* 0.	

Captain Dangerfield's *Memoires,* 1685

REWARD FOR A CHEAT

Whereas John Fairshomp, alias Greenfield, a Frenchman born, late a pretended merchant, a tall slender-bodied man, wears a light wig and clothes, thin and pale visage, pretty long straight-nosed, being found guilty of cheating of William Russel Turner in Long Lane, Southwark, of eleven hundred kid-skins, value 160 pounds has absconded from his usual abode. Whoever can give notice of the said Fairshomp alias Greenfield, so as he may be apprehended, to William Russel aforesaid, or John Snat, Leather-cutter in Tuttle Street, Westminster, shall have two guineas reward.   *Post Boy,* 16–18 July 1702

THE PILLORY AND OTHER PUNISHMENTS
Celia Fiennes says, about 1703,
the pillory indeed is to punish perjured persons, which is a great crime;

59. Punishments in the seventeenth century: whipping at the cart's tail; the pillory; and the gallows at Tyburn.

60. Branding.

61. Whipping outside the prison.

there is also whipping, some at the cart's tail, and for some crimes they are burnt in the hand or cheek as a brand of their evil, and if found again to transgress, that mark serves as a greater witness to their condemnation.

THE IMPOSTER REVEALED, 1704
There is now in their Workhouse in Bishopsgate Street, one Rob. Cunningham, a man of about forty years of age, who went begging up and down this City, and other places, with this paper following:

> To the Pious Reader
> Remember that God gave out the Law,
> To keep the people of the world in awe.
> Hope without Faith availeth not indeed,
> Faith without Works, you may be sure is dead;
> Without Charity there is no Salvation,
> Poverty causes a sorrowful Vexation.
> Excuse the Writer, if bold he seems to be,
> He is DEAF and DUMB, and desires Charity.
> He came last from Londonderry
> Where he lost his Speech and Hearing.
> The occasion may be told.
> It was Sickness, Famine and Cold.
> At last confined within the town,
> For a Dog's Head paid half a Crown.
> He does now for a pension wait,
> The which he is promised to get.
> But the old Proverb you may observe,
> While the Grass grows the Horse may Starve.
>   Rob Cunningham.

This man being committed to the Workhouse for begging in the City in the manner aforesaid, was there detected the 13th of this instant September before the Committee there present, he having no Infirmity in his Speech or Hearing, and he will shortly be sent a Soldier in Her Majesty's Service. He is the fourth pretended Dumb Person who hath been here lately detected.

DEATH SENTENCES
London, December 19. The Sessions at the Old Bailey did not end till Monday last; and it has not been known for many years, that so many persons received sentence of death at one time there being then condemned 23 persons, being 6 women, and 17 men, two of which are Richard Keele, and William Lowther, for the late notorious riot and

murder of Edward Perry, the late Turnkey at Clerkenwell-Bridewell; 7 for burglary, 5 for shop-lifting, 4 upon the late Statute for entering of houses, and stealing goods above the value of 40 shillings, and the rest for several capital offences.   *Post Boy,* 17–19 December 1713

Witchcraft

In the thirteenth century and onwards, witchcraft was an extreme heresy, one caused by a personal pact with Satan. This belief in the personal pact, in Devil's marks, familiars, covens, Sabbats, transvection, and spells, became widespread.

In 1484 Pope Innocent VIII, himself 'a man of scandalous life' according to a Catholic historian, in his bull, *Summis Desiderantes*, condemned witches as heretics including in his indictment the sin of hindering fertility in human beings. Jakob Sprenger and Heinrich Krämer, with his approval, produced *Malleus Maleficarum* (Hammer of Witches), containing much information on witchcraft, and the ecclesiastical rules for discovering, trying, and destroying witches. This terrifying, inquisitorial condemnation led to ceaseless persecution for over two hundred years.

After the Reformation, the Protestants' hatred of witches was stronger than ever before. In England, between 1542 and 1684, a thousand witches were executed, with imprisonment in the pillory for mild offences. For this heresy the most dangerous period was that from 1598 to 1607, when nearly half the accused witches were killed. Over the years, one in five of the accused were hanged. In Scotland the number executed was higher, and death was by burning. In Europe from the fifteenth to the eighteenth century over two hundred thousand died at the stake for witchcraft.

The power of this persecution lay not only in bigotry and intolerance but in the unwavering belief in the Fall of Man. Adam had sinned. His descendants were born as sinners. This was our burden of guilt. With guidance from the priest, with the aid of conscience and by repentance man could be saved from damnation by the Grace of God. Damnation meant Hell, eternal punishment. 'In Hell are more pains than are birds flying under Heaven.'

In those days, man was vividly conscious of the terrible punishments, the excruciating tortures put before him in many graphic illustrations of the cruelties of the Inquisition, of the trials and executions of witches. Dante's *Inferno* describes Hell as a graduated conical funnel leading to successive circles where all categories of sinners are imprisoned. The Church felt all outcries, all surges of rebellion against such penalties were of no importance standing against the inescapable facts and consequences of Original Sin.

Witchcraft remained a popular belief and witch-hunts a patriotic sport for many years, supported by the knowledge that many accused witches confessed to different crimes: worship of Satan, murder by wax images, the causing of real suffering. That such confessions followed severe torture, sleepless hours, and stretches of starvation was ignored. Witchcraft was kept before the eyes of many people by pamphlet, illustrations, drama, poetry, sermons, literary wars, law and conjuration. John Wesley, the famous religious reformer, wrote in his *Journal*, 25 May 1768, 'The giving up of witchcraft is in effect giving up the Bible.'

As early as 1584 Reginald Scot in his *Discoverie of Witches* resolutely denied the reality of witchcraft and the power of the Devil. Others followed his attack upon the witchcraft delusion: Thomas Ady, Sir Robert Filmer, George Gifford, Francis Hutchinson, John Webster. Sir John Holt, the most influential judge in the history of English witchcraft, Lord Chief Justice from 1689 to 1710, directed every jury under him to dismiss each case. This strength of will appeared in other courts, so that the last conviction in England, that of Jane Wenham in 1712, was followed by pardon and kindly protection. Belief in witchcraft lingered among the more credulous churchgoers, but in 1736 the statute of 1604 was repealed, and no longer now did the law punish witches. Prosecutions on the Continent and in the American colonies continued for some years, but some time in the eighteenth century the mania of witch-hunts disappeared.

AN ACT AGAINST CONJURATION, WITCHCRAFT, AND DEALING WITH EVIL AND WICKED SPIRITS, 1604

This statute was framed under the command of James I by some of the ablest men in England, including the Earl of Northumberland, the Bishop of Lincoln, the Chief Justice of the Court of Common Pleas, the Attorney General, and the Chief Justice of the King's Bench, and repealed the statute of Queen Elizabeth.

II   . . . be it further enacted by the authority aforesaid, that if any person or persons, after the said Feast of Saint Michael the Archangel next coming

   (a) shall use, practise, or exercise any invocation, or conjuration, of any evil and wicked spirit, or shall consult, covenant with, entertain, employ, feed, or reward any evil and wicked spirit to or for any intent or purpose; or

(b) take up any dead man, woman or child out of his, her, or their grave . . . to be employed or used in any manner of witchcraft, sorcery, charm, or enchantment; or

(c) shall use, practise, or exercise any witchcraft, enchantment, charm or sorcery, whereby any person shall be killed, destroyed, wasted, consumed, pined or lamed in his or her body, or any part thereof; that then every such offender or offenders their aiders . . . being of any the said offences duly and lawfully convicted and attainted, shall suffer pains of death as a felon or felons, and shall lose the privilege and benefit of clergy and sanctuary.

III   . . . to take upon him or them by witchcraft, enchantment, charm, or sorcery,

(a) tell or declare in what place any treasure of gold or silver should or might be found or had in the earth or other secret places, or where goods or things lost or stolen should be found or become; or

(b) to the intent to provoke any person to unlawful love; or

(c) whereby any chattel or goods of any person shall be destroyed, wasted, or impaired; or

(d) to hurt or destroy any person in his or her body, although the same be not effected and done;

that then all and every such person and persons so offending, and being thereof lawfully convicted, shall for the said offence suffer imprisonment by the space of one whole year, without bail or mainprize [surety], and once in every quarter of the said year shall in some market town, upon the market day or at such time as any fair shall be kept there, stand openly upon the pillory by the space of six hours, and there shall openly confess his or her error and offence.

IV   . . . every such offender, being of any the said offences the second time lawfully and duly convicted . . . shall suffer pains of death as a felon or felons, and shall lose the benefit and privilege of clergy and sanctuary. . . .

V   Provided always that if the offender in any of the cases aforesaid shall happen to be a peer of this realm, then his trial therein to be had by his peers, as is used in cases of felony or treason, and not otherwise.

EXECUTION OF WITCHES IN SCOTLAND

1608, December 1. The Earl of Mar declared to the Council that some women were taken in Broughton as witches, and being put to an assize and convicted, albeit they persevered constant in their denial to the end, yet they were burned quick [alive], after such a cruel manner that some of them died in despair, renouncing and blaspheming [God]; and others, half burned, brake out of the fire, and were cast quick in it again, till they were burned to the death.

Sir Thomas Hamilton, *Minutes of Proceedings in the Privy Council*, Edinburgh, 1608

PRESUMPTIONS OF GUILT

These 'at least probably and conjecturally note one to be a witch; and these are certain signs whereby the party may be discovered':

1.   Notorious defamation is a common report of the greater sort of people with whom the person suspected dwelleth, that he or she is a witch. This yieldeth a strong suspicion.

2.   If a fellow-witch or magician give testimony of any person to be a witch, either voluntary, or at his or her examination, or at his or her death.

3.   If after cursing there followeth death, or at least some mischief; for witches are wont to practise their mischievous acts by cursing and banning.

4.   If after enmity, quarrelling, or threatening, a present mischief doth follow.

5.   If the party suspected be the son or daughter, the manservant or maidservant, the familiar friend, near neighbour, or old companion of a known and convicted witch. [Guilt by association.]

6.   If the party suspected be found to have the devil's mark.

7.   If the party examined be inconstant or contrary to himself in his deliberate answers.

William Perkins, *A Discourse of the Damned Art of Witchcraft*, 1608

THE WHITE WITCH

For let a man's child, friend, or cattle be taken with some sickness or strangely tormented with some rare and unknown disease, the first thing he doth is to bethink himself and enquire after some wise man or wise woman, and thither he sends and goes for help. . . . And the party thus cured cannot say with David, 'The Lord is my helper,' but 'The Devil is my helper!' for by him he is cured. Of both these kinds of witches the present law of Moses must be understood.

Though the witch were in many respects profitable, and did not hurt, but procured much good, yet because he hath renounced God, his King and governor, and hath bound himself by other laws to the service of the enemies of God and his Church, death is his portion justly assigned him by God: he may not live.

William Perkins, *A Discourse of the Damned Art of Witchcraft*, 1608

THE LANCASHIRE WITCHES

In 1612, before Sir James Altham and Sir Edward Bromley, Barons of Exchequer, nineteen alleged witches were tried at Lancaster. The chapbook, a semi-official record, was written by Thomas Potts, the clerk of the court. This was 'carefully set forth and truly reported' and became the accepted guide for the holding of witch trials.

Mrs Elizabeth Sowthern, known as Old Demdike, confessed that she became a witch in 1560, when she declared her soul was received by 'a spirit or devil in the shape of a boy'. She soon made her friend, Mrs Ann Whittle, Old Chattox, join her in the 'most barbarous and damnable practices, murders, wicked and devilish conspiracies'. In a short time they recruited their daughters Elizabeth Device and Anne Redfearne, and several other relatives.

Old Chattox was a 'withered, spent, and decrepit creature', her sight almost gone. According to Potts, Old Demdike was the 'rankest hag that ever troubled daylight'. Elizabeth Device, her daughter,

> was branded with a preposterous mark in nature, even from her birth, which was her left eye standing lower than the other, the one looking down, the other looking up, so strangely deformed, as the best that were present in that honourable assembly and great audience did affirm, they had not often seen the like.

Because of suspicion among the neighbours, Old Demdike was taken before a local justice, Roger Nowell, in March 1612. Under questioning, she involved her grand-daughter Alison Device and Old Chattox. These were arrested, and all three tried at Lancaster. Alison confessed. Old Chattox was indicted:

> For that she feloniously had practised, used, and exercised divers wicked and devilish arts called witchcraft, enchantments, charms, and sorceries, in and upon one Robert Nutter of Greenhead, in the Forest of Pendle in the county of Lancaster, and by force of the same witchcraft feloniously had killed the said Robert Nutter.

It was also maintained that both Elizabeth Device and Anne Redfearne had bewitched Robert Nutter and that this led to his death.

Strange events were recorded. Elizabeth Device at Malking Tower in the Forest of Pendle, her mother's home, called a meeting of about eighteen women and several men to make plans to rescue her mother and other witches at Lancaster. At what may have been the first English Sabbat it was decided to kill the gaoler at Lancaster, and blow up the Castle. Another meeting was arranged. Roger Nowell called for action, and on 27 April another nine witches were arrested.

Elizabeth Device refused to confess. Then 'it pleased Gôd to raise up a young maid, Jannet Device, her own daughter, about the age of nine years, a witness unexpected, to discover all their practices, meetings, consultations, murders, charms and villainies'. When her other two children joined Jannet, Elizabeth made 'a very liberal and voluntary confession'. Later she withdrew this, but a confession had been made, and she was found guilty.

Jannet and her brother James referred to a brown dog, called Ball, which helped their mother to kill people. They told of clay figures being made, of a hare that spoke to them. These two children identified many of the witches who had been at the Sabbat at Malking Tower. On further information given, Potts described James 'as dangerous and malicious a witch as ever lived in these parts of Lancaster'.

Anne Redfearne was found not guilty of bewitching Robert Nutter to death, but she was convicted of causing the death of his father, Christopher Nutter – again on evidence which was merely gossip. It was gossip which led to the conviction, as a witch, of Mrs Alice Nutter, Robert's mother, supported by identification made by Jannet Device, who picked her out of a number of prisoners.

It was accepted that witches knew all about the activities of other witches, therefore their evidence should be accepted. The trial continued. Old Demdike died in gaol. Old Chattox confessed in tears. Nearly all the other accused pleaded innocence.

But in the end ten of those tried were hanged, among them Old Chattox and her daughter Anne Redfearne, Elizabeth Device, her son James, and her eleven-year-old daughter Alison, and Mrs Alice Nutter. Two others served one year in gaol. The remainder of the twenty were acquitted.

MARGARET AND PHILIPPA FLOWER
Specially arraigned and condemned before Sir Henry Hobart, and Sir Edward Bromley, judges of the assize, for confessing themselves actors in the destruction of Henry, Lord Rosse, with their damnable practices against others, the children of the Right Honourable Francis, Earl of Rutland.   *Wonderful Discovery*, 1619

The Flower sisters were executed at Lincoln in March 1618. Philippa's confession:
[She] brought from the Castle the right-hand glove of the Lord Henry Rosse, which she delivered to her mother, who presently rubbed it on the back of her spirit Rutterkin; and then put it into hot boiling water. Afterwards she pricked it often and buried it in the yard, wishing the Lord Rosse might never thrive. And so her sister Margaret continued with her mother, where she often saw the cat, Rutterkin, leap on her shoulder and suck her neck.

FAVERSHAM WITCHES
The following 'confession' of Joan Williford taken on 24 September 1645 led her to execution at Faversham, Kent, five days later.

She confessed that the Devil about seven years ago did appear to her in the shape of a little dog, and bid her to forsake God and lean to him. [She] replied that she was loath to forsake him. She confessed also that she had a desire to be revenged upon Thomas Letherland and Mary Woodruff now his wife. She further said that the Devil promised her that she would not lack, and that she had money sometimes brought her – she knew not whence – sometime one shilling, sometimes eight pence, never more at once. She called her devil by the name of Bunnie. She further saith that her retainer Bunnie carried Thomas Gardler out of a window, who fell into a backside [cesspool]. She further saith that near twenty years since she promised her soul to the Devil. She further saith that she gave some of her blood to the devil, who wrote the covenant betwixt them. She further saith that the devil promised to be her servant about twenty years, and that the time is almost expired. She further saith that Jane Holt, Elizabeth Harris, Joan Argoll were her fellows. She further saith that her devil told her that Elizabeth Harris, about six or seven years since, cursed the boat of one John Woofcott, and so it came to pass. She further saith that the devil promised her that she should not sink, being thrown into the water. She further said Goodwife Argoll cursed Mr Major, and also John Mannington, and said that he should not thrive. And so it came to pass. She likewise saith that the devil sucked her twice since she came into the prison; he came to her in the form of a mouse.

FAMILIARS
Matthew Hopkins saw the familiar spirits come to Elizabeth Clark, after keeping her awake for four nights:
1. Holt, who came in like a white kitling [kitten].
2. Jamara, who came in like a fat spaniel without any legs at all. she said she kept him fat, for she clapped her hand on her belly, and said he sucked good blood from her body.
3. Vinegar Tom, who was a long-legged greyhound, with an head like an ox, with a long tail and broad eyes, who when this discoverer spoke to and bade him go to the place provided for him and his angels, immediately transformed himself into the shape of a child of four years old without a head, and gave half a dozen turns about the house, and vanished at the door.
4. Sack and Sugar, like a black rabbit.
5. News, like a polecat. All these vanished away in a little time.
        Matthew Hopkins, *Discovery of Witches*, 1647

DIVINATION
This professional witch-finder caused the death of over two hundred persons.

He was paid twenty shillings or more by the authorities for each witch he found.
The said reputed witch finder acquainted Lieutenant Colonel Hobson
that he knew women, whether they were witches or no by their looks,
and when the said person was searching of a personable and good-like
woman, the said Colonel replied and said, Surely this woman is none
and need not be tried. But the Scotsman said she was, for the town said·
she was, and therefore he would try her. And presently in sight of all
the people, [he] laid her body naked to the waist, with her clothes over
her head, by which fright and shame, all her blood contracted into one
part of her body. And then he ran a pin into her thigh, and then
suddenly let her coats fall, and then demanded whether she had
nothing of his in her body and did not bleed. Then he put his hand up
her coats and pulled out the pin, and set her aside as a guilty person and
child of the Devil. And [he] fell to try others, whom he made guilty.

Lieutenant Colonel Hobson, perceiving the alteration of the foresaid
woman, by her blood settling in her right parts, caused that woman to
be brought again, and her clothes pulled up to her thigh, and required
the Scot to run the pin into the same place, and then it gushed out of
blood, and the said Scot cleared her, and said she was not a child of the
Devil.   Witch trial at Newcastle upon Tyne, 1649

DOCTOR LAMB'S DARLING

Dr Lamb was the Duke of Buckingham's physician, and experimented in
alchemy and magic till his death in 1640. Dr Lamb's 'darling' was his servant,
Mrs Anne Bodenham. She learnt alchemy from him, and studied a little book of
charms. After his death, she gained a reputation as a 'wise woman' – one who
knew a great deal about magic and medicinal herbs. About her neck she wore a
toad in a green bag. She moved to the village of Fisherton Anger in Wiltshire.
Here she met the family of Richard Goddard. Mrs Goddard was sure her two
daughters were trying to poison her. She tried to poison them and went to Anne
Bodenham for three packets of dried dill, dried vervain, and nail parings.

In 1653, a Mr Mason asked Mrs Bodenham about a lawsuit against his
father-in-law, Mr Goddard. She tried to divine the future. Her attempt is
described by Nathaniel Crouch in his Kingdom of Darkness, *1688.*
Anne Bodenham took her staff and therewith drew a circle about the
house, and then took of a book, carrying it over the circle with her
hands. After that, she laid a green glass on the book, and placed within
the circle an earthen pot of coals wherein she threw something which
caused a very noisome smell . . . and so calling Beelzebub, Tormentor,
Satan, and Lucifer [to] appear, there suddenly arose a very high wind
which made the house shake. And presently, the back door flying open,
there came five spirits . . . in the likeness of ragged boys, some bigger
than others, and ran about the house where she had drawn the staff;

and the witch threw upon the ground crumbs of bread which the spirits picked up, and leaped often over the pan of coals in the midst of the circle, and a dog and a cat of the witch's danced with them.

A servant-girl, Ann Styles, was the go-between in the dealings of Mrs Bodenham and the Goddards. She had bought arsenic to help Mrs Goddard in her poisoning. When the two daughters heard of this, Ann Styles, in fear, ran away, first stealing some silver. She was caught, and to avoid punishment accused Mrs Bodenham of witchcraft. She said Mrs Bodenham had changed herself into a black cat, had pricked her (Ann's) finger to wet a pen with blood, and had forced her to sign a red book full of the names of those who had sold their souls to the Devil.

At the trial the marks on Ann's finger were seen. The stolen silver was displayed. Then Ann fell into fits shouting about a headless black man who fought for her soul. The accused was searched. Witch marks were found, and so Mrs Bodenham was condemned and hanged at Salisbury in 1653.

THE DRUMMER OF TEDWORTH

Poltergeist performances continued from March 1662 to April 1663 in the home of John Mompesson, a magistrate of Tedworth in Wiltshire.

The performances started in March 1662 with the arrest of William Drury a vagrant drummer, who 'went up and down the country to show hocus-pocus, feats of activity, dancing through hoops and such like devices'. Drury was accused of forging documents to obtain money while on his way to Portsmouth. The local magistrate, John Mompesson, set him free but confiscated his drum. The strange events at Mompesson's house began after the taking away of the drum, and became more annoying after it had been destroyed. Drury moved about the country. He escaped hanging after trial at Gloucester. Early in 1663 he bought a new drum. On the next day he was tried by Mompesson for pig-stealing, and put in Salisbury jail. He was also charged with being a witch – this, however, was not proved. He was condemned to transportation to Virginia.

Revd Joseph Glanvill, chaplain to Charles II and a Fellow of the Royal Society, went to Tedworth to investigate. This is an extract from his Saducismus Triumphatus.

The noise of thumping and drumming was very frequent, usually five nights together, and then it would intermit three. It was on the outsides of the house, which is most of it board. It constantly came as they were going to sleep, whether early or late. After a month's disturbance without, it came into the room where the drum lay, four or five nights in seven, within half an hour after they were in bed, continuing almost two. The sign of it, just before it came, was . . . an hurling in the air above the house, and at its going off, the beating of a drum like that at the breaking up of a guard. . . .

On the fifth of November, 1662, it kept a mighty noise, and a servant observing two boards in the children's room seeming to move, he bid it give him one of them. Upon which the board came (nothing moving it that he saw) within a yard of him. The man added, 'Nay, let me have it in my hand.' Upon which, it was shoved quite home to him. He thrust it back, and it was driven to him again, and so up and down, to and fro, at least twenty times together, till Mr Mompesson forbade his servant such familiarities. This was in the daytime, and seen by a whole room full of people. . . .

Mr Mompesson perceiving that it so much persecuted the little children, he lodged them out at a neighbour's house, taking his eldest daughter, who was about ten years of age, into his own chamber, where it had not been a month before. As soon as she was in bed, the disturbance began there again, continuing three weeks drumming, and making other noises, and it was observed that it would exactly answer in drumming anything that was beaten or called for. After this, the house where the children were lodged out, happening to be full of strangers, they were taken home, and no disturbances having been known in the parlour, they were lodged there, where also their persecutor found them, but then only plucked them by the hair and night clothes without any other disturbance. . . .

After this, it was very troublesome to a servant of Mr Mompesson's, who was a stout fellow and of sober conversation. This man lay within, during the greatest disturbance, and for several nights something would endeavour to pluck his clothes off the bed, so that he was fain to tug hard to keep them on, and sometimes they would be plucked from him by main force, and his shoes thrown at his head. And now and then he should find himself forcibly held, as it were bound hand and foot, but he found that whenever he could make use of his sword, and struck with it, the spirit quitted its hold. . . .

The drummer was tried at the Assizes at Salisbury upon this occasion. He was committed first to Gloucester Jail for stealing, and a Wiltshire man coming to see him, he asked what news in Wiltshire. The visitant said he knew of none. 'No,' saith the drummer. 'Do you not hear of the drumming at a gentleman's house at Tedworth?' 'That I do enough,' said the other. 'I,' quoth the drummer, 'I have plagued him (or to that purpose) and he shall never be at quiet, till he hath made me satisfaction for taking away my drum.' Upon the information of this, the fellow was tried for a witch at Salisbury, and all the main circumstances I have related were sworn at the Assizes by the minister of the parish, and divers others of the most intelligent and substantial inhabitants, who had been eye and ear witnesses of them, time after time for divers years together.

STONE-THROWING DEVIL

'Lithobolia, or the Stone-Throwing Devil: Being an exact and exact and true account, by way of journal, of the various actions of infernal spirits, or – devils incarnate – witches, or both; and the great disturbance and amazement they gave to George Walton's family, at a place called Great Island [Newcastle] in the province of New Hampshire in New England, chiefly in throwing about by an invisible hand, stones, bricks and brickbats of all sizes, with several other things, as hammers, mauls, iron crows, spits, and other domestic utensils, as came into their hellish minds, and this for the space of a quarter of a year.'

About midnight (24 June 1682 while I was a guest at George Walton's house) two very great stones weighing about 30 pounds a piece (that used to lie in the kitchen, in or near the chimney) were, in the former wonted rebounding manner, let fly against my door and wall in the ante-chamber, but with some little distance of time. This thundering noise must needs bring up the men from below, as before (I need not say to wake me) to tell me the effect, which was the beating down several pictures, and displacing abundance of things about my chamber. But the repetition of this cannon-play by these great rumbling engines, now ready at hand for the purpose, and the like additional disturbance by four bricks that lay in the outer room chimney (one of which having been so employed the first Sunday night, as has been said) made me despair of taking rest and so forced me to rise from my bed.

Richard Chamberlain, Secretary of the Province of New Hampshire,
in a tract published in London in 1698

WITCH TRIAL AT YORK ASSIZES

A poor old woman had the hard fate to be condemned for a witch. *Some, that were more apt to believe those things than me,* thought the evidence strong against her, the boy that said he was bewitched falling into fits before the bench when he see her. But in all this it was observed that the boy had no distortion, no foaming at the mouth, nor did his fits leave him gradually, but all of a sudden; *so that the judge thought fit to reprieve her.*

However, it is just to relate this odd story. One of my soldiers, being upon the guard at eleven o'clock at night at Clifford Tower Gate the night the witch was arraigned, hearing a great noise at the Castle, came to the porch, and being there see a scroll of paper creep from under the door, which, *as he imagined by moonshine,* turned first into the shape of a monkey, then a turkey cock, which moved to and fro by him. Where upon he went to the gaol and called the under-gaoler, who came and see the scroll dance up and down and creep under the door, where there was scarce the room of the thickness of half a crown. *This I had from the mouth both of the soldier and gaoler.*

Sir John Reresby at the York Assizes in 1687

SALEM WITCHES

The English colonies attracted many different types of immigrants. Some were men of scholarship and education; others had considerable material resources, but the great majority came from the lower middle classes and had limited education. However, they often brought to the New World a burning religious faith and a capacity for hard work.

This was especially true in Massachusetts where, as the result of Archbishop Laud's persecutions, substantial immigration took place between 1630 and 1640. The colony seemed to offer a natural haven for Puritans, but, as the years passed, the faith began to show itself in many forms. Change of settlements were inevitable. Those who felt the church leadership to be overstrict followed Roger Williams to Rhode Island; those who considered it lax, moved to New Haven. The mass of settlers, distributed in villages and small townships, accepted church authority even when it was narrow and ill-informed. A pious but parochial society developed and, for lack of wider interests, a disrupting morality flourished. Neighbour observed neighbour, gossip took the place of discussion and whispered superstition was often a substitute for resolute faith. The astonishing climax to spiritual distortion was the Witches' Trials at Salem in 1692.

In that year a number of young women went into convulsions and screamed that their bodies were being pricked painfully by invisible pins.

Belief in the supernatural was unquestioned. The fundamental evil was the spectral evidence that the Devil used the bodies only of the wicked to torment or kill the innocent. In the hysteria produced by the Salem witch trials we find guilt by association with the Devil, and guilt by accusation. Hundreds of simple people were arrested and tried. It seemed as if the Puritans of New England still had the religious heresy of Matthew Hopkins, the English witch-finder in the middle of the seventeenth century, who was exposed and hanged as a sorcerer.

Before the truly shocking trials were over, nineteen people had been hanged between 10 June and 22 September, thirteen of them women.

Ten years after the trials, Judge Samuel Sewall confessed the guilt of the court, asking 'to take the blame and shame of it, asking pardon of men'.

News

2 December 1620 is the date of the first newspaper in the English language. The theme was 'the great Battel about Prague'; on the reverse of the sheet were the words, 'Imprinted at Amsterdam by George Veseler'. Each issue consisted of one leaf in small folio with the text in two columns on both sides. It was known as the 'Corrant', 'Courant', or 'Coranto', a description meaning 'a current relation of events'.

In 1621 Thomas Archer at Pope's Head Alley, Cornhill, was issuing 'Corantos'. Nicholas Bourne and Nathaniel Butter later joined him to publish them up to the Civil War.

In 1623 a newsletter, a *Newes from Spayne,* told the story of the journey to Spain made by Prince Charles and the Marquis of Buckingham, and the mock-serious wooing of the Spanish Infanta under the *noms-de-guerre* of Smyth and Browne. In February 1626 Thomas Archer published the first English advertisement. It was a notice of a bookseller's pamphlet on the marriage of Prince Charles with the French princess Henriette Marie, illustrated by 'a lively Picture of the Prince and the Lady cut in Brasse'.

By this time the dramatists, James Shirley, John Fletcher, and especially Ben Jonson, were jealous of this new printed journalism, following upon broadside ballads. They seized upon the name Nathaniel Butter and ridiculed the 'butter prints', 'butter papers', 'butter spread', 'stale Butter'. In 1632 the Star Chamber suppressed the 'Corantos', forbidding printing of news 'as well Butter's and Bourne's as others''. However, in 1638 Butter and Bourne received the monopoly of printing foreign news.

Illustrations were used, printed from blocks – a ship and two dolphins represented a naval battle. The first real topical illustration was startling. It was in a news pamphlet in 1623. An early attempt was to be made to assassinate the Duke of Buckingham. The illustration showed the weapon – 'a poysined Knife both in length and breadth, hauing foure edges'.

Samuel Pecke was a scrivener with a counter in Westminster Hall. In

January 1642 he wrote *A Perfect Diurnall of the Passages in Parliament* – the first English newspaper dealing with home and not foreign news. Diurnalls now replaced Corantos and were the beginning of a parliamentary press. In 1643 *Mercurius Aulicus,* the earliest royalist pamphlet, appeared. It was written by Sir John Berkenhead of Oriel and printed in Oxford. (Mercurius with a word added was a favourite name.) *Scottish Dove,* a venomous paper, was burned by the common hangman for insulting the French. *London Post,* an official paper, had a woodcut of the person who brought the news – the postman. These publications were called 'books'. The terms 'news-sheet' and 'newspaper' were not used.

Now journalism was pretty firmly established, and Cromwell used it much in the way of a modern dictator. In turn he himself was jeered at as 'King copper nose', 'red-nosed Noll', 'carrot nose', 'Beelzebub's chief ale-brewer'. *Mercurius Elenctius* said of the execution of the King: 'he yielded up his spotless Soul with that Alacrity, Courage, Constancy, Faith, Hope and Charity, which became the Justness of the Cause he dy'd in and the greatness of his royal Spirit'. One number of the weekly newsbook *Mercurius Publicus,* June 1660, contained Charles II's advertisement for his missing dog.

The first real newspaper, other than a newsletter, to be published in England was the *Oxford Gazette.* It appeared in 16 November 1665 at Oxford, the court being there owing to the Great Plague, and was started by the most famous of the seventeenth-century journalists, Henry Muddiman. He had issued *The Parliamentary Intelligencer* and *Mercurius Publicus* working under the direction of his patron Sir Joseph Williamson. Pepys writes: 'This day the first of the Oxford Gazettes come out, which is very pretty, full of news, and no folly in it.' Transferred to London in 1666, it became the *London Gazette,* and still exists as the oldest European newspaper with a continuous history.

ADVERTISEMENT ISSUED IN 1609 FOR VIRGINIA

It gives notices to all artificers, smiths and carpenters, coopers, shipwrights, turners, planters, fishermen, metalmen of all sorts, brickmakers, ploughers, weavers, shoemakers, sawyers, spinsters and labouring men and women who are willing to go to the said plantation of Virginia and inhabit there.

If immigrants will repair to Philpot Lane to Smith, Colony Treasurer, their names shall be registered and their persons esteemed a single share, i.e. 12 guineas. They shall be admitted to go as adventurers to Virginia, where they shall have houses to dwell in, gardens and orchards, food and clothing, at the common charge of the joint stock.

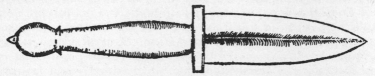

THis *is the true Portraiture of the poystned Knife both in length and breadth, having foure edges; with which a Iesuited* Vratine *was sent out of the Fort by* Monsieur de Thorax, *the Gouernour of that Iland, with an intent to haue killed his Excellence, but by* Gods Prouidence *was deliuered. His Grace hath vsed the French so nobly in all respects, that he rather deserued their loue, then any wayes o haue his life thus treacherously sought after, vnder the pretence that it was a meritorious act. Which Knife was brought ouer vnto* England, *by* Captaine Buckstone, *and by him deliuered vnto the Dutches of* Buckingham *her Grace on Monday night last.*

62. *The True Portraiture of the Poysined Knife.* Early topical illustration, from a news-pamphlet of 1623.

PATENTS
In 1626 a patent was granted to Thomas Rons and Abraham Cullen to use, exercise, practise, and put in use the art and feat of framing, working, and making of all and all manner of pot, jug, and bottle, commonly called or known by the name or names of stone pot, stone jug, and stone bottle.

In 1635 a patent was issued for the coal-firing process for the making and dying of all sorts of pantiles, stone jugs, bottles of all sizes . . . and other earthen commodities within this our realm, which now are made by strangers in foreign parts. . . .

CHARLES II ADVERTISES FOR HIS MISSING DOG
We must call upon you again for a black dog, between a greyhound and a spaniel, no white about him, only a streak, on his breast, and tail a little bobbed. It is His Majesty's own dog, and doubtless was stolen, for the dog was not born nor bred in England, and would never forsake his master. Whosoever finds him may acquaint any at Whitehall, for the dog was better known at Court than those who stole him. Will they never leave robbing his Majesty? Must he not keep a dog? This dog's place (though better than some imagine) is the only place which nobody offers to beg.   *Mercurius Publicus,* July 1660

CHINA-WARE
Of China-Ware I see but little imported in the year 1694, I presume by reason of the war and our bad luck at sea. There came only from Spain certain, and from India certain twice. 'Tis a curious manufacture, and deserves to be encouraged here, which without doubt money would

do; and Mr Dwoit at Fulham has done it, and can again in any thing that is flat; but the difficulty is, that if a hollow dish be made, it must be burnt so much, that the heat of the fire will make the sides fall. He tells me that our clay will very well do it; the main skill is in managing the fire. By my consent, the man that would bring it to perfection, should have for his encouragement 1000 1. from the public, though I helped to pay a tax towards it.

Of Tea-Pots, there came but 10, and those from Holland. To our credit be it spoken, we have about Vauxhall (as I have been informed) made a great many, and I cannot gainsay, but they are as good as any came from abroad.

The next are Tobacco-pipes, of which came from Holland, gross 110, chests 4. I have seen some very long ones, and also small from thence, that truly are very fine. If there comes no more, they'll do us no great hurt. I think they must be permitted to be patterns to set our people on work, and if our smokers would use none but fine ones, I question not but we should make as fine as any body.

Now for Tobacco-pipe Clay; a good sort whereof is gotten at or nigh Pool, a port town in Dorsetshire, and there dug in square pieces, of the bigness of about half a hundred weight each; from thence 'tis brought to London, and sold in peaceable times at about eighteen shillings a ton, but now in this time of war is worth about three and twenty shillings.

The ordinary pipes are sold for eighteen pence the gross, and the glazed ones for two or three shillings.

Extracts from leading articles in Houghton's 'Collection' of
13 March 1695/6 and 12 January 1693/4

LOST: SERVANT, WIFE, AND HORSE

Run away from Neats Court on the Island of Sheppy, Kent, about the 6th Instant, one Will. Greenfeild and his wife, with a considerable sum of money; he is a man of a middle stature, aged about 40, sandy beard, longish chin, wears a wig, and at present looks meagre and sickly: rode away on a truss dark brown nag, about 13 hands high without any mark, with new bridle and saddle: his wife is middle-sized, black eyed, lost an upper tooth before, and very big with child. Whoever secures the said Will. Greenfeild, and given notice to Mr John Edwin in Austin Friars, London, shall receive 10 1. reward and reasonable charges; for his wife 5 1. and for the horse one guinea.   *Post Boy,* 19–21 March 1702

GUINEA REWARD FOR INDIAN BLACK SERVANT

Went away from his master's house in Drury-Lane upon Monday the 6th instant, and has been since seen at Hampstead, Highgate, and

Tottenham-Court, an Indian black boy with long hair, about 15 years of age, speaks very good English; he went away in a brown fustian frock, a blue waistcoat, and scarlet shag breeches, and is called by the name of Morat: Whoever brings him to, or gives notice of him, so as he may be brought to Mr Pain's House in Prince's Court, Westminster, shall have a guinea reward, and the boy shall be kindly received.

Flying Post, 11–14 July 1702

ADVERTISEMENT FOR *THE SECRET MERCURY*

Tomorrow will be published,

A new paper, entitled, *The Secret Mercury,* or the Adventures of Seven Days. To be continued weekly, in as many parts. The author on his Sundays Adventure, criticizes upon the parson both Conformist and Dissenter, and rallies the misbehaviour of the audience on Monday, he peeps into the music houses on Tuesday, he discovers the cheats of the town and the romantic news on Wednesday, he searches the Playhouse on Thursday, he rambles after lewd women, and relates his conferences with them and place of abode on Friday, he visits Bridewell, Newgate, and Bedlam, etc. and on Saturday (having surveyed the town) he takes a trip into the country to find out the intrigues of the clowns and bumpkins. Sold by E. Mallet, near Fleet-bridge.

Flying Post, 5–8 September 1702

PETS FOR SALE

Choice singing Canary Birds, mottled, white, and all other sort of colours; as also Wistling Birds, all sorts of fine Pigeons, choice Turtle-Doves, and a great quantity of Pheasants of all colours: Parrot-Keats [Parakeets] and fine talking Parrots; one Mamozel Monkey, and one sweet Monkey that Wistles like a Bird; fine Italian Grey-hounds, fine Peacocks and Peahens, and all sorts of other Fowls, you may be furnished with at reasonable rates, at David Randal's a Bird-Merchant at his House in Channel-Row, over-against the Rising Sun in Westminster. There is a great many that sells birds in my name, as I know nothing of, so that if any Person or Persons Quality, or Gentlemen, will come to me, they shall be kindly dealt with.

Flying Post, 7–9 March 1704

TWO SHILLINGS FOR BUGG

LOST the 20th Instant between St James's Square and the Old Palace-Yard, a little cross shaped dog, of the lurcher kind, of a yellow brown colour. 'Twas taken up by an ill looked fellow, a notorious dog-stealer, and led by a blue string towards York-Building. He answers to the name of Bugg, and leaps over a stick. Whoever brings him next door to the great house in Dean's Yard, shall have two shillings reward. NB. He will never be worth a George to those who have him, his marks being known.   *Flying Post*, 22–24 May 1712

Famous People

SIR FRANCIS BACON

Yet there happened, in my time, one noble speaker, who was full of gravity in his speaking. His language (where he could spare, or pass by a jest) was nobly censorious. No man ever spake more neatly, more precisely, more weightily, or suffered less emptiness, less idleness, in what he uttered. No member of his speech, but consisted of his own graces: his hearers could not cough, or look aside from him, without loss. He commanded where he spoke; and had his judges angry, and pleased at his devotion. No man had their affections more in his power. The fear of every man that heard him, was, lest he should make an end.   Ben Jonson, *Timber: or, Discoveries*, 1640

GUY FAWKES

Last of all [at the execution] came the great devil of all, Fawkes, *alias* Johnson, who should have put fire to the powder. His body being weak with torture and sickness, he was scarce able to go up the ladder, but yet, with much ado, by the help of the hangman, went high enough to break his neck with the fall; who made no long speech, but, after a sort, seeming to be sorry for his offence, asked a kind of forgiveness of the King and the state for his bloody intent; and with his crosses and idle ceremonies, made his end upon the gallows and the block.
    Harleian Miscellany; quoted in David Jardine's *Criminal Trials*, 1832

BEN JONSON

He can set Horoscopes, but trusts not in them, he with the consent of a friend Cousened a lady, with whom he had made an appointment to meet one old astrologer in the suburbs, which she kept and it was himself disguised in a long gown and a white beard at the light of a dim burning candle up in a little cabinet reached unto by a ladder.

He hath consumed a whole night in lying looking to his great toe, about which he hath seen Tartars and Turks, Romans and Carthaginians fight in his imagination.

                              William Drummond of Hawthornden, 1618

234

63.   'Praise God Barebones.'

WILLIAM LAUD

Amongst his human frailties, choler and passion most discovered itself.
In the Star-Chamber (where if the crime not extraordinary, it was fine
enough for one to be sued in so chargeable a Court) he was observed
always to concur with the severest side, and to infuse more vinegar than
oil into all his censures, and also was much blamed for his severity to his
predecessor easing him against his will, and before his time, of his
jurisdiction. . . .

He was very plain in apparel, and sharply checked such clergymen
whom he saw go in rich or gaudy clothes, commonly calling them of the
Church-Triumphant. Thus as Cardinal Wolsey is reported the first
Prelate, who made silks, and satins fashionable amongst clergy-men; so
this Archbishop first retrenched the usual wearing thereof. Once at a
visitation in Essex, one in orders (of good estate and extraction)
appeared before him very gallant in habit, whom Dr Laud (then
Bishop of London) publicly reproved, showing to him the plainness of

his own apparel. My Lord (said the Minister) *you have better clothes at home and I have worse*, whereat the Bishop rested very well contented.
                          Thomas Fuller, *The Church-History of Britain*, 1648

THE DUKE OF BUCKINGHAM
He had no principles of religion, virtue, or friendship. Pleasure, frolic, or extravagant diversion was all that he laid to heart. He was true to nothing, for he was not true to himself. He had no steadiness nor conduct: he could keep no secret, nor execute any design without spoiling it. . . . He was bred about the King: and for many years he had a great ascendent over him: but he spoke of him to all persons with that contempt, that at last he drew a lasting disgrace upon himself. And he at length ruined both body and mind, fortune and reputation equally.   Bishop Burnet, *History of His Own Time*, 1724–1734

WILLIAM PRYNNE
His manner of study was thus: he wore a long quilt cap, which came 2 or 3, at least, inches over his eyes, which served him as an umbrella to defend his eyes from the light. . . .

64.   An early print of the buccaneer Sir Henry Morgan, 1635–1688.

Upon the opening of the Parliament . . . he girt on his old long rusty sword (longer than ordinary). Sir William Waller marching behind him (as he went to the House), W. Prynne's long sword ran between Sir William's short legs, and threw him down, which caused laughter.

He was of a strange saturnine complexion. Sir C.W. said once that he had the countenance of a witch.   John Aubrey, *Brief Lives*, 1813

SIR KENELM DIGBY

Sir Kenelm Digby was held to be the most accomplished cavalier of his time. . . . He was such a goodly handsome person, gigantic and great voice, and had so graceful elocution and noble address, etc., that had he been dropped out of the clouds in any part of the world, he would have made himself respected. . . . He was a person of very extraordinary strength. I remember one at Sherbourne . . . protested to us that as he, being a middling man, being set in [a] chair, Sir Kenelm took him up, chair and all, with one arm.   John Aubrey, *Brief Lives*, 1813

GEORGE MONCK

He was of a very comely personage, his countenance very manly and majestic, the whole fabric of his body very strong, his constitution very healthful and fitted for business, before his sickness; he was never known to desire meat or drink till called to it, which was but once a day, and seldom drank but at his meal: he was of a great natural force; his eyes were a little deficient at a distance, but near hand very excellently useful, being able to the last to read the worst handwriting without spectacles; his ears were so quick that it was dangerous to whisper in the room without you would have him privy to your discourse; his judgment was slow but sure, he was very cogitative, and of great natural prudence and cunning in his own affairs. . . .

His temperance was remarkable . . . I have known him fast from eating and drinking above thirty hours many times upon the obligation of necessary and important affairs, and constantly made but one meal a day, and in that was not over curious, having been accustomed to the hardships of a soldier's life in his younger years. He was the most watchful person that you have heard of, four hours sleep was to him sufficient and full satisfaction. . . .

All his pleasure was walking and conferring with a trusty friend in a spacious room, but if any the least business invited, he applied to it.

Thomas Gumble, *Life of General Monck, Duke of Albemarle*, 1671

JOHN MILTON

One that had often seen him, told me he used to come to a house where he lived, and he has also met him in the street, led by Millington, the

same who was so famous an aucioneer of books about the time of the
Revolution, and since. This man was then a seller of old books in *Little
Britain,* and Milton lodged at his house. This was 3 or 4 years before he
died. He then wore no sword that my informer remembers, though
probably he did, at least it was his custom not long before to wear one
with a small silver-hilt, and in cold weather a grey camblet coat. . . .

I have heard many years since that he used to sit in a grey coarse cloth
coat at the door of his house, near Bun-Hill Fields without Moor-gate,
in warm sunny weather to enjoy the fresh air, and so, as well as in his
room, received the visits of people of distinguished parts, as well as
quality, and very lately I had the good fortune to have another picture
of him from an ancient clergyman in Dorsetshire, Dr Wright; he found
him in a small house, but thinks but one room on a floor; in that, up one
pair of stairs, which was hung with a rusty green, he found John
Milton, sitting in an elbow chair, black clothes, and neat enough, pale,
but not cadaverous, his hands and fingers gouty, and with chalk stones.
Among other discourse he expressed himself to this purpose; that he
was free from the pain this gave him, his blindness would be tolerable.

. . . besides what affliction he must have from his disappointment on
the change of the times, and from his own private losses, and probably
cares for subsistence, and for his family; he was in perpetual terror of
being assassinated, though he had escaped the talons of the law, he
knew he had made himself enemies in abundance. He was so dejected
he would lie awake whole nights. He then kept himself as private as
could. This Dr Tancred Robinson had from a relation of Milton's, Mr
Walker of the Temple. And this is what is intimated by himself,
VII.26.
> On Evil Daies though fall'n and Evil Tongues,
> in Darkness, and with Dangers compast round,
> and Solitude.

Mr Bendish has heard the widow or daughter or both say it, that soon
after the Restoration the King offered to employ this pardoned man as
his Latin Secretary, the post in which he served Cromwell with so much
integrity and ability; (that a like offer was made to Thurlow is not
disputed as ever I heard) Milton withstood the offer; the wife pressed
his compliance. *Thou art in the right* (says he) *You, as other women, would
ride in your coach; for me, my aim is to live and die an honest man.*

Other stories I have heard concerning the posture he was usually in
when he dictated, that he sat leaning backward obliquely in an easy
chair, with his leg flung over the elbow of it, that he frequently
composed lying in bed in a morning ('twas winter sure then) I have
been well informed, that when he could not sleep, but lay awake whole
nights, he tried; not one verse could he make; at other times flowed *easy*

his unpremeditated verse, with a certain impetus and aestro, as himself seemed to believe. Then, at what hour soever, he rung for his daughter to secure what came. I have been also told he would dictate many, perhaps 40 lines as it were in a breath, and then reduce them to half the number.   Jonathan Richardson

Some people have lately nicknamed me 'the Lady'. But why do I seem to them too little of a man? I suppose because I have never had the strength to drink off a bottle like a prize-fighter; or because my hand has never grown horny with holding a plough handle; or because I was not a farm hand at seven, and so never took a midday nap in the sun – last perhaps because I never showed my virility the way those brothellers do. But I wish they could leave playing the ass as readily as I the woman.   John Milton, *Vocation Exercise*, 1628

THOMAS FULLER
He undertook once in passing to and fro from Temple-bar to the furthest conduit in Cheapside, at his return again to tell every sign as they stood in order on both sides of the way, repeating them either backward or forward, as they should choose, which he exactly did, not missing or misplacing one, to the admiration of those that heard him.

But that which was most strange, and very rare in him, was his way of writing, which something like the Chinese, was from the top of the page to the bottom: the manner thus. He would write near the margin the first words of every line down to the foot of the paper, then would be beginning at the head again, fill up every one of these lines, which without any interlineations or spaces but with the full and equal length, would so adjust the sense and matter, and so aptly connect and conjoin the ends and beginnings of the said lines, that he could not do it better, as he hath said, if he had writ all out in a continuation.   *Anonymous*

GIRLHOOD OF LUCY HUTCHINSON
For my father and mother fancying me then beautiful, and more than ordinarily apprehensive, applied all their cares, and spared no cost to improve me in my education, which procured me the admiration of those that flattered my parents. By the time I was four years old I read English perfectly, and having a great memory, I was carried to sermons; and while I was very young could remember and repeat them exactly, and being caressed, the love of praise tickled me, and made me attend more heedfully. When I was about seven years of age, I remember I had at one time eight tutors in several qualities, languages, music, dancing, writing, and needlework; but my genius was quite averse from all but my book, and that I was eager of, that my mother

thinking it prejudiced my health, would moderate me in it; yet this rather animated me than kept me back, and every moment I could steal from my play I would employ in any book I could find, when my own were locked up from me. After dinner and supper I still had an hour allowed me to play, and then I would steal into some hole or other to read. My father would have me learn Latin, and I was so apt that I outstripped my brothers who were at school, although my father's chaplain, that was my tutor, was a pitiful dull fellow. My brothers, who had a great deal of wit, had some emulation at the progress I made in my learning, which very well pleased my father; though my mother would have been contented if I had not so wholly addicted myself to that as to neglect my other qualities. As for music and dancing, I profited very little in them, and would never practise my lute or harpsichords but when my másters were with me; and for my needle I absolutely hated it. Play among the other children I despised, and when I was forced to entertain such as come to visit me, I tired them with more grave instructions than their mothers, and plucked all their babies to pieces, and kept the children in such awe, that they were glad when I entertained myself with elder company; to whom I was very acceptable, and living in the house with many persons that had a great deal of wit, and very profitable serious discourses being frequent at my father's table and in my mother's drawing-room, I was very attentive to all, and gathered up things that I would utter again, to great admiration of many that took my memory and imitation for wit.

Lucy Hutchinson, *Life of Mrs. Lucy Hutchinson*

THE EARL OF LAUDERDALE

He made a very ill appearance: he was very big: his hair red, hanging oddly about him. His tongue was too big for his mouth, which made him bedew all that he talked to: and his whole manner was rough and boisterous, and very unfit for a Court. He was very learned, not only in Latin, in which he was a master, but in Greek and Hebrew. He had read a great deal of divinity, and almost all the historians ancient and modern: so that he had great materials. He had with these an extraordinary memory, and a copious but unpolished expression. He was a man, as the Duke of Buckingham called him to me, of a blundering understanding. He was haughty beyond expression, abject to those he saw he must stoop to, but imperious to all others.

Gilbert Burnet, *History of His Own Time*, 1724–1734

EVELYN'S INTEREST

13 September 1661. I presented my *Fumifugium*, dedicated to his Majesty, who was pleas'd I should publish it by his special commands.

[A treasure on the abolition of the smoke nuisance in London.]

24 November 1661. This night his Majesty fell into discourse with me concerning bees, &c.

10 January 1662. Being call'd into his Majesty's closet with Mr Cooper, the rare limner, was crayoning of the King's face and head, to make the stamps for the new mill'd money now contriving, I had the honour to hold the candle whilst it was doing, he choosing the night and candle-light for the better finding out the shadows. During this his Majesty discoursed with me on several things relating to painting and graving.

22 August 1662. I din'd with my Lord Brouncker and Sir Robt. Mornay, and then went out to consult about a new model'd ship at Lambeth, the intention being to reduce that art to as certain a method as any other part of architecture.   John Evelyn, *Diary*

JOHN BUNYAN

He appeared in countenance to be of a stern and rough temper, but in his conversation mild and affable, not given to loquacity or much discourse in company, unless some urgent occasion required it, observing never to boast of himself . . . but rather seem low in his own eyes.

As for his person, he was tall of stature, strong-boned though not corpulent, somewhat of a ruddy face with sparkling eyes, wearing his hair on the upper lip after the old British fashion, his hair reddish, but in his latter days sprinkled with grey; his nose well-set, but not declining or bending, and his mouth moderately large, his forehead something high, and his habit always plain and modest.

George Cokayne, *A Contribution of Mr. Bunyan's Life . . .*, 1666

JOHN DRYDEN

The two cavaliers had now approached within the throw of a lance, when the stranger desired a parley, and, lifting up the vizor of his helmet, a face appeared from within, which, after a pause, was known for that of the renowned Dryden. The brave Ancient [i.e. the poet Virgil] suddenly started, as one possessed with surprise and disappointment together; for the helmet was nine times too large for the head, which appeared situate in the hinder part, even like the lady in a lobster, or like a mouse under a canopy of state, or like a shrivelled beau, from within the pent-house of a modern periwig; and the voice was suited to the visage, sounding weak and remote.

Jonathan Swift, *The Battle of the Books*, 1704

SIR CHRISTOPHER WREN

He was in his person low and thin; but by temperance and skilful management, for he was proficient in anatomy and physic, he enjoyed a good state of health and prolonged his life to an unusual length. For this, however, he might probably be indebted to his remarkable cheerfulness and equanimity.

Francis Wrangham, The British Plutarch, 1810

SAMUEL PEPYS

1703, May 26. This day died Mr Samuel Pepys, a very worthy, industrious and curious person, none in England exceeding him in knowledge of the navy, in which he had passed through all the most considerable offices, Clerk of the Acts and Secretary of the Admiralty, all which he performed with great integrity. When King James II went out of England, he laid down his office, and would serve no more; but withdrawing himself from all public affairs, he lived at Clapham with his partner, Mr Hewer, formerly his clerk, in a very noble house and sweet place, where he enjoyed the fruit of his labours in great prosperity. He was universally beloved, hospitable, generous, learned in many things, skilled in music, a very great cherisher of learned men of whom he had the conversation. His library and collection of other curiosities were of the most considerable, the models of ships especially.

John Evelyn, Diary

SIR ISAAC NEWTON

His carriage then was very meek, sedate and humble, never seemingly angry, of profound thought, his countenance mild, pleasant and comely. I cannot say I ever saw him laugh but once. . . . He always kept close to his studies, very rarely went a-visiting, and had as few visitors. . . . I never knew him to take any recreation or pastime either in riding out to take the air, walking, bowling, or any other exercise whatever, thinking all hours lost that was not spent in his studies, to which he kept so close that he seldom left his chamber except at term time, when he read in the schools as being Lucasianus Professor, where so few went to hear him, and fewer that understood him, that oftimes he did in a manner, for want of hearers, read to the walls. So intent, so serious upon his studies, that he ate very sparingly, nay oftimes he has forgot to eat at all . . . of which, when I have reminded him, he would reply – 'Have I?' and then making to the table, would eat a bite or two standing, for I cannot say I never saw him sit at table by himself. . . . I cannot say I ever saw him drink either wine, ale, or beer, excepting at meals, and then but very sparingly. He very rarely went to dine in hall, except on some public days, and then if he has not been minded, would go very carelessly, with shoes down at heels, stockings untied, surplice on, and his head scarcely combed.

Humphrey Newton, *Letters* written in 1728 to John Conduit,
Master of the Mint

GEORGE JEFFREYS
His friendship and conversation lay much among the good fellows and humorists; and his delights were, accordingly, drinking, laughing, singing, kissing, and all the extravagances of the bottle. He had a set of banterers, for the most part, near him; as, in old time, great man kept fools to make them merry. . . . When he was in temper, and matters indifferent came before him, he became his seat of justice better than any other I ever saw in his place. . . . He had extraordinary natural abilities, but little acquired, beyond what practice in affairs had supplied. He talked fluently, and with spirit; and his weakness was that he could not reprehend without scolding; and in such Billingsgate language as should come out of the mouth of any man.

Roger North, *Life of . . . Francis North, Baron Guilford*, 1742

EVELYN MEETS GRINLING GIBBONS
18 January 1671. This day I first acquainted his Majesty with that incomparable young man Gibbon, whom I had lately met with in an obscure place by meere accident as I was walking neere a poore solitary thatched house, in a field in our parish, neere Sayes Court. I found him shut in; but looking in at the window I perceived him carving that large cartoon or crucifix of Tintoret, a copy of which I had myselfe brought from Venice, where the original painting remains. I asked him if I might enter; he open'd the door civilly to me, and I saw him about such a work as for the curiosity of handling, drawing, and studious exactnesse, I had never before seene in all my travells. I questioned him why he worked in such an obscure and lonesome place; he told me it was that he might apply himselfe to his profession without interruption, and wondred not a little how I had found him out. I asked if he was unwilling to be made knowne to some greate man, for that I believed it might turn to his profit, he answer'd he was yet but a beginner, but would not be sorry to sell off that piece; on demanding the price, he said £100. In good earnest the frame was worth the money, there being nothing in nature so tender and delicate as the flowers and festoons about it, and yet the worke was very strong; in the piece were more than 100 figures of men, &c. I found he was likewise musical, and very civil, sober, and discreete in his discourse. There was onely an old woman in the house. So desiring leave to visite him sometimes, I went away.

John Evelyn, *Diary*

JOHN CHURCHILL, DUKE OF MARLBOROUGH

He is a man of birth: about the middle height, and the best figure in the world: his features without fault, fine sparkling eyes, good teeth, and his complexion such a mixture of white and red that the fairer sex might envy: in brief, except for his legs, which are too thin, one of the handsomest men ever seen. . . . He expresses himself well, and even his very bad French is agreeable; his voice is harmonious, and as a speaker in his own language he is reckoned among the best. His address is most courteous, and while his handsome and well-graced countenance engages everyone in his favour at first sight, his perfect manners and his gentleness win over even those who start with a prejudice or grudge against him.

Sicco van Goslinga, *Mémoires* quoted by Sir Winston Churchill
in *Marlborough*

ROBERT HARLEY, FIRST EARL OF OXFORD

He was a cunning and dark man, of too small ability to do much good, but of all the qualities requisite to do mischief and to bring on the ruin and destruction of a nation. The mischievous darkness of his soul was written in his countenance, and plainly legible in a very odd look, disagreeable to everybody at first sight, which, being joined with a constant awkward motion or rather agitation of his head and body, betrayed dishonesty within, even in the midst of all those familiar and jocular bowing and smiling, which he always affected to cover what would not be covered.

Sarah, Duchess of Marlborough, *An Account of the Conduct of
the Duchess of Marlborough*; quoted in
English Historical Documents, 1660–1714

DOCTOR HENRY SACHEVERELL

He had a haughty insolent air, which his friends found occasion often to complain of; but it made his presence more graceful in public.

His person was framed well for the purpose, and he dressed well. A good assurance, clean gloves, white handkerchief well-managed, with other suitable accomplishments, moved the hearts of many at his appearance [at his impeachment for seditious libels].

Everybody knows that he was afterwards sent about several counties; where, with his usual grace, he received as his due the homage and adulation of multitudes. . . .

Sarah, Duchess of Marlborough, *Private Correspondence*, 1838

Historic Events

THE DISCOVERY OF TOBACCO

There is a herb which is sowed apart by itself, and is called by the inhabitants Uppowoc; in the West Indies it has different names according to the places and countries where it grows and is used. The Spaniards generally call it Tabacco. The leaves being dried and brought into powder, they use to take the fume or smoke thereof, by sucking it through pipes made of clay, into their stomach and head; from whence it openeth all the pores of the body: by which means the use thereof not only preserveth the body from obstructions but also (if any be, so that they have not been of too long continuance) in short time breaketh them. Whereby their bodies are notably preserved in health, and know not many grievous diseases, wherewith we in England are often times afflicted.

This Uppowoc is of so precious estimation amongst them, that they think their gods are marvellously delighted therewith. Whereupon sometime they make hallowed fires, and cast some powder therein for a sacrifice. Being in a storm upon the waters, to pacify their gods, they cast some up into the air and into the water. So a pond for fish being newly made, they cast some therein and into the air. After an escape from danger they cast some into the air likewise: but all done with strange gestures, stamping, sometimes dancing, clapping of hands, holding up of hands, and staring up into the heavens, uttering therewithal and chattering strange words and noises.

We ourselves, during the time we were there, used to suck it after their manner, as also since our return, and have found many rare and wonderful experiments of the virtues thereof.

Thomas Heriot, from Hakluyt's *Principal Voyages*, 1600

A COUNTERBLAST TO TOBACCO

As every human body, dear countrymen, how wholesome soever, is notwithstanding subject to some sorts of diseases, so there is no Commonwealth or Body-Politic that lacks popular errors and corruptions. For remedy whereof, it is the King's to purge it of disease, by Medicines meet for the same.

Now surely in my opinion, there cannot be a more base and hurtful corruption in a country than is the vile use of taking Tobacco in this Kingdom. Now how you are by this custom disabled in your goods, let the gentry of this land bear witness, some of them bestowing three, some four hundred pounds a year upon this precious stink. Is it not both great vanity and uncleanness, that at table, a place of respect, of cleanliness, of modesty, men should not be ashamed, to sit tossing of tobacco pipes and puffing of the smoke of tobacco one to another, to exhale athwart the dishes, and infect the air, when very often men that abhor it are at their repast? Surely smoke becomes a kitchen far better than a dining chamber, and yet it makes a kitchen also oftentimes in the inward parts of men, soiling and infecting them with an unctuous and oily kind of soot, as hath been found in some great Tobacco takers, that after their death were opened.

Are you not guilty of sinful and shameful lust? That although you be troubled with no disease, but in perfect health, yet can you neither be merry at an Ordinary, nor lascivious in the Stews, if you lack Tobacco to provoke your appetite to any of those sorts of recreation, lusting after it as the children of Israel did in the wilderness after Quails?

Mollicies and delicacy were the wrack and overthrow, first of the Persian, and next of the Roman Empire. Have you not reason then to be ashamed, and to forbear this filthy novelty, so basely grounded, so foolishly received, and so grossly mistaken in the right use thereof? In your abuse thereof sinning against God, and taking also thereby the marks and notes of Vanity upon you. A custom loathsome to the eye, hateful to the nose, harmful to the brain, dangerous to the lungs, and in the black stinking fume thereof, nearest resembling the horrible Stygian smoke of the pit that is bottomless.

James I, *A Counterblast to Tobacco*, 1604

THE PLOT THAT FAILED

I confess, that a practice in general was first broken unto me, against his Majesty for relief of the Catholic cause, and not invented or propounded by myself. And this was first propounded unto me about Easter last was twelve months beyond the seas, in the Low Countries by Thomas Winter. He came thereupon with me into England. There we imparted our purpose to three other gentlemen, namely, Robert Catesby, Thomas Percy and John Wright. All five consulting together of the means how to execute the same, and taking a vow among ourselves for secrecy. Catesby propounded to have it performed by gunpowder, and by making a mine under the upper House of

65.   A Dutch engraving of the execution of those who took part in the Gunpowder Plot.

Parliament, which place we made a choice of the rather because religion having been unjustly suppressed there, it was fittest that justice and punishment should be executed there.

This being resolved amongst us, Thomas Percy hired a house at Westminster for that purpose, near adjoining to the Parliament House, and there we began to make our mine about the 11 of December 1604.

The five who first entered into the work were Thomas Percy, Robert Catesby, Thomas Winter, John Wright and myself. Soon after we took another unto us, Christopher Wright having sworn him also, and taken the sacrament for secrecy.

When we came to the very foundation of the wall of the House, which was about three yards thick, and found it a matter of great difficulty, we took unto us another gentleman, Robert Winter, in like manner with oath and sacrament as afore said.

It was about Christmas when we brought our mine unto the wall. About Candlemas we had wrought the wall half through. Whilst we were working, I stood as sentinel to descry any man that came near, whereof I gave them warning, and so they ceased until I gave notice again to proceed.

All we seven lay in the House, and had shot and powder being resolved to die in that place before we should yield or be taken. As they were working upon the wall they heard a rushing in the cellar of removing of coals, whereupon we feared we had been discovered. They sent me to go to the cellar, who finding that the coals were a-selling and that the cellar was to be let, viewing the commodity thereof for our purpose, Percy went and hired the same for yearly rent.

We had before this provided and brought into the House twenty barrels of powder, which we removed into the cellar, and covered the same with billets and faggots, which were provided for that purpose.

About Easter, the Parliament being prorogued till October next, we dispersed ourselves. I retired into the Low Countries by advice and direction of the rest, as well as to acquaint Owen with the particulars of the Plot, as also lest by my longer stay I might have grown suspicious, and so have come in question.

In the meantime, Percy, having the key of the cellar, laid in more powder and wood into it. I returned about the beginning of September next. Then receiving the key again of Percy, we brought powder and billets to cover the same again, and so I went for a time into the country till the 30 of October.

It was a further resolve amongst us that the same day that this act should have been performed, some other of our confederates should have surprised the person of Lady Elizabeth the King's eldest daughter, who was kept in Warwickshire at Lord Harrington's house. Then presently have her proclaimed as Queen. We had a project of a Proclamation ready for that purpose, wherein we made no mention of altering of Religion, nor would have avowed the deed to be ours, until we should have had power enough to make our party good, and then we would have avowed both.

Concerning Duke Charles, the King's second son, we had sundry consultations how to seize on his person. But because we found no means how to compass it (the Duke being kept near London, where we had not forces enough) we resolved to serve our turn with the Lady Elizabeth.

The True Copy of the Declaration of Guido Fawkes of Nov. 17th taken in the presence of the Councillors

THE VOYAGE OF THE MAYFLOWER

And I may not omit here a special work of God's Providence. There was a proud and very profane young man, one of the seamen; of a lusty able body, which made him the more haughty. He would always be contemning the poor people in their sickness, and cursing them daily with grievous execrations, and he did not let to tell them, That he hoped to help to cast half of them overboard before they came to their journey's end; and to make merry with what property they had. And if he were by any gently reproved, he would curse and swear most bitterly.

But it pleased God, before they came half the sea over, to smite this young man with a grievous disease; of which he died in a desperate manner. And so he was himself the first that was thrown overboard. Thus his curses lighted on his own head; and it was an astonishment to all his fellows; for they noted it to be just hand of God upon him.

After they had enjoyed fair winds and weather for a season, they were encountered many times with cross winds; and met with many fierce storms; with which the ship was shrewdly shaken, and her upper works made very leaky. . . . In sundry of these storms, the winds were so fierce and the seas so high, as they could not bear a knot of sail: but were forced to hull for divers days together.

And in one of them, as they thus lay at hull, in a mighty storm, a lusty young man, called John Howland, coming upon some occasion above the gratings, was with the seel [sudden heeling over] of the ship thrown into the sea: but it pleased God that he caught hold of the top sail halliards, which hung overboard and ran out at length; yet he held his hold, though he was sundry fathoms under water, till he was hauled up, by the same rope, to the brim of the water; and then, with a boathook and other means, was got into the ship again, and his life

66.   The Commons in session, 1624.

saved. And though he was something ill with it, yet he lived many years after; and became a profitable member, both in Church and Common Wealth.

William Bradford MS. Taken from *The Story of the Pilgrim Fathers*

THE MURDER OF THE DUKE OF BUCKINGHAM
A letter from Dudley Lord Carleton to Queen Henrietta Maria.
Saturday, 23rd of August, 1628

Madam,
I am to trouble your Grace, with a most lamentable relation. This day betwixt nine and ten of the clock in the morning, the Duke of

Buckingham, then coming out of a parlour into a hall to go to his coach and so to the King (who was four miles off), having about him diverse Lords, Colonels, and Captains, and many of his own servants, was by one Felton (once a Lieutenant of this our army) slain at one blow, with a dagger-knife.

In his staggering he turned about, uttering only this word, 'Villain!' and never spoke a word more. But presently plucking out the knife from himself, before he fell to the ground, he made towards the traitor, two or three paces, and then fell against a table although he were upheld by divers that were near him. They (through the villain's close carriage in the act) could not perceive him hurt at all, but guessed him to be suddenly over-swayed with some apoplexy, till they saw the blood come gushing from his mouth and the wound, so fast, that life, and breath, at once left his begored body.

Madam, you may easily guess what outcries were then made, by us that were Commanders and Officers there present, when once we saw him thus dead in a moment, and slain by an unknown hand. For it seems that the Duke himself only knew who it was that had murdered him, and by means of the confused press at the instant about his person, we neither did nor could.

In the meantime Felton passed the throng, which was confusedly great, not so much as marked or followed, in so much that not knowing where, nor who he was that had done that fact, some came to keep guard at the gates, and others went to the ramparts of the town. In all which time the villain was standing in the kitchen of the same house. After inquiry made by a multitude of captains and gentlemen then pressing into the house and court, and crying out amain, 'Where is the villain? Where is the butcher?' he most audaciously and resolutely drawing forth his sword, came out and went among them, saying boldly, 'I am the man, here I am.' Upon which divers drew upon him, with the intent to have dispatched him. But Sir Thomas Morton, myself, and some others, used such means (though with much trouble and difficulty) that we drew him out of their hands. And by order of my Lord High Chamberlain, we had the charge of keeping him from any coming to him until a guard of musketeers were brought to convey him to the Governor's House, where we were discharged.

My Lord Chamberlain and Mr Secretary Cooke, that were then at the Governor's House, did there take his examination of which as yet there is nothing known. Only whilst he was in our custody I asked him several questions to which he answered. He said he was a Protestant in Religion. He also expressed himself that he was partly discontented for want of eighty pounds pay which was due to him. And that he being Lieutenant of a company of foot, the company was given over his head unto another, and yet, he said, that did not move him to this resolution, but that he reading the Remonstrance of the house of Parliament it came into his mind that in committing the act of killing the Duke he should do his country great good service. I then asked him at what church, and to what purpose. He told me at a church by Fleet-Street-Conduit, and, for a man much discontented in mind.

But to return to the screeches made at the fatal blow given, the Duchess of Buckingham and the Countess of Anglesey came forth into the Gallery which looked into the Hall where they might behold the blood of their dearest Lord gushing from him. Ah, poor ladies, such were their screechings, tears, and distractions, that I never in my life heard the like before, and hope never to hear the like again. His Majesty's grief for the loss of him was expressed to be more than great, by the many tears he shed for him, with which I will conclude this sad and untimely news.

Felton had sewn a writing in the crown of his hat, half within the lining, to show the cause why he put this cruel act in execution; thinking he should have been slain in the place: and it was thus: 'If I be slain, let no man condemn me, but rather condemn himself; it is for our sins that our hearts are hardened, and become senseless, or else he had not gone so long unpunished.'

'John Felton.'

'He is unworthy of the name of a gentleman, or soldier, in my opinion, that is afraid to sacrifice his life for the honour of God, his King and Country.'

'John Felton.'

EXECUTION OF KING CHARLES I

While an undergraduate at Christ Church, Oxford, Philip Henry had leave to go to London, and there saw, when he was just over seventeen years old, the execution of Charles I.

At the later end of the year 1648 I had leave to go to London to see my father, and during my stay there at that time at Whitehall it was that I saw the beheading of King Charles the First. He went by our door on foot each day that he was carried by water to Westminster, for he took barge at Gardenstairs where we lived and once he spoke to my father and said Art thou alive yet! On the day of his execution, which was Tuesday, January 30, I stood amongst the crowd in the street before Whitehall gate where the scaffold was erected, and saw what was done, but was not so near as to hear any thing. The blow I saw given, and can truly say with a sad heart, at the instant wherof, I remember well, there was such a groan by the thousands then present as I never heard before and desire I may never hear again. There was according to Order one

67. Trial of Charles I
in Westminster Hall.

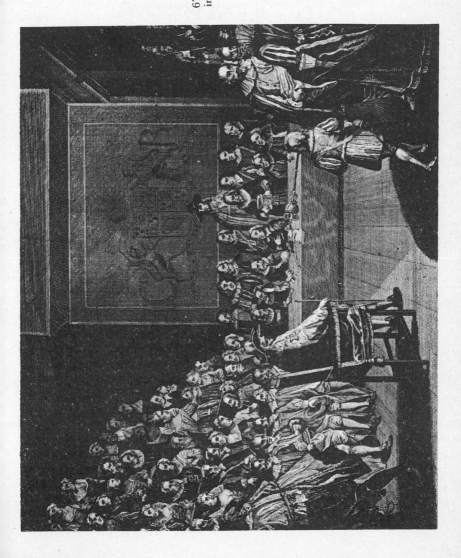

68. An eighteenth-century engraving of the death warrant of Charles I.

69. A Dutch engraving showing the execution of Charles I in Whitehall on 30 January 1649.

70. This engraving of Boscobel House, Shropshire, made early in the eighteenth century by Michael van der Gucht, shows details of what happened to Charles II after his escape from the battle of Worcester, 1651. In Boscobel Wood is the Royal Oak in which 'his Majesty and Col. Carlos' hid while the enemy were searching round about. In the left-hand corner His Majesty's Troop are marching from White Ladies.

Troop immediately marching from Charing Cross to Westminster and another from Westminster to Charing Cross purposely to master the people, and to disperse and scatter them, so that I had much ado amongst the rest to escape home without hurt.   Philip Henry, *Diary*

THE FAMOUS ESCAPE OF PRINCE CHARLES
From the 3 of September at Worcester to the 15 of October at Brightthelmston, being one and forty days, he passed through more dangers than he travelled miles, of which yet he traversed in that time only near three hundred . . . sometimes on foot with uneasy shoes; at other times on horseback, encumbered with a portmanteau and which was worse, at another time, on the gall-back'd slow paced miller's horse; sometimes acting one disguise in coarse linen and a leather doublet; sometimes another of almost as bad a complection; one day he is forced to skulk in a barn at Madely; another day sits with Colonel Carlos in a tree, with his feet extremely surbated [bruised], and at night glad to lodge with William Penderel in a secret place at Boscobel which never

71.   A satirical Royalist engraving. The Royal Oak, bearing the long-known laws of this country, is being cut down. The hypocritical Cromwell, standing at the entrance to Hell, quotes from the Bible to comfort his conscience.

was intended for the dormitory of a King. Sometimes he was forced to shift with coarse fare for a belly-full; another time in a wood, glad to relieve the necessities of nature with a mess of milk served up in an homely dish by good-wife Yates, a poor countywoman. Then again for a variety of tribulation, when he thought himself almost out of danger, he directly meets some of those rebels, who so greedily sought his blood, yet by God's providence had not the power to discover him.

Thomas Blount, Boscobel, 1651

CROMWELL BURIED AT TYBURN

4 December 1660. This day the Parliament voted that the bodies of Oliver, Ireton, Bradshaw, &c., should be taken up out of their graves in the Abbey, and drawn to the gallows, and there hanged and buried under it: which (methinks) do trouble me that a man of so great courage as he was, should have that dishonour, though otherwise he might deserve it enough.

30 January (Fast Day) 1661. To my Lady Batten's; where my wife and she are lately come back again from being abroad, and seeing of Cromwell, Ireton and Bradshaw hanged and buried at Tyburn.

Samuel Pepys, Diary

THE GREAT PLAGUE, 1665

Honoured Sir,   London, July 18th, 1665.

Blessed be the Lord I got to London safe on Wednesday by eleven of the clock: and there is but very little notice took of the sicknesses here in London though the bills are very great, there died threescore and 18 in St Giles in the fields since the bill; and 5 in one hour, in our parish since, it spreads very much; I went by many houses in London that were shut up; all over the city almost; nobody that is in London fears to go anywhere but in St Giles's: they have a bellman there with a cart; there die so many that the bell would hardly ever leave ringing and so they ring not at all: the citizens begin to shut up apace; nothing hinders them from it for fear of the houses breaking open: my father's has been shut up about a week; but there is hardly an house open in the Strand: nor the exchange: the sickness is at Tottenham High Crosse but Mr Moyse would not have you let his son know. It is much at Hogsden [Hoddesdon]; so I saw them as I went in the road, lie in a small thatched house, and I believe all most starved so great a dread it strikes into the people: I tarried in London till Thursday in the afternoon, because the tide would not serve, but then went to Windsor. . . . It is very credibly reported that de Ruyter is beat and taken or sunk. One Wednesday night such news came from Hampton Court. The sickness is at Richmond and we believe the King will reside not there long.

72. Oliver Cromwell orders the Commons to leave in 1653. The owl, wearing glasses, stands for the stupidity of the members. This is a Dutch print.

Thus with my humble service to you and Mr Blithe Jun.
I rest your obedient pupil
Sam: Herne
For his Honoured Tutor
Mr Samuel Blithe fellow of
Clarehall In Cambridge.

ADVANTAGE BROUGHT BY THE CIVIL WAR
Thomas Sprat said in 1666:
The late times of Civil War, and confusion, to make recompense for
their infinite calamities, brought this advantage with them, that they
stirred up men's minds from the long ease, and the lazy rest, and made
them active, industrious and inquisitive: it being the usual benefit that
follows upon tempests, and thunders in the State, as well as in the sky,
that they purify, and clear the air, which they disturb. . . . Now there is a
universal desire, and appetite after knowledge, after the peaceable, the
fruitful, the nourishing knowledge.

THE POPISH PLOT, 1678
For my own part, I must own, that the first public matter I can
remember I took any distinct notice of, was the discovery of the Popish
Plot. . . . The discovery of this plot put the whole kingdom into a new
fermentation, and filled people universally with unspeakable terror.

To see the posts and chains put up in all parts of the city, and a
considerable number of the Trained Bands drawn out, night after
night, well armed, watching with as much care as if a considerable
insurrection was expected before morning; and to be entertained from
day to day with the talk of massacres designed, and a number of bloody
assassins ready to serve such purposes, and recruited from abroad to
support and assist them (which thing were the general subjects of all
conversation) was very surprising. The murder of Sir Edmund Bury
Godfrey . . . with the black Sunday that followed soon after it, when it
grew so dark on a sudden, about eleven in the morning, that ministers
could not read their notes in their pulpits without the help of candles;
together with the frequent execution of traitors that ensued and the
many dismal stories handed about continually, made the hearts, not
only of the younger, but elder persons to quake for fear. Not so much
as a house was at that time to go met with, but what was provided with
arms nor did any be to rest at night without apprehensions of somewhat that was very tragical might happen before morning. And this was
then the case, not for a few weeks or months only, but for a great while
together.

Though I was at that time but young, yet can I not forget how much I

73.   Playing cards illustrate some events in the Popish Plot, 1678.

S.ʳ E.B.Godfree takeing D.ʳ Oates his depoſitions.

Titus Oates gives his evidence to Sir Edmund Godfrey.

D.ʳ Oates diſcouereth y̆ Plot to y̆ King and Ccuncell.

He repeats it to the King and Council.

Coleman drawn to his execution.

Father Coleman is drawn to his execution.

The Execution of the 5 Ieſuitts.

Five Catholic priests are executed for plotting to kill the King.

was affected with seeing several that were condemned for this plot, such as Pickering, Ireland and Grove, etc. go to be executed at Tyburn; and at the pageantry of the mock processions on the 17th of November. . . . In one of them . . . there were carried in pageantry upon men's shoulders through the chief streets of the city, the effigies of the Pope, with the representative of the Devil behind him, whispering in his ear and wonderfully soothing and caressing him (though he after-wards deserted him and left him to shift for himself, before he was committed to the flames), together with the likeness of the dead body of Sir Edmund Bury Godfrey, carried before him by one that rode on horseback, designed to remind people of his execrable murder. And a great number of dignitaries, in their copes, with crosses, monks, friars, and Jesuits, and Popish Bishops in their mitres, and with all their trinkets and appurtenances. Such things as these very discernibly heightened and inflamed the general aversion of the nation from Popery.   Edmund Calamy D.D., *An Historical Account of My Own Life*

MONMOUTH'S REBELLION, 1685

July 4 we marched to Kings Sedgemoor, marching eight miles in the moor so far as Middlesey; where being alarumed. . . .

July 6. The Rt Honourable the Earl of Pembroke Lord Lieutenant in great haste came riding to the house where his Honour Colonel Windham was quartered, it being between twelve and one of the clock in the morning, calling out Colonel Windham, Colonel Windham the enemy is engaged, and asking for his drums. The Colonel's answer was that he was ready, and so forthwith prepared himself.

When the alarum was beaten by Adam Wheeler in Middlesey accord-ing to the Lord Lieutenant's command the regiment marched through Weston into Weston Moor with as much expedition as possible could be, where they were drawn up three deep in order to engage if occasion required.

The aforesaid sixth of July the fight began very early in the morning, which battle was over within the space of two hours, and the enemy received a total rout.

Here Adam Wheeler (being then at his post) was one of those of the right wing of his Honour Colonel Windham's regiment who after the enemy began to run desired leave of his Honour to get such pillage in the field as they could find. But his Honour's answer and command was: That upon pain of death not a man of his regiment should move from his post saying that if the enemy should rally together again, and the regiment be in disorder, every man of them might lose his life.

The battle being over the Right Honourable the Earl of Feversham, General of his Majesty's army, came to the head of Colonel Windham's

74. A Dutch engraving showing the excitement as the seven bishops are taken to the Tower, 1688.

75. William III and Mary set sail for England, 1688.

regiment and gave him many thanks for his readiness, saying, his Majesty should not hear of it by letter, but by word of mouth, and that he would certify the King himself of it. . . .

July 9. This is the best account I can give your Honour of that successful march, and do humbly beg your Honour's pardon for this presumption and with leave subscribe myself, Sir,

Your Honour's most dutiful Drum, and most humble
and obedient servant,
Adam Wheeler
Adam Wheeler, His Account of 1685

PETER THE GREAT AT SAYES COURT

9 June 1698. I went to Deptford to see how miserably the Czar [Peter the Great] had left my house after 3 months making it his Court. I got Sir Christopher Wren the King's surveyor, and Mr London his gardener, to go and estimate the repairs, for which they allowed 150 *l.* in their report to the Lords of the Treasury.   John Evelyn, *Diary*

76.   A meeting of Quakers in 1699. Before it begins, the chairman verifies that the doors are locked and no intruders are present.

ENGLAND AND SCOTLAND UNITED

Westminster, March 6. Her Majesty came this day to the House of Peers; and being in her royal robes seated on the throne, with the usual solemnity, Mr Aston, Deputy Gentleman-Usher of the Black Rod, was sent with a message from Her Majesty to the House of Commons, requiring their attendance in the House of Peers. The Commons being come thither accordingly, Her Majesty was pleased to give the Royal Assent to

An Act for an Union of the Two Kingdoms of
England and Scotland. . .

After which Her Majesty made a most gracious speech to both Houses, which follows:

My Lords and Gentlemen,

It is with the greatest satisfaction, that I have given my assent to a Bill for Uniting England and Scotland into one Kingdom.

I consider this Union, as a matter of the greatest importance to the wealth, strength, and safety, of the whole Island, and at the same time as a work of so much difficulty, and nicety in its own nature, that till now all attempts, which have been made towards it in the course of above a hundred years, have proved ineffectual; and therefore I make no doubt but it will be remembered, and spoke of hereafter to the honour of those who have been instrumental in bringing it to such a happy conclusion.

I desire and expect from all my subjects of both Nations, that from henceforth they act with all possible respect and kindness to one another, that so it may appear to all the world, they have hearts disposed to be one people.

This will be a great pleasure to me, and will make us all quickly sensible of the good effect of this Union.

And I cannot but look upon it as a peculiar happiness, that in my reign so full a provision is made for the peace and quiet of my people, and for the security of our religion, by so firm an Establishment of the Protestant Succession throughout GREAT BRITAIN . . .

London Gazette, 6–10 March 1706/7

ROYAL UNION COFFEE-HOUSE OPENS

London, 8 March 1706. On Thursday last the Queen went to the House of Lords, and gave the Royal Assent to the UNION BILL, on which day was opened a large new Coffee-house against the Royal Exchange in Cornhill, named the ROYAL UNION COFFEE-HOUSE, the sign of which is the three Protestant Queens, *viz.* Queen Elizabeth, the late Queen Mary, and our present Gracious Sovereign QUEEN ANN, curiously painted. The House kept by Mr Aylmer.   *Post Boy*, 6–8 March 1706/7

DANIEL DEFOE ON THE SCOTTISH UNION

I have a long time dwelt on the subject of a Union; I have happily seen it transacted in the Kingdom of Scotland; I have seen it carried on there through innumerable oppositions, both public and private, peaceable and unpeaceable; I have seen it perfected there, and ratified, sent up to England, debated, opposed, and at last passed in both Houses, and having obtained the Royal Assent, I have the pleasure, just while I am writing these lines, to hear the guns proclaiming the happy conjunction from Edinburgh Castle.

A Review of the State of the British Nation, 29 March 1707

POPE BURNED IN EFFIGY

The Effigies being prepared accordingly, the Pope dressed in his *Pontificalibus* was placed in a chair covered with red; and the Pretender on his left, in a French dress, with a wooden shoe hanging on his left arm, and in his right hand a candle, which he held to the Pope and the Devil, as proper emblems of the blessings we are to expect from one, bred up in the idolatry of Rome, and the tyranny of France. Behind those two, was placed the Effigies of the Devil, as the sole author of the spiritual and temporal tyranny, which is put in execution by the scarlet coloured whore, and such kings and princes of the earth, as she intoxicates with her cup of fornication. The Pope and the Devil were represented grinning, and their young pupil smirking, to express their different way of looking at this nation. Instead of laying any marks of state upon his shoulder, it was thought more proper to have a little French ware strung about his neck, of half a score turnips and onions. And the following motto writ on his breast,

Magna Spec altera Romae,

In English thus,

With Pope and Devil here I come.

The other Hope of Mighty Rome.

The gentlemen who met at the Three Tuns, took due care to provide constables for keeping the peace, and having all things in readiness, the Devil, the Pope, and the Pretender, were carried three times round the fire with great solemnity, and thrown into it, with loud acclamations of the spectators, who vied with one another who should give most blows to the effigies of those three Grand Enemies to Christianity and Human Liberty. . . .

All this passed without the least disorder, till at last the wicked souls of the Jacobites being grieved at this Protestant solemnity, they sent a parcel of their emissaries to break the Queen's Peace. . . .

These disciples of the Pope, the Devil, and the Pretender, had laid some mobs in ambuscade to assault the people about the fire, and sallying from their lurking holes wounded one of the constables, and some others, with long staves, brickbats, etc., but were soon knocked down and dispersed, and one of their leaders, who had the impudence to cry out, *No Hanover*, was soundly buffeted for his pains, and made to cry out, *God Bless the Illustrious House of Hanover.* . . .

Flying-Post, 7–10 February 1712/13

TREATY OF UTRECHT SIGNED

London, April 4. Yesterday the Hon. Geo. St John, Esq., brother to the Right Honourable the Lord Viscount Bolingbroke, arrived here express, with the agreeable news of signing the Peace, attended by Mr Beckley, one of Her Majesty's Messengers; this Express left Utrecht at 10 of the clock on Tuesday night last, landed at 8 of the clock on Thursday night, at Aldborough, and yesterday between 11 and 12 of the clock in the morning, was at Whitechapel, and between 12 and 1, waited on Her Majesty at Her Royal Palace at St James's, with the following advices.

Utrecht, April 11. N.S. This morning, the Ministers of France came to my Lord Privy-Seal's House; and between 3 and 4 of the clock in the afternoon signed the Treaty of Peace between Her Majesty and the King their Master; as did, immediately after, the Ministers of Savoy, with the Ambassadors of France; after which, the Earl of Strafford entertained at dinner the same Ministers, and those of Portugal, and Prussia, and the States-General. All the abovesaid Ministers have actually signed, this evening, their respective Treaties of Peace at his Lordship's House, except the Dutch.

Whilst Mr St John was at the Brill, the following express was sent to him.

Utrecht, April 12. N.S. This morning between two and three of the clock, the States of Holland's Plenipotentiaries signed the Treaty of Peace; after which, the Plenipotentiaries of the several Powers congratulated each other, with mutual joy, upon this great and good undertaking. About 3 days hence, is expected here the Duke d'Ossuna, the King of Spain's Plenipotentiary, to sign the same.

Post Boy, 2–4 April 1713

REWARD FOR THE CAPTURER OF THE PRETENDER

London, September 18. On Thursday last a Proclamation was publish'd by Order of the Lords Justices, setting forth, That whereas by an Act of Parliament, made in the last session of Parliament, intituled, *An Act for the better Support of His Majesty's Household, and of the Honour and Dignity of the Crown of Great Britain,* reciting, That Her late Majesty Queen ANNE, of Blessed Memory, being fully convinced of the imminent

Dangers which threatened Her Kingdoms and the Protestant Succession in the House of *Hanover*, as well as from a just Resentment of the Indignities offered to Her said Majesty by the Pretender's remaining in *Lorrain*, in Defiance of Her repeated Instances for his Removal, and of the Treasonable Practices committed by inlisting Her said late Majesty's Subjects in the Service of the Pretender, was pleased to issue Her Royal Proclamation, promising a Reward of Five Thousand Pounds to such Person who should apprehend the Pretender; and that the Commons of Great Britain . . . did . . . assure Her said late Majesty, that they would assist Her, by granting . . . the Sum of One Hundred Thousand Pounds, as a further Encouragement and Reward for apprehending the Pretender, whenever he should land, or attempt to land in any of Her said late Majesty's Dominions. . . .

Post Boy, 16–18 September 1714

Warfare

Sir Edward Cecil said in 1628 how very hard it was to get volunteers when they were badly needed: 'We disburthen the prison of thieves, we rob the taverns and alehouses of tosspots and ruffians, we scour both towns and country of rogues and vagabonds.' Such men would find their commanders unconvincing soldiers also. Buckingham after a visit to Madrid involved this country in a war with Spain in 1624, which proved to be a fiasco. He also led England into a second and even more senseless war with France. After a final defeat at La Rochelle, Charles made peace with Spain and France as quickly as possible. It has been said that at this time Englishmen did not know the difference between a free fight for all and a battle fought by professional armies.

Within two generations this had changed. The armed rabble had gone. Milton, having lived through the Civil War, describes in *Paradise Regained* trained cavalry in action:

> All Horsemen, in which fight they most excel;
> See how in warlike muster they appear,
> In Rhombs and wedges, and half moons, and wings.

Muskets and pistols replace the bow and arrow. Cannon now fire metal shot. The besieged town is threatened by the bomb, a 'devilish invention which was hatched in Hell'. Prince Rupert's vivid cavalry rides through the countryside; and above all there is Cromwell's New Model Army. E. L. Woodward points out: 'At the beginning of the war each side seems to have thought vaguely that matters would be settled after a single battle. After this forecast had been proved wrong, neither party had any plan for winning outright.' Cromwell saw what should be done. After Edgehill in 1642 he said to John Hampden:

> Your troops are most of them old, decayed serving-men and tapsters, theirs are gentlemen's sons. . . . Do you think that the spirits of such base and mean fellows will ever be able to encounter gentlemen that have courage, honour, and resolution in them? You must get men of a spirit that is likely to go on as far as gentlemen will go, or you will be beaten still.

Once again we see the influence of the Dutch, for in their particular method the New Model was trained by officers who had served abroad.

This efficient army, however, produced no desire in the English to turn their country into a military state. To many people, army meant power and power meant tyranny. It was seen that the weaknesses of Charles I brought positive action against him. Men on both sides felt it should never have come to war. The political rule of the army under Cromwell lasted only ten years. After that the English hated a standing army. By a gradual process there was a turning away from the bearing of arms. Officers still came from the upper class. Common soldiers were treated with indifference by the governing powers. For many years the fear of military despotism remained.

In these difficult conditions with this unpromising material, Marlborough won his four great victories. In 1704 he made his famous march up the Rhine and across country in Bavaria to defeat the French at Blenheim, which proved to be the turning point of the war. Addison celebrates the victory in *The Campaign*:

'Twas then great Marlborough's mighty soul was proved . . .
Calm and serene he drives the furious blast;
And, pleased th' Almighty's orders to perform,
Rides in the whirlwind, and directs the storm.

The character of war had been revolutionized since the time of Cromwell by the invention of the ring bayonet. This made each soldier a pikeman as well as a musketeer. Battles were won not only by the brilliance of command but by the steadiness of the foot regiments. Marlborough's outstanding success as diplomat and general brought the War of the Spanish Succession to an end in 1713 with the treaty at Utrecht.

A HORSE! A HORSE!

April 1639. I am infinitely sorry to hear the Scots continue in there stubbornness, for I fear if they come to blows the business will not be easily ended, but we must refer all to God. I have been a little too negligent of getting my arms . . . where and when I shall have my pistols . . . I pray you send me your opinion whither I had not best bespeak a waggon presently and what other provisions I had best make. I should be loath to be utterly unprovided. You that are so near and know more, may judge better of it than I can, therefore I humbly crave your advice. I confess I say not this that I am at all fond of the journey, or that I can say I shall leave your affairs here in so good order as that I may conveniently come. I hope if need be you can furnish me with an horse, that will be readier than any that can be brought by me.

Ralph Verney to his father Sir Edmund, who was with the
King in the Scotch war

THE PURITAN PARTY

The King had upon his heart the dealings both of England and Scotland with his mother, and harboured a secret desire of revenge upon the godly in both nations, yet had not courage enough to assert his resentment like a prince, but employed a wicked cunning he was master of, and called king-craft, to undermine what he durst not openly oppose, – the true religion; this was fenced with the liberty of the people, and so linked together, that it was impossible to make them slaves, till they were brought to be idolators of royalty and glorious lust; and as impossible to make them adore these gods, while they continued loyal to the government of Jesus Christ.

The payment of civil obedience to the king and the laws of the land satisfied not; if any durst dispute his impositions in the worship of God, he was presently reckoned among the seditious and disturbers of the public peace, and accordingly persecuted; if any were grieved at the dishonour of the kingdom, or the griping of the poor, or the unjust oppressions of the subject, by a thousand ways, invented to maintain the riots of the courtiers, and the swarms of needy Scots the king had brought in to devour like locusts the plenty of this land, he was a puritan; if any, out of mere morality and civil honesty, discountenanced the abominations of those days, he was a puritan, however he conformed to their superstitious worship; if any showed favour to any godly honest person, kept them company, relieved them in want, or protected them against violent or unjust oppression, he was a puritan; if any gentleman in his Country maintained the good laws of the land, or stood up for any public interest, for good order or government, he was a puritan: in short, all that crossed the views of the needy courtiers, the proud encroaching priests, the thievish projectors, the lewd nobility and gentry – whoever was zealous for God's glory or worship, could not endure blasphemous oaths, ribald conversation, profane scoffs, sabbath breaking, derision of the word of God, and the like – whoever could endure a sermon, modest habit or conversation, or anything good, – all these were puritans; and if puritans, then enemies to the King and his government, seditious, factious hypocrites, ambitious disturbers of the public peace, and finally, the pest of the Kingdom.

Memoirs of Colonel Hutchinson (1639–41)

LADY SUSSEX TO DEFEND GORHAMBURY, HER HOME

July 1642. I must beseech you to get some body to buy six carbines for me and some twenty pounds of powder I hope that will be enough to defend us here if it be not powder enough, as much as you think fit, for I would fain have you and your lady as safe here as at London, which truly I believe you will.   Lady Sussex to Ralph Verney

THE BATTLE OF EDGEHILL, 1642

On Sunday last I saw the Battle which was the bloodiest I believe the oldest soldiers in the field ever saw. We have routed utterly their horse and slain & chased away so considerable a party of their foot, that the enemy is very weak. Though we have lost some, yet few of eminency, save some prisoners. The Earl of Lindsey, Willoughby, and Colonel Lunston, the Lord St John, with the Lord Fielding are slain, with many others. My Lord of Essex escaped us by being in an alehouse. We have his coach and much money in it. There needs no more to assure any understanding man we had the day, than to tell them (which is true) we had all their ordnances in the field and fetched them out next morning in their sight. They are so weak they have entrenched themselves, and we are now going on our intended march to Oxford, having only gone backward on Sunday to bestow this breathing on them. We have taken about five colours and cornets, and lost about five or six colours, but never a cornet. The King hath five hundred of their horse alive, and of eighteen hundred not one horse is left them. At the beginning of the fight, two double troops came over to the King's party commanded by Sir Faithfeill Fortescue and Mr Gervase Pain, & fought on that side. It is commonly reported the Earl of Essex his soldiers ran away daily. Three hundred prisoners are taken, among which is Sergeant Major Barrey, a recusant of the Irish. My Lord Albany is slain on the King's side, and Dr Lake. The King gave fire to the first piece, the Lord General having first demanded the word, which was '*Go in the name of God and I'll lay my bones with yours.*' Marquis Hartford is now on the march with ten thousand men armed out of Wales, and intends to meet the King at Oxford. Sir R. Hopton and Mr Rogers bring as many from the West Country.   C.H.

A letter from C.H. to Sancroft of Emmanuel College, Cambridge, later Archbishop of Canterbury

LETTER AFTER EDGEHILL

27 October, 1642. For all our great victory I have had the greatest loss by the death of your noble father that any friend did, which next to my wife and master was the greatest misfortune that by death could have fallen to me. He himself killed two with his own hands, whereof one of them had killed poor Jason, and broke the point of his standard at push of pike before he fell, which was the last account I could receive of any of our own side of him. The next day the king sent a herald to offer mercy to all that would lay down arms, and to enquire for my Lord of Linsey, my Lord Willoughby and him. He brought word that my Lord Linsey was hurt, your father dead, and my Lord Willoughby only prisoner. He would neither put on arms or buff coat the day of battle,

the reason I know not. The battle was bloody on your side, for your horses ran away at the first charge, and our men had the execution of them for three miles; it began at three a clock and ended at six. The king is a man of the least fear and the greatest mercy and resolution that ever I saw, and had not been in the field, we might have suffered. My Lord of Essex is retired in great disorder to Warwick, for the next morning he suffered his cannon to be taken away within musket shot of his army, and never offered to hinder them; it is said there was killed and run away since eight thousand of his army. This day the king took in bamberie our army daily increases. God in mercy send us peace, and although your loss be as great as a son can lose in a father, yet God's children must bear with patience what affliction soever he shall please to lay upon them.   Sir Edward Sydenham to Ralph Verney

DURING THE CIVIL WAR

We that had till that hour lived in great plenty and great order, found ourselves like fishes out of the water, and the scene so changed that we knew not at all how to act any part but obedience, for from as good a house as any gentleman in England had, we came to a baker's house in an obscure street, and from rooms well furnished, to be in a very bad bed in a garret, to one dish of meat, and that not the best ordered, no money, for we were as poor as Job, nor clothes more than a man or two brought in their cloak bags: we had the perpetual discourse of losing or gaining towns and men; at the windows the sad spectacle of war, sometimes plague, sometimes sickness of other kinds, by reason of so many people being packed together, as I believe, there never was before of that quality; always in want, yet I must needs say that most bore it with a martyr-like cheerfulness. For my own part, I began to think we should all, like Abraham, live in tents all the days of our lives.   *Lady Fanshawe's Memoirs*

THE FALL OF DUDLEY CASTLE
To Mr Ashurst and Mr Swinfen touching the surrender of Dudley Castle.
                                                                13 May 1646
Sirs, This day the strong Castle of Dudley was delivered unto me, whereunto we entered about one of the clock. The conditions for the surrender whereof were sent unto you by the last which I shall not now repeat but shall give you this further account touching this place.
    There marched out of the Castle near 300 Foot of the cannon soldiers besides Horse and near 40 reformade [left without a command] officers marched out with their horses and arms. They were well furnished with beer and plentifully with water so as if that God (which by the sounding of rams horns and seven times compassing the walls of

Jericho brought down those strong walls) had not also taken away their courage and divided them against themselves this might have been a tedious and expensive work and one of the last reduced garrisons in the kingdom. I desire the whole honour and glory may be ascribed to God with whom it is easy to deliver up the strongest as the weakest holds.... Sir William Brereton

AFTER NASEBY

Confusion after the battle of Naseby was felt in many villages. For the year 1647 the Constables' Accounts *of Fillongley, Warwickshire, have these entries:*

Spent for quartering soldiers	1s.	6d.
Paid for carriage for the foot soldiers that laid in our town	15s.	0d.
Spent when I went to quarter Sir Tho. Fairfax's soldiers being unruly	2s.	0d.

THE BATTLE OF DUNBAR

For the Honourable William Lenthall, Esquire, Speaker of the Parliament of England: These.

Dunbar, 4th September, 1650.

Sir,

... The Enemy lying in the posture before mentioned, having those advantages; we lay very near him, being sensible of our disadvantages, having some weakness of the flesh, but yet consolation and support from the Lord himself to our poor weak faith, wherein I believe not a few amongst us stand: That because of their numbers, because of their advantages, because of their confidence, because of our weakness, because of our strait, we were in the Mount, and in the Mount of the Lord would be seen; and that He would find a way of deliverance and salvation for us:– and indeed we had our consolations and our hopes.

... The Enemy made a gallant resistance, and there was a very hot dispute at sword's point between our horse and theirs. Our first foot, after they had discharged their duty (being overpowered with the Enemy) received some repulse, which they soon recovered. For my own regiment, under the command of Lieutenant-Colonel Goffe and my Major, White, did come seasonably in; and, at the push of pike, did repel the stoutest regiment the Enemy had there, merely with the courage the Lord was pleased to give. Which proved a great amazement to the residue of their foot; this being the first action between the foot. The horse in the meantime did, with a great deal of courage and spirit, beat back all oppositions; charging through the bodies of the Enemy's horse, and of their foot; who were, after the first repulse given, made by the Lord of Hosts as stubble to their swords. . . .

The best of the Enemy's horse being broken through and through in less than an hour's dispute, it became a total rout; our men having the chase and execution of them near eight miles. We believe that upon the place and near it were about Three-thousand slain. . . .

Thus you have the prospect of one of the most signal mercies God hath done for England and His people, this war. . . .

Beseeching you to pardon this length, I humbly take leave; and rest,

Sir,

Your most obedient servant,

Oliver Cromwell

DROGHEDA, 1649

During five days the streets ran with blood. A thousand unresisting victims were immolated together within the walls of the great church. This was on 11 and 12 September but on 4 November Ralph wrote: 'I am yet between hope and fear concerning dear dear Mun', and it was not till 8 November that Mr Buck sent him word of the death of

your brother and my dear friend, Sir Edmund Verney, who behaved himself with the greatest gallantry that could be – he was slain at Drogheda three days after quarter was given him as he was walking with Cromwell by way of protection. One Ropier, who is brother to the Lord Ropier, called him aside in a pretence to speak with him, being formerly an acquaintance, and instead of some friendly office which Sir Edmund might expect from him, he barbarously ran him through with a tuck [sword], but I am confident to see this act once highly revenged. The next day after, one Lieutenant Colonel Boyle, who had quarter likewise given him, as he was at dinner with my Lady More, sister to the Earl of Sunderland, in the same town, one of Cromwell's soldiers came and whispered him in the ear to tell him must presently be put to death, who rising from the table, the lady asked him whither he was going, he answered, Madam to die, who no sooner stepped out of the room but he was shot to death. These are cruelties of those traitors, who no doubt will find the like mercy when they stand in need of it.

Memoirs of the Verney Family, 1649

LETTER TO SOLDIER-HUSBAND

Since my dear encourages me to the only pleasure I have or ever can think of in your absence, which is by expressing my kindness by all opportunities, you need not fear but I'll trouble you every post, though at the same time I am sorry I have nothing to repeat but still constant assurances of my being ever yours. And that sound is so extreme pleasing to me from you, that I will not doubt but it has the same effect from me to you.

My sister and I being now alone, we sit working all day long in their room and sup there sometimes, musing in the fire till our eyes are burnt out of our heads, and then that moves my spleen to laugh to think if any of our town acquaintances could see us. I believe if I were dying I could not help a jocose [jest] now and then.

. . . Adieu, my dear; make me happy as soon as you can, for with you I can have no doubts nor fears: and without you there never was, nor never can be, any real satisfaction to her who is most faithfully, my dearest, ever yours.

An English wife, in the year before Blenheim, wrote to her absent
husband, 1703

THE BATTLE OF BLENHEIM, 1704

We have cut off great numbers of them, as well in the action as in the retreat, besides upwards of twenty squadrons of the French, which I pushed into the Danube, where we saw the greater part of them perish. Monsieur Tallard, with several of his general officers being taken prisoners at the same time, and in the village of Blenheim, which the enemy had entrenched and fortified, and where they made the greatest opposition, I obliged twenty-six entire battalions, and twelve squadrons of dragoons, to surrender themselves prisoners at discretion. We took likewise all their tents standing, with their cannon and ammunition, as also a great number of standards, kettle-drums, and colours in the action, so that I reckon the greatest part of Monsieur Tallard's army is taken or destroyed.

The bravery of all our troops on this occasion cannot be expressed, the Generals, as well as the officers and soldiers, behaving themselves with the greatest courage and resolution. The horse and dragoons were obliged to charge four or five several times. The Elector and Monsieur de Marsin were so advantageously posted, that Prince Eugene could make no impression on them, till the third attack, near seven at night, when he made a great slaughter of them. But being near a woodside, a great body of Bavarians retired into it, and the rest of that army retreated towards Lawringen, it being too late, and the troops too much tired to pursue them far.

I cannot say too much in praise of that Prince's good conduct, and the bravery of his troops on this occasion. You will please to lay this before her Majesty and his Royal Highness, to whom I send my Lord Tunbridge with the good news. I pray you likewise inform yourself, and let me know her Majesty's pleasure, as well relating to Monsieur

Tallard and the other general officers, as for the disposal of near one thousand two hundred other officers, and between eight and nine thousand common soldiers, who being all made prisoners by her Majesty's troops, are entirely at her disposal: but as the charge of subsisting these officers and men must be very great, I presume her Majesty will be inclined that they be exchanged for any other prisoners that offer.

I should likewise be glad to receive her Majesty's directions for the disposal of the standards and colours, whereof I have not yet the number, but guess there cannot be less than one hundred, which is more than has been taken in any battle these many years.

You will easily believe that, in so long and vigorous an action, the English, who had so great a share in it, must have suffered as well in officers as men; but I have not the particulars. I am, Sir,

Your most obedient,
humble servant,
Marlborough.
From the camp at Hochstet, 4 August (old style) 1704

AFTER BLENHEIM

My dearest soul I love you so well, and have set my heart so entirely on ending my days in quiet with you, that you may be so far at ease as to be assured that I never venture myself but when I think the service of my queen and country requires it. Besides I am now at an age when I find no heat in my blood that gives me temptation to expose myself out of vanity; But as I would deserve and keep the kindness of this army, I must let them see that when I expose them, I would not exempt myself. Marlborough, to his wife, 6 August 1705

THE DUKE OF MARLBOROUGH AT RAMILLIES, SUNDAY, 23 MAY 1706

Major-General Murray, who was posted on the left of the second line, was so happy visibly to save the Duke of Marlborough, who fulfilled that day all the parts of a great captain, except in that he exposed his person as the meanest soldier. The attack being to be made by the Dutch on our left against the enemy's right where all the King's household and their best troops were, the Duke put himself at the head of the Dutch horse; and the guards du corps, Mousquetaires, and gendarmes, happening to encounter them, ten of the Dutch squadrons were repulsed, renversed and put in great disorder. The Duke, seeing this, and seeing that things went pretty well elsewhere, stuck by the weak part to make it up by his presence, and led up still new squadrons there to the charge, till at last the victory was obtained. It was here where those squadrons being renversed and in absolute deroute and the French mixed with them in the pursuit, the Duke, flying with the crowd, in leaping a ditch fell off his horse and some rode over him. Major-General Murray, who had his eyes there and was so near he could distinguish the Duke in the flight, seeing him fall, marched up in all haste with two Swiss battalions to save him and stop the enemy who were hewing all down in their way. The Duke when he got to his feet again saw Major-General Murray coming up and ran directly to get in to his battalions. In the meantime Mr Molesworth quitted his horse and got the Duke mounted again, and the French were so hot in the pursuit that some of them before they could stop their horses ran in upon the Swiss bayonets and were killed, but the body of them, seeing the two battalions, shore off to the right and retired.

Colonel Cranstoun, Portland Papers

OUDENARDE, 1708

In short, small shot continued very brisk and smart on both sides, with several sore assaults and repulses, from about three in the afternoon till past nine at night, before it was fully ceased, or the dispute decided. In which time, with much to do, to speak the truth, we drove the enemy from ditch to ditch, from hedge to hedge, and from out of one scrub to another, and wood, in great hurry, disorder, and confusion; so that the night being approached, the enemy, as often before, most joyfully embraced the shade of its canopy, under which they retired from the place or field of battle, one very great expedition, disorder, and confusion.

John Millner, Sergeant in the Honourable Royal Regiment
of Foot of Ireland, Journal

SOLDIER'S WIFE, SIEGE OF GHENT, 1708

My husband in the siege was one of the forlorn hope, a body of men ordered to lay the ropes and to direct the cutting of the trenches: we seldom expect to see any of them return again; and here the danger was greater than customary, as the night was clear, and they were soon descried by the sentinels; and so remarkably expeditious were our men, that they were all covered before the enemy had got their forces together to oppose them. As I always accompanied my husband, however dangerous it was, I, as usual followed him this time, but Colonel Hamilton stopping me, and saying, 'Dear Kit, don't be so forward,' I lost sight of him and was for some time hunting before I could find him; for the ropes being lain, he with his companions were retired into a turnip field, and lay flat on their bellies, expecting the trench, which the workmen were throwing up, to cover them. Major

Irwin told me where he was; and both the major and Lieutenant Stretton begged hard of me for some beer; but as I had but three flasks, and feared my husband might want, I had no pity for anyone else: as the night was very cold and the ground wet, I had also provided myself with a bottle of brandy, and another of gin, for my dear Richard's refreshment. When I left these officers, I met a lieutenant known by the nick-name of 'A— and Pockets' a spent musket-ball had grazed on, and scratched his forehead, which his fright magnified to a cannon-ball. He desired I would show him to a surgeon; but his panic was so great, that I believe, had he been examined at both ends, he stood more in need of having his breeches shifted than his wound dressed. I went to the turnip field, where I found my husband in the front rank, to whom my liquors were very comfortable.

(Mrs) Christian Davies, *Life and Adventure*

England and the Sea

The Elizabethan idea of sea power came to an end in the reign of James I. The badly-led Navy of Charles I was humiliated when Buckingham led a disastrous expedition to Cadiz, and later failed ignominiously at La Rochelle. For these failures the English seamen never forgave the King. With the Navy behind him, London, the Puritan stronghold, would have collapsed under the blockade of the Thames estuary bringing royalist victory in the Civil War.

England's greatest rival for sea power in the seventeenth century was Holland. The Dutch controlled the spice trade with the Far East, and traded with China and Japan. They founded colonies in America, secured control of the herring fishery in the North Sea, and became the 'waggoners of all seas' – carrying goods from one port to another all over Europe.

After the Civil War England and Holland were on the verge of war. In 1651 the Rump Parliament passed the Navigation Act. This ordered all goods imported into England to be brought in English ships or in the ships of the country where the goods were actually produced. Dutch success up to this time had been gained by the number of their ships and the efficiency of their widespread organization. This Act hit their carrying trade very hard.

Disputes continued and led to war. In 1652 Robert Blake defeated Tromp off Dover, and routed De Witt in the same year. A further engagement off Dungeness caused him to withdraw into the Thames. He decisively defeated Tromp in 1653 at the battle of Portland. Off the African coast a number of English sailors had been captured by the Bey of Tunis. Blake sailed into the Mediterranean and wrote: 'We judged it necessary for the honour of our fleet, our nation, and our religion, seeing that they would not deal with us as friends, to make them feel us as enemies.' He attacked the shore batteries and destroyed the Bey's fleet in the harbour. Blake's most brilliant victory was at Santa Cruz where in 1656 he destroyed a Spanish fleet, and saved Portugal from invasion. Though an English fleet failed to take San Domingo, the capture of Jamaica was a consolation.

281

After the Restoration a Dutch fleet under De Ruyter sailed up the Medway, burnt English ships off Chatham, and fired a fort at Sheerness. But by now Dutch supremacy had been curbed and England had recovered her position. Another great power now threatened, the France of Louis XIV. The sea powers, England and Holland, 'turned together in their ancient role to defend liberty against a second military dictatorship'.

Louis XIV planned a great invasion of England, but the English and Dutch fleets under Sir George Rooke won the battle of La Hogue, 1692, and all fear of invasion was over. 'During several days the bells of London pealed without ceasing. Flags were flying in all the steeples. Rows of candles were in all the windows. Bonfires were at all the corners of the street. And three lords took down with them £37,000 in coin to distribute among the sailors.' How this victory must have delighted Samuel Pepys, secretary to the Admiralty till 1688, who laboured hard to provide the country with a really efficient fleet. 'In his long service,' as J. A. Williamson tells us, 'he accumulated knowledge and wisdom and helped to carry the Navy interest to an inner place in the counsels of the great.'

As compared with the Army, the Navy was universally popular. J. A. Williamson clearly indicates how sea power was a 'veritable limb and member of the nation' when he says:

> So long as ships-of-war were built and equipped with the same timber, cordage, and canvas as the merchantman, fashioned by the same shipwrights and manned by the same seamen, the State expenditure on the Navy vitalized the same trades, crafts, and callings that produced the mercantile marine and, by definition of 1651, 'the safety and welfare of this Commonwealth'. Sea power was both combatant and productive, and the two aspects were inseparable. . . . The men who fought the French in war carried the wares of England all over the world in peace.

PREPARING TO SAIL FROM BRISTOL TO VIRGINIA

Certain of the Chief Merchants of the City of Bristol induced thereto by the inducements of Master Richard Hakluyt, resolve to set forth a voyage for the further discovery of the northern parts of Virginia. . . . They prepared a small ship called the *Speedwell,* of about 50 tons, manned with thirty men and boys, and a bark called the *Discoverer* of 26 tons with thirteen men and a boy, victualled for eight months, and furnished with certain merchandise to trade with the people of the country; as hats of divers colours, apparel of coarse kersey and canvas ready-made, stockings, shoes, saws, pickaxes, hooks, knives, scissors, bells, beads, looking-glasses, thimbles, needles, thread and suchlike. They set sail from Milford Haven on the 10th April.

Samuel Purchas, *Purchas His Pilgrims,* 1625

FIGHTING THE ROUGH AND BOISTEROUS OCEAN

For it is not enough to be a seaman, but it is necessary to be a painful seaman; for a seabred man of reasonable capacity may attain to so much art as may serve to circle the earth's globe about; but the other, wanting the experimental part, cannot. For I do not allow any to be a good seaman that hath not undergone the most offices about a ship, and that hath not in his youth been both taught and inured to all labours. For to keep a warm cabin and lie in sheets is the most ignoble part of a seaman. But to endure and suffer, as a hard cabin, cold and salt meat, broken sleeps, mouldy bread, dead beer, wet clothes, want of fire, all these are within board; besides boat, lead, top-yarder, anchor-moorings and the like.

Luke Fox of Hull, *North-West Fox; or Fox from the North-West Passage*, 1635

77.   A Dutch print showing an English warship of the mid seventeenth century.

BATTLE OF LOWESTOFT, 3 JUNE 1665

When his Royal Highness began the aforesaid close engagement, at the same time I let fall my mainsail and bore up upon the enemy (putting abroad my blue flag on the mizzen peak, a sign for my squadron to follow me) and we pressed sore upon them and made some of them give way. Others endeavouring to keep their luff ran foul one of the other insomuch as 4 sail of brave ships (as they say that had upward of 1000 men in them) were entangled, into whom we poured our broadsides as we passed by and left them to the mercy of that part of our fleet that followed us. One of these was the ship Kouverdine, Tromp['s] Vice Adml., another the Prince Maurice, then the Stadt Utrecht, the Steden. His Royal Highness (as I am told) ordered a fireship to burn them if they would not yield, which was presently put in execution and all destroyed, not above 100 men saved, that were taken out of the sea by our ships' boats as they passed by. Here happened a strange accident, one of the 4 ships burning, when her powder took fire, blew up, and that same force struck away the mast and rigging of one of the rest (of about 40 guns). The hull of which ship not being much possessed by the fire, the men extinguished it and sheered off their ship and were towed away by another ship of theirs after our whole fleet had passed by. But whether the ship was towed into harbour or not, we know not.

At the same time when I bore up, Prince Rupert and his squadron very bravely fell in upon the enemy, who giving way before us and bearing up by degrees, endeavoured to have clapped by a wind the other way and so have weathered us; but the Prince Rupert, most bravely pressing them and preserving still the weather gage of them, made them downright bear up before the wind and run with studding sails, cutting off their boats and using all advantages of flight, so that the Prince and his squadron to the westward and I and mine to the eastward (pari passu) abreast one of the other pursued the enemy about 6 oclock in the evening, in the beginning of which pursuit the Marseveen, the Tergoes and Capt Kuyper's ship keeping their luff more than the rest to engage my ship and hinder our chase, I bore up unto him and after some dispute made him bear up round and so sheer aboard his two consorts, and being fast together and well paid they struck their colours unto me and gave over shooting; but I left them to the ships in the rear who might have preserved and secured them, but one Gregory in a fireship of Prince Rupert's squadron went and set fire on them and they were all destroyed but 100 saved in a boat and some few taken up out of the water. This cruel fact was much detested by us as not beseeming Christians and his Royal Highness ordered the Judge Advocate to examine the matter, in order to have the judgment of a Court Martial thereupon. We continued our chase, but I was much hindered by having my main topsail shot to pieces, so that I was fain to bring a new one to the yard as we sailed along. About 9 oclock at night his Royal Highness came up with me and I fell astern of him, that he might direct our course all night, which he altered more to the eastward, to cut them off from the shore and going into the Texel, the success whereof follows in the next day's proceedings.

Dutch ships taken in the fight and next morning:– Mars –46, Zelandia –44, Carolus Quintus –53. Delph –32, Negelboome –52, Younge Prince –36, Hilversome –60, Ruyter –18, Black Bull. Some affirm they saw Dutch ships sink down, but I have yet nothing credible thereof.

English slain and wounded:– Of the Red 117, 199, of the White 109, 84, of the Blue 57, 157. Total 283, 440

Great persons slain:– Earl of Marlborough, Earl of Portland, Earl of Falmouth, Lord Muskerry, Mr Boyle, son of the Earl of Burlington, Commanders:– Rear Admiral Sansum, Capt Ableson, Capt Kirby.

The Earl of Sandwich, *Journal*, 1659–1665

PRESS-GANG

30 June 1666. Mightily troubled all this morning with going to my Lord Mayor, (Sir Thomas Bludworth, a silly man I think,) and other places, about getting shipped some men that they have these two last nights pressed in the City out of houses: the persons wholly unfit for sea, and many of them people of very good fashion, which is a shame to think of, and carried to Bridewell they are, yet without being impressed with money legally as they ought to be. But to see how the King's business is done; my Lord Mayor himself did scruple at this time of extremity to do this thing, because he had not money to pay the pressed-money to the men. I did out of my own purse disburse 15 *l.* to pay for their pressing and diet last night and this morning; which is a thing worth record of my Lord Mayor. Busy about this all the morning, and about the getting off men pressed by our officers of the fleet into the service; even our own men that are at the office, and the boats that carry us.

Samuel Pepys, *Diary*

DIET OF THE FLEET

Our beef and pork is very scant,
I'm sure of weight, one half it want:
Our bread is black, and maggots in it crawl,
That's all the fresh meat we are fed withal.
When we these things to Sir John Harman say,
Our purser mends the matter for a day,
Thinking to make us weary of complaining,

But he upon our bellies still is gaming;
A little rice we get instead of fish,
Which to you well is known, but a poor dish,
Except good spice to put in it you had,
For with a good sauce a deal board is not bad.
Our drink it is but vinegar and water,
Four-shilling beer in England's ten times better,
So that when sailors gets good wine,
They think themselves in Heaven for the time.
    A Seaman sailing under Sir John Harman, 1669–1671
                            in the Mediterranean

MUTINY IN 1674
On Thursday last about 100 seamen in a body did in a mutinous manner march with a black flag before them through the City of London as far as Guildhall assaulting all press mariners and rescuing of pressed men.
    Samuel Pepys, *Journal of the Admiralty*, 10 January 1673/74

FEASTING NAVAL OFFICERS, 1675
Henry Teonge, a Navy chaplain, wrote off Lisbon,
our noble Captain feasted the officers of his small squadron with 4 dishes of meat, viz., 4 excellent hens and a piece of pork boiled, in a dish; a gigget [leg] of excellent mutton and turnips; a piece of beef of 8 ribs, well seasoned and roasted; and a couple of very fat green geese; last of all a great Cheshire cheese.
They drank
canary, sherry, rhenish, claret, white wine, cider, ale, beer and punch.

WHIPPED WITH A CAT, 1675
Henry Teonge records punishment: boys who had misbehaved were 'whipped with a cat with nine tails for their misdemeanours, by the boatswain's mate'. Two men and a boy had 'an iron pin clapped close into their mouths and tied behind their heads, and there they stood a whole hour . . . an excellent cure for swearers'.

SHARP, BUCCANEER, IN COQUIMBO, CHILE, 1679–80
The 3d Being Fryday in the morning an hour before day wee Landed with 35 men and Travelled for the Towne of Coquimbo we had not gone above one League before we met with about 250 horsmen who gave us Battle but we soone cleared the ffield of them soe we stayed for the rest of our Party which came about one houre afterwards and then we marched on our way together and came into the Towne about 8 of

the Clock with 100 men this is a very large towne about ¾ of a mile every way here is all sorts of English fruite allso corne wine and oyle in great abundance it is a mighty pleasant place and from this place is Transported a Bundance of Copper which they take out of a Hill. The inhabitants of this Towne of Coquimbo findeing our small Armes a little too hoot for them left us the Towne to refresh our selves in the 4th of this instant in the morning I had a consultacon with the Governor about the Redempcon of it ther was a way made between each party he came with 5 men and I met him with 2 his party contained 500 men and mine about 120 we agreed for 100000 pieces of Eight but they were falce to their word and soe the Towne was burnt and we fought our way through:/

Decemb

the 6th Being Munday we came on Board againe about 4 of the clock in the afternoone with the Loss of never a man onely wounded in the Body not mortally whilst we were gon the spaniards had like to set our ship on fier but by good ffortune our men soone espied it and Extinguished it:/ *Bartholomew Sharp's South Sea Voyage*, 1679–80

SLAVE TRADE

By this means they can fill the Plantations with *Blacks* and have Stock enough to furnish the *Spaniard*, which at this time make Overtures to them, and to shew what a Trade it might be, take the following Account.

The *Spaniards* treated with the Royal *African Company* of *England* for 5000 whole Pieces of *India* the Year for 7 Years to be delivered at some of the Islands.

But to make this good, the Company were to ship from *Africa* 7 or 8000 Pieces, out of which the *Spaniards* were to chuse 5000 whole Pieces, and the Company to dispose of the rest.

A whole Piece of *India* was according to the Ages of the *Negroes*, Male or Female. Those between 15 and 45 or 35 were a whole Piece; between 4 and 8, were 2 for 1; between 8 and 15, or above 45 or 35, were 3 for 2, and those under 4, were cast in with the Mother.

Now considering the Allowances, there were to be ship'd from *Africa* yearly about 10000 Persons in 7 Years 70000.

The *Spaniards* not being in good Credit, negotiated this by *Augustino Lomelino* and other *Genoeses* Bankers at *Madrid*, in and about 1664, and transferr'd it to *Signor Ferini* at *Amsterdam*; But the *Dutch* War in 1665 broke all off.

This I have from a Gentleman who had the Perusal of a Book of the Letters and Negotiations of the Treaty.

Such a Trade as this made by an Act of Parliament for 99 Years certain, wou'd much improve all our Western Plantations, and by degrees perhaps find as good Mines in *Carolina* as in *Potosi*; 'twoud encrease Seamen and Ships of Strength for our use at home, and encourage Growths and Manufactures here great, 'twill bring us in Gold apace to make Guineas with, and the Goods from the Plantations will fetch us in Silver, besides the Silver is gotten for the *Blacks*: And this is what I verily believe might have been already done had not our Misunderstandings hinder'd in; and I do think I shall never meet with the Man that can and will fairly gainsay it. But perhaps this is not best for us: For if Jessuron shou'd wax fat, he won'd kick his Maker: Therefore God thinks fit to let us be divided, which will keep us poor, and perhaps more humble.

Extract from a Leading Article in Houghton's 'collection', 14 February 1695/6

PIRATE KIDD ATTEMPTS A BLUFF

And the 23rd day of October 1697 at ten at night we got to Calicut, finding no ship there: but the pirate Kidd had been there and sent ashore to demand wood and water; and told Mr Penning, the Chief there, that he was sent out by the King of England and had his commission to take pirates or French. But he turned pirate himself. He had got a commission with the King's hand to it, but how he came by it is best known by them that procured it for him; and he designed to do mischief and no good with it. But the Chief would not send him anything aboard, taking him to be no other than what he was. Yet Kidd could send him word ashore that for denying that civil request he would make it known at Whitehall when he arrived in England.

Edward Barlow, *Journal*, 1659–1703

Colonies

O my America! my new-found-land.

Great events of the reigns of the first two Stuarts were the successful founding of colonies in Virginia, New England, and the West Indian Islands, and the establishment of trading stations on the coast of Northern India, the Great Mogul Empire.

A daring soldier and adventurer, Captain John Smith, with his companions, colonized Virginia in 1606. In the early days, he is said to have been rescued from the Indians by their princess Pocahontas, who married a colonist, John Rolfe, and later came to England. Smith became governor of Virginia in 1608; he explored and so named New England in 1616.

These important emigrations were financed by London Companies – Virginia Company and Massachusetts Bay Company. The objects of the men who found the money were to earn on the investment they had made, to find new markets for English goods, and to introduce to England the products of the colonies, for example, tobacco from Virginia, potatoes from Carolina. Shakespeare said: 'Let the skie raine Potatoes.'

In *The Early Stuarts*, Godfrey Davies informs us that between 1630 and 1643 England spent £200,000 to take 20,000 people in 200 ships to New England. Another 40,000 emigrants sailed on these difficult voyages to Virginia and other places on the North American coast.

Though the promoters of these expeditions were themselves wealthy, the colonists came mainly from the lower classes. Some, such as the Pilgrim Fathers who sailed in 1620, were Puritan exiles, anxious to have religious freedom, but the greater number left England to improve their way of life – and this meant to obtain land. As G. M. Trevelyan says, 'It was a period of land-hunger in England'. Land was hard to get, and younger sons felt this particularly. 'Free land, not free religion was the promise held out in the pamphlets issued by the Companies promoting the emigration.' Fathers seized this opportunity to deal with the son who did little but get into trouble. Though a young member of a distinguished family, Thomas Verney was often mixed up

289

in quarrels which led to duels; he was always short of money. So he went out to Virginia. Very soon he returned. In 1638 he went to Barbados. Many others, however, were successful in these lands of promise, which gave full scope to private enterprise.

Colonists brought with them wide knowledge of the agricultural life, of craftsmanship which self-sufficing villages and small towns had demanded. For hundreds of years the work of peasants and yeomen had been creative. They were well equipped to build new villages and to farm the land anywhere in the known world. These colonists had courage, versatility, and endurance. They were able to absorb the convicts sent during the Civil Wars, and to use slaves from Africa to work on the plantations in Virginia and in the West Indian Islands. Villages were extended into townships, and life became ordered with sensible intelligence. John Harvard, a pensioner of Cambridge University, settled in Charlestown, Massachusetts, and founded a new college at another Cambridge in 1638, to be known as Harvard University.

These American colonies, founded by private enterprise, expressed a spirit of independence which was shown in the communal self-government. When Cromwell took Jamaica from Spain, and Charles II took from the Dutch what were renamed New York, New Jersey, and Pennsylvania, there is the sign of imperial development in the future.

> And those unchristened countries call our own
> Where scarce the name of England hath been known.

The East India Company traded most successfully in the Far East. The large, impressive 'East Indiamen' ships fought tenaciously against the Portuguese, Dutch, and pirates in the Indian Ocean and beyond. Charles II's marriage with Catherine of Braganza brought the Portuguese possession of Bombay as part of her dowry. Factories at Bombay, Madras, and Hugli linked trade with Canton. Indian trade, producing 'great ships and expert mariners', brought to England silk, saltpetre (for gunpowder), and bitter aromatic spices – with vast quantities of pepper. As there were no root crops on which to feed cattle and sheep they were killed and salted in early autumn. These spices were to preserve and season meat throughout the winter months.

After the Restoration the number of imports grew rapidly. Tea and coffee were now fashionable drinks. 'As tea begins to come into use by some of the people, we expect some jars of Chinese as well as Japanese tea with every ship.' Coffee was not now taken to be 'black as soote, and tasting not much unlike it'. For exotic drinks, exotic cups were fitting. Barlow, serving as chief mate and China pilot on the *Fleet Frigate*, wrote: 'and having all things ready on Monday the 1st day of February 1702–3, we set sail from a place called "Whampow" in the river of

Canton in China, praying God for a good passage to England, being a full ship and laden with goods, namely: 205 chests of China and Japan ware, porcelain . . . and a great deal more loose China and Japan earthenware.' Other goods were Indian and Chinese silk, Persian carpets, Turkish rugs, also carpets made at Agra and Lahore.

In 1672 the Royal African Company was established by Charter with the sole privilege of trading the long coast of Africa from Salee to the Cape of Good Hope for the term of one thousand years. This 'sole privilege' caused bitter feelings. So, in 1697 African trade was made free to all English merchantmen.

Peter Mundy, the traveller, wrote 'one of the seven things wherein England may be said to excel, traffic and discoveries, viz. so many incorporated companies of merchants for foreign trade, who employ their study and means for the increase thereof, by adventuring their goods and sundry fleets and ships into most parts of the known world'.

ALEXANDER SELKIRK
Captain Woodes Rogers, commander of two privateer ships, sailed to the island of Juan Fernandez in 1709. He describes how they found on this island:
a man clothed in goat-skins, who seemed wilder than the original owners of his apparel. His name was Alexander Selkirk, a Scotsman, who had lived alone on the island for four years and four months. He had with him his clothes and bedding, with a firelock and some powder and bullets, some tobacco, a knife, a kettle, a bible, with some other books, and his mathematical implements. He diverted himself and provided for his sustenance as well as he could; but had much ado to bear up against melancholy for the first eight months, and was sore distressed at being left alone in such a desolate place. He built himself two huts, thatched with long grass and lined with goat skins. He employed himself in reading, praying and singing psalms, so that he said he was a better Christian during his solitude than he had ever been before. When his clothes were worn out, he made himself a coat and cap of goat-skins, which he stitched together with thongs of the same, cut out with his knife, using a nail by way of a needle or awl. . . . At his first coming on board, he had so much forgotten his language, for want of use, that we could scarcely understand him, as he seemed to speak his words by halves.
                    Woodes Rogers, *A Cruizing Voyage round the World*, 1712
Selkirk's experiences formed the basis of Defoe's Robinson Crusoe.

THE CHARTER TO THE VIRGINIAN COLONIES, 1606
10 April 1606
James, by the grace of God, &c. Whereas our loving and well-disposed

subjects Sir Thomas Gates and Sir George Somers, knights, Richard Hakluyt, clerk, prebendary of Westminster, gentlemen, and divers others of our loving subjects, have been humble suitors unto us, that we would vouchsafe unto them our licence to make habitation, plantation, and to deduce a colony of sundry of our people into that part of America commonly called Virginia, and other parts and territories in America, either appertaining to us or which are not now actually possessed by any Christian prince or people; and to that end, and for the more speedy accomplishment of their said intended plantation and habitation there, are desirous to divide themselves into two several colonies and companies, the one consisting of certain knights, gentlemen, merchants and other adventurers of our city of London and elsewhere which are and from time to time shall be joined unto them which do desire to begin their plantations in some fit and convenient place, between four-and-thirty and one-and-forty degrees of the said [north] latitude, all along the coast of Virginia and coasts of America aforesaid; and the other consisting of sundry knights of our cities of Bristol and Exeter and of our town of Plymouth and of other places which do join themselves unto that colony, which do desire to begin their plantations in some fit and convenient place between eight-and-thirty and five-and-forty degrees of the said latitude, all along the said coast of Virginia and America as that coast lieth:

We, greatly commending and graciously accepting of their desires for the furtherance of so noble a work, which may, by the providence of Almighty God, hereafter tend to the glory of his divine Majesty, in propagating of Christian religion to such people as yet live in darkness and miserable ignorance of the true knowledge and worship of God, and may in time bring the infidels and savages living in those parts to humane civility and to a settled and quiet government, do, by these our letters patents, graciously accept of and agree to their humble and well-intended desires.   *Pat. Roll, 4 Jac. i. pt 19*

VIRGINIA, 1607

On the nineteenth of December, 1606, we set sail from Blackwall, but by unprosperous winds were kept six weeks in the sight of England; all which time Master Hunt, our preacher, was so weak and sick that few expected his recovery. Yet although he were but twenty miles from his habitation (the time we were in the Downs), and notwithstanding the stormy weather, nor the scandalous imputations (of some few, little better than atheists, of the greatest rank amongst us) suggested against him; all this could never force from him so much as a seeming desire to leave the business, but he preferred the service of God in so good a voyage, before any affection to contest with his godless foes, whose disastrous designs (could they have prevailed) had even then over-thrown the business, so many discontents did then arise, had he not with the water of patience, and his godly exhortations (but chiefly by his true devoted examples) quenched those flames of envy and dissension.

We watered at the Canaries, we traded with the savages at Dominica, three weeks we spent in refreshing ourselves amongst those West India Isles; in Gaudelupe we found a bath so hot, as in it we boiled pork as well as over the fire. And at a little isle called Monica we took from the bushes with our hands near two hogsheads full of birds in three or four hours. In Nevis, Mona and the Virgin Isles we spent some time, where, with a loathsome beast like a crocodile called gwayn, tortoises, pelicans, parrots, and fishes, we daily feasted.

Gone from thence in search of Virginia, the company was not a little discomforted, seeing the mariners had three days passed their reckoning and found no land; so that Captain Ratcliffe (Captain of the Pinnace) rather desired to bear up the helm to return for England than make further search. But God, the guider of all good actions, forcing them by an extreme storm to hull all night, did drive them by his providence to their desired port, beyond all their expectations; for never any of them had seen that coast.

The first land they made they called Cape Henry; where thirty of them, recreating themselves on shore, were assaulted by five savages, who hurt two of the English very dangerously. . . .

Until the thirteenth of May they sought a place to plant in; then the Council was sworn, Master Wingfield was chosen president, and an oration made, why Captain Smith was not admitted of the council as the rest.

Captain John Smith, *The Generall Historie of Virginia*, 1624

IN THE COLONIES

This day the people of the country came aboard of us, seeming very glad of our coming, and brought green tobacco, and gave us of it for knives and beads. They go in deer skins loose, well dressed. They have yellow copper. They desire clothes, and are very civil. They have great store of maize or Indian wheat, whereof they make good bread. The country is full of great and tall oaks. . . . Our men went on land there, and saw great store of men, women, and children, who gave them tobacco at their coming on land. So they went up into the woods, and saw great store of very goodly oaks and some currants. For one of them came aboard and brought some dried, and gave me some, which were sweet and good. This day many of the people came aboard, some in mantles of feathers, and some in skins of divers sorts of good furs.

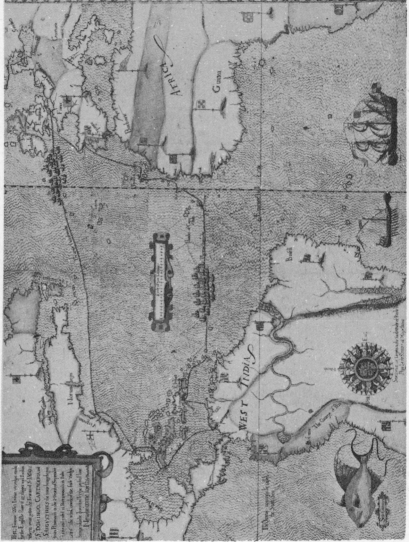

78. Francis Drake's route to the West Indies, 1583–1586. The flags indicate the possessions of different countries.

Some women also came to us with hemp. They had red copper tobacco pipes, and other things of copper they did wear about their necks.

The Third Voyage of Master Henry Hudson, written by Robert Juet, of Lime-house, 1609

USEFUL DIRECTIONS TO NEW SETTLERS

Now because I expect your coming unto us with other of our friends, whose company we much desire, I thought good to advertise you of a few things needful. Be careful to have a very good bread-room to put your biscuits in, let your cask for beer and water be iron-bound for the first tyre if not more. Let not your meat be dry salted, none can better do it than the sailors. Let your meal be so hard trod in your cask that you shall need an adze or hatchet to work it out with. Trust not too much on us for corn at this time, for by reason of this last company that came, depending wholly on us, we shall have little enough till harvest. . . .

Bring juice of lemons, and take it fasting, it is of good use; for hot waters, aniseed water is the best, but use it sparingly. If you bring any thing for comfort in the country, butter or salad oil, or both is very good. Our Indian corn, even the coarsest, maketh as pleasant meal as rice, therefore spare that unless to spend by the way. Bring paper, and linseed oil for your windows, with cotton yarn for your lamps. Let your shot be most for big fowls, and bring store of powder and shot. I forbear further to write for the present, hoping to see you by the next return, so I take my leave, commending you to the Lord for a safe conduct unto us. Resting in him.

Your loving friend.
E.W.
[Edward Winslow]

Plimmouth in New-England
this 11. of December 1621

A PEACE TREATY WITH KING MASSASOYT, NEW ENGLAND, 1622

They could not well express in English what they would, but after an hour the King came to the top of an hill over against us, and had in his train sixty men, that we could well behold them, and they us: we were not willing to send our governor to them, and they unwilling to come to us, so Squanto went again unto him, who brought word that we should send one to parley with him, which we did, which was Edward Winslow, to know his mind, and to signify the mind and will of our governor, which was to have trading and peace with him. We sent to King a pair of knives, and a copper chain, with a jewel at it . . . our messenger made a speech unto him, that King James saluted him with words of love and peace, and did accept him as his friend and ally, and that our governor desired to see him and to truck with him, and to confirm a peace with him, as his next neighbour: he liked well of the speech and heard it attentively, though the interpreters did not well express it. . . . Captain Standish and master Williamson met the King at the brook, with half a dozen Musketeers, they saluted him and he them, so one going over, the one on the one side, and the other on the other, conducted him to an house then in building, where we placed a green rug, and three or four cushions, then instantly came our governor with drum and trumpet after him, and some few Musketeers. After salutations, our governor kissing his hand, the King kissed him, and so they sat down. The governor called for some strong water, and drunk to him, and he drunk a great draught . . . he called for a little fresh meat, which the King did eat willingly. . . . Then they treated of peace, which was:

1. That neither he nor any of his should injure or do hurt to any of our people.

2. And if any of his did hurt to any of ours, he should send the offender, that we might punish him.

3. That if any of our tools were taken away when our people were at work, he should cause them to be restored, and if ours did any harm to any of his, we would do the like to them.

4. If any did unjustly war against him, we would aid him; if any did war against us, he should aid us.

5. He should send to his neighbour confederates, to certify them of this, that they might not wrong us, but might be likewise comprised in the conditions of Peace.

6. That when their men came to us, they should leave their bows and arrows behind them, as we should do our pieces when we came to them.

Lastly, that doing thus, King **James** would esteem of him as his friend and ally: all which the King seemed to like well, and it was applauded of his followers. . . .

G. Mourt, *A Relation of the English Plantation at Plymouth in New England*

VIRGINIA

The next day came divers boats [to our settlement], and in one of them the king's brother, with forty of fifty men, proper people, and in their behaviour very civil; his name was Granganameo, the king is called Wingina, the country Wingandacoa. Leaving his boats a little from our ships, he came with his train to the point, where spreading a mat he sat down. Though we came to him well armed, he made signs to us to sit down without any show of fear, stroking his head and breast, and also ours, to express his love.

After he had made a long speech unto us, we presented him with divers toys, which he kindly accepted. He was greatly regarded by his people, for none of them did sit nor speak a word, but four, on whom we bestowed presents also, but he took all from them, making signs all things did belong to him.

The king himself, in a conflict with a king, his next neighbour and mortal enemy, was shot in two places through the body and the thigh, yet recovered: whereby he lay at his chief town six day's journey from thence.

A day or two after showing them what we had, Granganameo taking most liking to a pewter dish, made a hole in it, hung it about his neck for a breastplate: for which he gave us twenty deer skins, worth twenty crowns: and for a copper kettle, fifty skins, worth fifty crowns. Much other truck we had, and after two days he came aboard, and did eat and drink with us very merrily. Not long after he brought his wife and children; they were of mean stature, but well favoured and very bashful. She had a long coat of leather, and about her forehead a band of white coral, and so had her husband; in her ears were bracelets of pearl, hanging down to her middle, of the bigness of great peas. The rest of the women had pendants of copper, and the noblemen five or six in an ear; his apparel as his wives', only the women wear their hair long on both sides, and the men but on one; they are of colour yellow, but their hair is black, yet we saw children that had very fair chestnut coloured hair.

After that these women had been here with us, there came down from all parts great store of people, with leather, coral, and divers kinds of dyes, but when Granganameo was present, none durst trade himself and them that wore red copper on their heads, as he did. Whenever he came, he would signify by so many fires he came with so many boats, that we might know his strength. Their boats are but one great tree, which is but burnt in the form of a trough with gins and fire, till it be as they would have it. For an armour he would have engaged us a bag of pearl, but we refused, as not regarding it, that we might the better learn where it grew. He was very just of his promise, for oft we trusted him, and he would come within his day to keep his word. He sent us commonly every day a brace of bucks, conies, hares and fish, sometimes melons, walnuts, cucumbers, peas and divers roots. This author saith, their corn groweth three times in five months; in May they sow, in July reap; in June they sow, in August reap; in July sow, in August reap. We put some of our peas in the ground, which in ten days were fourteen inches high.

The soil is most plentiful, sweet, wholesome, and fruitful of all other; there are about fourteen several sorts of sweet smelling timber trees;

the most parts of the underwood, bays and such like, such oaks as we, but far greater and better. . . .

This discovery was so welcome into England that it pleased her Majesty to call this country of Wingandacoa, Virginia.

> Captain John Smith, *The Generall Historie of Virginia*, 1624

JOHN WINTHROP, A SUFFOLK MAN, FIRST GOVERNOR OF MASSACHUSETTS

1630. This year it pleased God, of his rich grace, to transport over into the bay of the Massachusetts, divers honorable personages, and many worthy Christians, whereby the Lord began in a manifest manner and way to make known the great thoughts which he had of planting the gospel in this remote and barbarous wilderness, and honouring his own way of instituted worship, causing such and so many to adhere thereunto, and fall upon the practice thereof; – among the rest, a chief one amongst them was that famous pattern of piety and justice, Mr John Winthrop, the first Governor of the jurisdiction, accompanied with divers other precious sons of Sion, which might be compared to the most fine gold.

> *New England's Memorial* by Nathaniel Morton, 1669

TO VIRGINIA

Tom Verney is leaving for Virginia in 1634. He hears from his mother, Lady Verney, and her agent tells him what preparations he must make.

Bring up with him feather bed, blankets and three pairs of sheets, it is but a spare pack horse needed to bring them. Although many households in Virginia are so well provided as to entertain a stranger with all things necessary for the belly, yet few or none are better provided for the back than will serve their own turn. He must take some corn, lest there should happen a scarcity in the country, which sometimes doth fall out, through the covetousness of the planters, that strive to plant much tobacco and little corn. I have already bought the flour, the fowling pieces, the strong waters and the grocery wares; if he settle a plantation for himself, he should have some seasoned men of his own.

> *Memoirs of the Verney Family during the Seventeenth Century*

VIRGINIA, 1649

Worthy Captain Matthews, an old planter of above thirty years standing, one of the Council, and a most deserving Commonwealthsman, I may not omit to let you know this gentleman's industry.

He hath a fine house, and all things answerable to it. He sows yearly store of hemp and flax, and causes it to be spun. He keeps weavers, and hath a tan-house, causes leather to be dressed, hath eight shoemakers employed in their trade, hath forty negro servants, brings them up to trades in his house. He yearly sows abundance of wheat, barley, etc. The wheat he selleth at four shillings the bushel; kills store of beeves, and sells them to victual the ships when they come thither: hath abundance of kine, a brave dairy, swine great store, and poultry. He married the daughter of Sir Thomas Hinton, and in a word, keeps a good house, lives bravely, and a true lover of Virginia; he is worthy of much honour.

> A perfect Description of Virginia . . . sent from Virginia, at the request of a Gentleman of worthy note, who desires to know the true state of Virginia as it now stands. 1649

SLAVE-TRADING BY THE ROYAL AFRICAN COMPANY

Charles the Second, To all whom these presents shall come, greetings. Whereas all and singular the regions [known] as Guynny [Guinea], Binny [Benin], and South Barbary . . . are the undoubted rights of us . . . Now know ye that we . . . have of our special grace [etc.] given and granted and by these presents give and grant unto [large number of persons, influential in Court, Parliament, and Trade] the regions beginning at the Port of Sally [Sallee] in South Barbary inclusive and extending from thence to Cape de bona Esperanza with all the islands near adjoining to those coasts and comprehended within the limits aforesaid. And therefore for the setting forward [of the trade] of our further and more ample grace [we incorporate the above named] by the name of the Company of Royal Adventurers of England trading into Africa.

[Power that the Company may set to sea ships etc. with ordnance etc.] and shall for ever hereafter have use and enjoy all mines of gold and silver which are or shall be found in all or any the places above mentioned and the whole entire and only trade [to those parts] for buying and selling, bartering and exchanging of for or with any negroes, slaves, goods, wares, and merchandise whatsoever to be vented or found at or any of the cities, etc.

> Charter of 10 January 1662–3

PROSPERITY OF THE COLONIES

The commodities of the production growth and manufacture of New England are, all things necessary for shipping and naval furniture in great abundance, as excellent oak, elm, beech, fir, pines for masts the best in the world, pitch, tar, hemp, and iron . . . clapboards, pipestaves, planks and dealboards, so that his Majesty need not be beholden to other nations for naval stores. . . .

[Exports] to Virginia, Jamaica and Maryland beef and pork salted, pease, flour, biscuit, codfish, and salt mackerel.

To Barbados, Nevis, St Christopher, and the other islands, the above commodities, together with horses, deal-boards, pipestaves, and houses ready framed.

To Spain, Portugal, and the Straits, Madeira, and Canary Islands, fish and timber, pipestaves, and dealboards.

To England, masts and yards for ships, fir and oak planks, with all sorts of peltry [fur-skins].

The Commodities imported from the plantations are tobacco, sugar, indigo, cotton wool, ginger, logwood, fustic [wood yielding yellow dye], cacao and rum, the which are again transported to other parts.

Mr Edward Randolph's Narrative 20 September and 12 October 1676

THE SLAVE TRADE

I arrived here in the *Margaret* . . . the 14 April and thought to have found Mr Thurloe [agent of the Royal African Company at James Island, Gambia] but he not only being dead, but Mr Phelps then agent lay very sick and 19th he died, no factors on the island but myself and Mr Cleave . . . the *Laurel* arrived under Capt Plumer [an Interloper] and made a stop to trade so that I could not buy a slave of the merchants.

[Ibid., 23 May, 1681]

I am apt to believe that in a short time the French will venture to go up the River, now I only want your order signed to bear me harmless for preventing them, and you shall find I will keep them in subjection if I sink burn or destroy ships or men that shall go past the Castle [the fort on James Island].   *Letter Book*, 2 March 1681

EAST INDIA COMPANY'S TRADE IN INDIA
27 December 1682

This day I spent wholly in seeing . . . what store of silk etc. was now in the Company's Godowns [warehouses] where I found the quantity of more than 500 bales of silk not yet prized [priced], which I caused to be . . . prized whilst I was there, which was accordingly done, Mr Charnock [Company's official at Cassumbazaar] promising 500 great bales and 200 chests of silk should follow me in 10 or 15 days at farthest. And this night . . . we took boat for Hugly.

The Diary of William Hedges (Agent in Bengal 1681–1687)

TRADE AT CASSUMBAZAAR
6 May 1683

At Cassumbazaar I saw the taffetas and atlasses [satins] in the warehouse, and gave directions concerning their various colours and stripes ordering Mr Charnock to . . . increase their quantity; the Honourable Company writing very earnestly for yours this year, which I fear he will not be able to perform by reason of the great prejudice the weavers have received against him by taking 2 per cent of them to price their goods favourably, and paying of them with light money. . . . In Mr Charnock's Company I saw divers patterns of good pieces of prunella and other sorts of silks, as black, blue, yellow and green taffetas . . . as well as of raw silk. I conceive, if 3 or 4 master weavers and as many able dyers were sent out with 5 or 6 boys apiece to be their apprentices, the trade of this place might be improved, to the Company's great advantage or at least if the said master weavers and dyers were but obliged for one or two years to instruct the natives.

The Diary of William Hedges (Agent in Bengal 1681–1687)

FRENCH COMPETITION AT HUDSON'S BAY AFTER 1680

The ports and places within Hudson's Bay in America were first discovered by the subjects of the Imperial Crown of this Kingdom.·. . . The petitioners were trading into those parts above twenty years and in that time have expended near two hundred thousand pounds sterling in erecting forts and factories there and in settling a trade and other necessaries thereunto within the limits of their charter, and have now arrived to a very considerable trade therein . . . and never were disturbed until the year 1682 when private merchants of Canada without any commission or colour of authority from his most Christian Majesty or from the governor of Canada did set out ships and in a piratical manner disturb and annoy the petitioners in their factories and settlements at Port Nelson and did burn their houses and robbed them of their trade there, to all of which though several memorials were sent to the Court of France by his late Majesty of ever blessed memory on behalf of the petitioners demanding satisfaction for the same, yet none was obtained. . . . That within these two months the petitioners have received advices . . . whereby it appears that the French of Canada this year have in a piratical manner taken and totally despoiled the petitioners of three of their forts and factories [Moose Factory, Fort Rupert, and Fort Albany] in the bottom of Hudson's Bay, three of their ships, fifty thousand beaver skins, and a great quantity of provisions . . . laid up for many years trade.

[Counter Memorials from the French were received by the English Government, and a Commission was appointed to settle the boundary question.]   Petition of 1686

PENNSYLVANIA, THE CHARTER OF PRIVILEGES, 1701

I the said William Penn do declare, grant and confirm, unto all the

Freemen, Planters and Adventurers, and other inhabitants of this province and Territories, these following liberties, franchises and privileges. . . .

First.

Because no people can be truly happy, though under the greatest enjoyment of civil liberties, if abridged of the freedom of their consciences, as to their religious profession and worship: I do hereby grant and declare, That no person or persons, inhabiting in this province or territories, who shall confess and acknowledge one almighty God, the creator, upholder and ruler of the world; and profess him or themselves obliged to live quietly under the Civil Government, shall be in any case molested or prejudiced, in his or their person or estate. . . .

And that all persons who also profess to believe in Jesus Christ, the Saviour of the World, shall be capable . . . to serve this Government in any capacity, both legislatively and executively, he or they solemnly promising, when lawfully required, allegiance to the King as sovereign and fidelity to the proprietary and governor. . . .

The Federal and State Constitutions

PLANTATION FOR SALE IN BARBADOS

These are to give Notice, that the undivided moiety of a Plantation in Barbados, late the estate of Nathaniel Rous of London, merchant, is to be sold by Richard Meriweather, Esq., and Capt Thomas Wharton . . . assignees of the said Mr Rous's Estate. The said Plantation consists of a new built Mansion-House, which cost above 2000 *l.* building, besides the Out-Houses, Sugar-Houses, and Distil-Houses, &c. furnished with all suitable and convenient Coppers, Stills, and other Utensils; 332 Acres of Land, all well planted; 180 Negroes; 100 Head of Cattle; the Situation very commodious for Shipping.

Flying Post, 30 April–2 May 1713

SELECT BIBLIOGRAPHY

Ashley, M., *England in the Seventeenth Century* (Penguin)

Churchill, Winston S., *Marlborough, His Life and Times* (Harrap)
Clark, G. N., *The Later Stuarts* (Oxford)
Cole, G. D. H., and Postgate, R. W., *The Common People* (Methuen)
Craven, W. F., *The Southern Colonies in the Seventeenth Century* (Baton Rouge)
Cunnington, C. W., and P., *English Costume in the Seventeenth Century*

Davies, G., *The Early Stuarts 1603–1660* (Oxford)
Dutton, R., *The English Interior 1500 to 1900* (Batsford)

Fastnedge, R., *English Furniture Styles* (Penguin)
Fussell, G. E., *The English Rural Labourer* (Batchworth)

Haller, W., *The Rise of Puritanism* (New York)
Hammond, J. L., and L. B., *The Village Labourer* (Longmans)
Hammond, J. L., and L. B., *The Skilled Labourer* (Longmans)
Hill, C., *The Century of Revolution 1603–1714* (Nelson)
Hole, C., *England Home-Life 1500–1800* (Batsford)
Hole, C., *Witchcraft in England* (Batsford)

Manning, B., *Life in Stuart England* (Batsford)
Mitchell, R. J., and Leys, M. D. R., *A History of London Life* (Longmans)

Newton, A. P., *The Colonizing Activities of the English Puritans* (New Haven)
Notestein, W., *The English People on the Eve of Colonization 1603 to 1630* (Harper)

Prothero, R. E., *English Farming, Past and Present* (Heinemann)

Stuart, D. M., *London through the Ages* (Methuen)
Summerson, J. N., *Architecture in Britain 1530–1830* (Penguin)

Trevelyan, G. M., *English Social History* (Longmans)
Trevelyan, G. M., *The English Revolution* (Oxford)
Trevelyan, G. M., *England in the Reign of Queen Anne* (Longmans)

Waterhouse, E., *Painting in Britain 1530–1790* (Penguin)
Watson, F., *The English Grammar Schools to 1660* (Cambridge)
Willey, B., *The Seventeenth Century Background* (Chatto)

Yarwood, D., *The English Home* (Batsford)

Biographies

JOSEPH ADDISON (1672–1719), essayist, poet, politician, was the son of Dean of Lichfield. Close friendship with Swift, Steele, and other writers. Produced the periodical essay the *Spectator*. Dr Johnson said: 'Whoever wishes to attain an English style, familiar but not coarse; and elegant but not ostentatious, must give his days and nights to the volumes of Addison.'

NICHOLAS ASSHETON (1590–1625), of Downham, Lancashire. Wrote a country social diary, a lively record of sport, pleasures and Puritan religious life in Lancashire.

JOHN AUBREY (1626–1697), antiquary and folklorist. Only his quaint *Miscellanies* printed in his lifetime; but left large mass of materials. Could 'conjure a living-being out of a mere list of facts'. Last years passed in 'danger of arrests' with Hobbes, Ashmole, and other protectors.

EDWARD BARLOW (*b.* 1642) of Prestwich, Lancashire. Sea diary, 1659–1703; in King's ships, East and West Indiamen, and other merchantmen; excellent account of sailor's life at sea and ashore.

RICHARD BAXTER (1615–1691), a Presbyterian divine, military chaplain on parliament side during the Civil War. Saintsbury calls him 'a pious, useful, irrepressible heresiarch'. Disputed face to face with John Tombes, another divine.

NATHANIEL BOTELER (*fl.* 1625–1627), sea-captain, with considerable knowledge of the internal economy of ships of war. His remarks in *Six Dialogues about Sea Services Between an High Admiral and a Captain at Sea* are very incisive and instructive.

WILLIAM BRADFORD (1590–1657), historian and administrator, of Austerfield, Yorkshire. Sailed on the *Mayflower* to Plymouth, New

England, elected Governor pretty regularly for next thirty years. Gave account of the colony.

SIR WILLIAM BRERETON (1604–1661), of Handforth, Cheshire. Diary, topographical and social, of Puritan's travels in Holland, Scotland, Ireland, through north and southwest England.

NICHOLAS BRETON (1545?–1626?), poet and satirist, son of a London merchant. Prolific author, best work in *England's Helicon*. *The Fantasticks* is a collection of observations on men and things arranged to the calendar.

JOHN BRÍNSLEY THE ELDER (*fl.* 1663), at Ashby-de-la-Zouch he propounded, in his *Ludus Literarius*, a new mode of translation, and declared the importance of teaching grammar.

JOHN BULWER (*fl.* 1654), Puritan pamphleteer, in his *Anthropometamorphosis* 'collected all the stories, ancient and modern, of savages' adornments and mutilations, to show how men disgrace what was made in God's image'.

JOHN BUNYAN (1628–1688), religious writer of Elstow near Bedford, son of a 'brasever' or tinker. Served in the parliamentary army, joined the Nonconformists, opposed the Quakers. Turned to religious books. 'I was never out of the Bible either by reading or meditation.' Preached without a licence, twelve years in prison, where he wrote nine of his books. During brief imprisonment, 1673, began *Pilgrim's Progress*, an allegory of extraordinary appeal.

GILBERT BURNET (1643–1715), Bishop of Salisbury, popular preacher, historian. Remonstrated with Charles II for his profligacy. Took active part in controversies of the time. His *History of my Own Times* has authority.

ROBERT BURTON (1577–1640), of Lindley, Leicestershire, a Student of Christ Church. Anthony Wood says of him: 'He was an exact mathematician, a curious calculator of nativities, a general real scholar, a thro'paced philologist. His company was very merry, facete, and juvenile.' His unique *Anatomy of Melancholy* is a farrago of quotations.

SAMUEL BUTLER (1612–1680), son of a Worcestershire farmer. As attendant on the Countess of Kent, became acquainted with John

Selden. He was later secretary to the Earl of Carbery. *Hudibras*, his mock-heroic poem, ridiculing the Puritans, 'took extremely', and Lord Chancellor Hyde 'had his picture in his Library over the Chimney'.

WILLIAM BYRD (1543–1623), composer, organist of Lincoln Cathedral, joint-organist with Tallis of the Chapel Royal. Wrote music for church services as well as madrigals, songs, and music for strings.

EDMUND CALAMY (1599–1666), Presbyterian divine, one of the five authors of *Smectymnuus*, a pamphlet attacking episcopacy. (The name is made up of the initials of the authors.) Calamy is reported to have died of melancholy caused by the Great Fire of London.

WILLIAM CAMDEN (1551–1623), antiquary and historian, born in the Old Bailey, London. Headmaster of Westminster School. *Britannia* is a survey of the British Isles. His *Annales* is also in Latin, later translated into English.

RICHARD CAREW (1555–1620), translator and antiquary, born in Cornwall, high sheriff in 1586. His *Survey of Cornwall* is a diligent and valuable piece of work.

SIR DUDLEY CARLETON, VISCOUNT DORCHESTER (1573–1632), ambassador to The Hague. Thomas Carew, the Cavalier lyrist, was for a time his secretary.

EDWARD CHAMBERLAYNE (1616–1703), antiquary, tutor to Prince George of Denmark. His *Angliae Notitia, or the Present State of England*, a handbook of social and political conditions, had immediate success.

EDWARD HYDE, EARL OF CLARENDON (1609–1674), statesman and historian. From 1641 onwards one of the chief advisers of the King. Lord Chancellor to Charles II from 1658. The future James II married his daughter. His *History* gave a most valuable account of contemporary events. From the profits of this work the Oxford University Press built the Clarendon Buildings and took the name of the Clarendon Press.

JOHN CLAVEL (1603–1642), highwayman, first robbery at Gad's Hill. Wrote *A Recantation of an Ill-led Life; or a Discoverie of the Highway Law* in verse.

LADY ANNE CLIFFORD, COUNTESS OF PEMBROKE (1590–1676), her domestic diary is a valuable and attractive record of her married life and troubles, of clothes, amusements, piety, and of the management of her estates.

GEORGE COKAYNE (1619–1691), divine of St Pancras. Anthony Wood said he was 'a prime leader in his preachings in Oliver's time'. He wrote *Divine Astrologie*.

CHARLES COTTON (1630–1687), poet and translator, of Beresford Hall, Staffordshire; a friend of Izaak Walton, he wrote the dialogue between 'Piscator' and 'Viator' in the *Compleat Angler*, also burlesque of Virgil and translation of Montaigne's *Essays*.

OLIVER CROMWELL (1599–1658), Lord Protector, 1653–1658; celebrated as great general, for his religious toleration, and strong foreign policy.

CAPT. THOMAS DANGERFIELD (1650?–1685), highwayman; his diary recounts the travels and adventures of a rogue through England; inns, expenses. Printed while in Newgate.

DANIEL DEFOE (1660?–1731), journalist, novelist, pamphleteer; born in St Giles, Cripplegate. Took part in Monmouth's rebellion; joined William III's army in 1688. Became tradesman-publicist, secret agent, political hack. His *Robinson Crusoe* had immediate and permanent success. Other fiction shows astounding versatility. His love of liberty is 'the real mark of a tribune of the people'.

THOMAS DEKKER (1570?–1632), dramatist, pamphleteer; lived mainly in London. Suffered from poverty, long in prison for debt, yet a kindly, warm-hearted man. His prose pamphlets give vivid impressions of London.

THOMAS DELONEY (1543?–1600?), ballad-writer and pamphleteer; by trade a silk-weaver. In the story of 'Simon Eyre' and other works he gives vivid pictures of London.

SIR KENELM DIGBY (1603–1665), diplomat, writer, had interest in physical science – discovered need of oxygen to life of plants. Defeated the French and Venetian fleets in Scanderoon harbour, 1628. Wrote part of *Private Memoirs* under disguised names.

JOHN DONNE (1572–1631), poet, satirist, dean of St Paul's. Great popularity as a preacher. Ben Jonson said he was 'the first poet in some things'. He was certainly the greatest of the 'metaphysical' poets, fusing thought and passion, maintaining the separate and warring identity of the conceit.

JOHN DRYDEN (1631–1700), poet, dramatist, critic, born at Ald-winkle Rectory, Northamptonshire. *Astraea Redux* in honour of the Restoration showed his mastery of the heroic couplet; *Absalom and Achitophel* showed his satirical power. He was appointed poet laureate and later historiographer. He was buried in Westminster Abbey in Chaucer's grave.

JOHN EARLE (1601?–1665), Bishop of Salisbury; was tutor to Charles II. Learned and eloquent, he wrote *Microcosmographie*, a collection of character sketches such as a plain country fellow, a modest man, a She-precise hypocrite, a coward.

JOHN EVELYN (1620–1706), diarist and author, 'helped to advance English civilization'. Much at court after the Restoration. Let Sayes Court to Admiral Benbow who sublet it to Peter the Great (a 'right nasty' inmate). Active, intelligent, God-fearing; wrote on architecture, politics, morals, gardening, and commerce. His brilliant diary, cover-ing his whole life, was found in an old clothes-basket at Wotton in 1817.

ADAM EYRE (1614?–1661), yeoman of Haslehead, Yorkshire. His diary describes country life round Peniston; farming, fishing, amuse-ments, religion.

LADY ANNE FANSHAWE (1625–1680), 'hoyting girl in her youth'; from 1644, her *Memoirs* tell of incessant struggle and sacrifice, and her heroic courage – whether on deck facing a 'Turk's man of war', or beneath her husband's prison window at Whitehall. Later with him, ambassador, in Portugal and Spain.

GUY FAWKES (1570–1606), born in York, became a Roman Catholic. Fanatical zeal for his religion led him with Catesby and others into the Gunpowder Plot. Taken with match in his possession, tried, and executed.

OWEN FELLTHAM (1602–1668), published, when eighteen years of age, *Resolves*, which established 'the essay's right to add sacred topics to the moral topics discussed by Bacon'.

CELIA FIENNES (1662–1741), of Newton Toney, a manor house near Salisbury, daughter of a Cromwellian colonel. During her leisurely journeys she explored every English county. 'Artless but charming, prim but adventurous, censorious and often caustic . . . she reacted to everything with liveliest curiosity and enthusiasm.'

HENRY FITZGEFFERY (*fl.* 1617), a writer of satires and epigrams.

ELIZABETH FREAKE (1641–1714) of County Cork. Domestic diary gives account of misfortunes of married life in Ireland; household work and inventories, health and home medicine.

THOMAS FULLER (1608–1661), of Aldwinkle St Peter's in Northamptonshire, divine and antiquary, 'chaplain in extraordinary' to Charles II. His *Worthies of England* is a miscellany about the counties of England and their notable men. Coleridge says of him: 'He was incomparably the most sensible, the least prejudiced great man in an age that boasted a galaxy of great men.'

EDMUND GIBSON (1669–1748), church jurist, Bishop of London. Translated Camden's *Britannia*. Best known for his *Codex iuris ecclesiastici Anglicani*.

THOMAS GUMBLE (*d.* 1676), biographer. Vicar of Chipping Wycombe, Buckinghamshire; later rector of East Lavant, Sussex. Wrote *Life of General Monck*.

JOSEPH HALL (1574–1656), divine, Bishop of Norwich. Impeached, imprisoned in the Tower. His *Characters of Virtues and Vices*, designed with a moral purpose, were the first imitation of Theophrastus; *Virgidemiarum Sex Libri* (six Books of Stripes) introduced Juvenalian satire in English.

LADY ANN HALKETT (1622–1699), Royalist and writer on religious subjects. Met Charles II at Dunfermline where she lived. Did much to educate children of persons of rank.

PHILIP HENRY (1631–1696), divine and diarist. Playmate to princes Charles and James. Favourite pupil of Busby at Westminster School. Gave graphic description of the execution of Charles I.

PAUL HENTZER, German traveller; in *A Journey into England* he describes this country as a sort of woman's paradise, says of English women that 'they are as it were men', sharing with men the toils of country life.

EDWARD HERBERT (1583–1648), first Baron Herbert of Cherbury, philosopher, historian, diplomatist, and poet; elder brother of George Herbert. Active life, traveller, soldier, ambassador. His *Autobiography* is a picture of contemporary manners.

THOMAS HEYWOOD (1574?–1650), dramatist; a Lincolnshire man. Strength lay in domestic drama, spectacle, and municipal pageants.

NICHOLAS HILLIARD (1537–1619), court goldsmith and miniaturist. Worked for Elizabeth and James I, and founded English school of miniature painting.

SIR EDWARD HOBY (1560–1617), diplomatist and controversialist; of Bisham, Berkshire, where he frequently entertained James I.

RANDLE HOLME (1627–1699), his *The Academy of Armory* has 'extraordinary glossaries of terms used in every conceivable art, trade, and domestic employment'.

ROBERT HOOKE (1635–1703), chemist and physicist. He anticipated the invention of the steam-engine, formulated the simplest theory of the arch, the extension and compression of elastic bodies. The balance-spring of watches, and the anchor-escapement for clocks, Gregarian telescope and microscope are among his inventions.

J. HOUGHTON (*d.* 1705), writer on agriculture and trade. Apothecary and dealer in tea, coffee, chocolate and other luxuries, against the Ship Tavern in St Bartholomew Lane.

JAMES HOWELL (1594?–1666), pamphleteer and letter-writer. Royalist spy, at Restoration became historiographer-royal. Chiefly remembered for his *Epistolae Ho-elianae: Familiar letters* and *Londinopolis; an Historical Discourse or Perlustration of the City of London.*

EDMOND HOWES (*fl.* 1607–1631), wrote a continuation of Stow's *Annals*, dealing, in part, with London playhouses.

LUCY HUTCHINSON (1620–1676?), biographer, daughter of Sir

Allan Apsley, Lieutenant of the Tower of London, wife of Colonel Hutchinson. Her life of her husband reveals a delightful picture of a distinguished Puritan family during the Civil War.

WILL KEMP (*fl.* 1600), comic actor and dancer. His *Kemps Nine Daies Wonder* describes his dance from London to Norwich.

DR EDWARD LISTER (1556–1620), of Wakefield, Yorkshire. Physician in ordinary to Elizabeth and James I.

WILLIAM LITHGOW (1582–1645?), traveller; born at Lanark. Claimed to have tramped thirty-six thousand miles over Europe in nineteen years. He gave account in *Rare Adventures and Paineful Peregrinations.*

EDMUND LUDLOW (1617?–1692), Puritan general and regicide; author of valuable *Memoirs.*

DONALD LUPTON (*d.* 1676), his *London and the Countrey Carbonadoed* shows how he was touched with the fascination of London streets.

THOMAS MACE (1620?–1710?), lay clerk of Trinity College, Cambridge. Wrote *Musick's Monument* on church music, lute, and viol.

SIR GEORGE MACKENZIE (1636–1691), Scottish lawyer and writer. Criminal prosecutor in persecution of the Covenanters; known as 'Bluidy Mackenzie'. Works include *A Moral Essay Preferring Solitude to Public Employment* and *Memoirs of the Affairs of Scotland.*

GERVASE MARKHAM (1568–1637), poet, translator, writer on agriculture and horsemanship. Said to have been the first to import an Arab horse into England. He wrote *Cavelarice, Country Contentments,* and *A Way to Get Wealth.*

THOMAS MIDDLETON (1570?–1627), dramatist. Known for satirical and romantic comedies, pageants and masques for city ceremonials. Wrote in collaboration with other dramatists.

JOHN MILTON (1608–1674), epic poet. Long preparation for his vocation as a poet. During the Commonwealth, Latin Secretary to the newly formed Council of State. By 1652, completely blind. After bitter disappointment at the Restoration, composed *Paradise Lost, Paradise Regained,* and *Samson Agonistes.* Died from 'gout struck in', buried in St Giles, Cripplegate, London.

FYNES MORYSON (1566–1617?), traveller; of Cadeby, Lincolnshire. Travelled over Europe and the Levant. Appears as an impartial, as well as candid, observer in his *Itinerary*.

THOMAS NASHE (1567–1601), satirist; lived in continuing poverty; hated the Puritans. His lively writing calls to mind Rabelais. His *Unfortunate Traveller* steps towards the novel of adventure.

SIR ISAAC NEWTON (1642–1727), mathematician, scientist, philosopher. Lucasian Professor of Mathematics at Cambridge, President of the Royal Society, Master of the Mint. 'By propounding the binomial theorem, the differential calculus, and the integral calculus, he began the series of discoveries in pure mathematics, optics, and physics which place him in the first rank of the scientists of all time.' His *Principia Mathematica* is, perhaps, the greatest achievement of the seventeenth century.

ROGER NORTH (1653–1734), lawyer and writer. Wrote interesting biographies of his brothers: one Keeper of the Great Seal, another the great Turkey merchant, the third master of Trinity College, Cambridge. He had many interests including music, mathematics, and sailing. When an old man he wrote two essays: *Memoirs of Musick* and *The Musicall Gramarian*.

JOHN OLDMIXON (1673–1742), historian, a prolific pamphleteer. Received a place in *The Dunciad*. Wrote *The British Empire in America*.

WILLIAM OLDYS (1696–1761), antiquary. Presents many interesting facts on literary history.

DOROTHY OSBORNE (1627–1695), married Sir William Temple. Her letters to him are among the best of their kind.

SIR THOMAS OVERBURY (1581–1613), courtier, poet, essayist. Opposed marriage of Robert Carr (afterwards Earl of Somerset) with the divorced Countess of Essex. Sent to the Tower. Slowly poisoned by agents of Lady Essex. Chiefly remembered for *Characters* – sketches in the manner of Theophrastus.

HENRY OXINDEN (1609–1670), poet, of Little Maydekin, Kent. Rector of Radnage, Buckinghamshire. Wrote *Jobus Triumphans*.

HENRY PEACHAM (1576?–1643?), author with varied interests. His work included *Graphice* on art, *The Compleat Gentleman*; from this Dr Johnson derived all the definitions on heraldry in his dictionary.

JOHN PECHEY (1655–1716), medical writer. Practised in London. Methods of apothecary rather than a doctor. Wrote *A Collection of Chronical Diseases*, and *The Compleat Herbal of Physical Plants.*

SAMUEL PEPYS (1633–1703), diarist, Secretary of the Admiralty (through patronage of the Earl of Sandwich, his father's cousin). He was a man of business, of pleasure; skilled in music and a collector of books, pictures, and manuscripts. His unique diary, in cipher, gives an eye-witness account of the life of his time, and unreserved self-revelation.

SIR WILLIAM PETTY (1623–1687), political economist, studied at Caen, Utrecht, Amsterdam, Leyden, Paris, and Oxford. Executed the 'Down Survey' of forfeited lands in Ireland. Original member of the Royal Society. Inventor of copying-machine and double-keeled sea-boat. Precursor of Adam Smith in political economy, wrote *A Treatise on Taxes*, and *Political Arithmetic.*

SIR HUGH PLATT (1552?–1611?), spoken of as the most ingenious husbandman of his times. He corresponded with all the lovers of agriculture and gardening throughout England. Chiefly remembered for his *Jewell House of Art and Nature.*

JOHN RAY (1627–1705), naturalist, son of a blacksmith at Black Notley, Essex. Became a fellow of Trinity College, Cambridge. Travelled across Europe, studying botany and zoology. His classification of plants founded the 'Natural System'; his zoological works called by Cuvier the basis of all modern zoology.

SIR JOHN RERESBY (1634–1689), governor of York. His *Memoirs* tell of political life of a Royalist at court, gossip and quarrels, talks with Charles II. Record of a 'self-praising hanger-on'.

JONATHAN RICHARDSON (1665–1745), a London portrait-painter, and writer on art.

JOHN WILMOT, SECOND EARL OF ROCHESTER (1648–1680), poet and notorious libertine. Showed courage at sea in the Dutch War. Favourite of Charles II; patron of several poets. Best work *A Satire Against Mankind.*

SAMUEL ROWLANDS (1570?–1630?), writer mainly of satirical tracts in prose and verse. *Greene's Ghost* is on coney-catchers. Later works are: *Doctor Merryman his Medicines Against Melancholy Humors*, and *Martin Mark-all*, about thieves.

PETER PAUL RUBENS (1577–1640), great painter of the Flemish school. Came to England in 1629 on a mission to Charles I.

EDWARD MONTAGU, FIRST EARL OF SANDWICH (1625–1672), admiral. Divided command of the fleet with Blake from 1653. Diaries give events in his naval career from the Restoration to Bergen-op-Zoom in the Dutch War.

JOHN SELDEN (1584–1654), eminent lawyer and bencher of the Inner Temple. Won fame as an orientalist on *De Diis Syris*. Collection of oriental manuscripts passed into the Bodleian Library. His *Table Talk* reported his remarks over twenty years composed by his secretary, Richard Milward.

CAPTAIN JOHN SMITH (1580–1631), went with the Virginia colonists in 1606. Taken prisoner by the Indians and said to have been rescued by Pocahontas. A man of verve and piquancy, became head of the colony. Author of a *General History of Virginia, New England, and the Summer Isles*.

SAMUEL SORBIERE: in 1663 this French traveller speaks of the vast number of booksellers' shops he had seen in London, especially in St Paul's churchyard and Little Britain, 'where there is twice as many as in the Rue St Jacques in Paris'.

SIR HANS SLOANE (1660–1753), physician; born at Killyleagh, County Down. In Jamaica collected a herbarium of eight hundred species. President of the Royal Society. His museum and large library formed the nucleus of the British Museum.

SIR RICHARD STEELE (1672–1729), essayist, dramatist, and politician. Born in Dublin. At Charterhouse with Addison. His missionary and reforming spirit shown in the *Tatler* and the *Spectator*.

JOHN   STRYPE   (1643–1737),   ecclesiastical   historian;   formed collection of original documents now in the Harleian and Landsdowne MSS. Enlarged Stow's *Survey of London.*

JOHN TAYLOR (1580–1653), the 'water poet' of Gloucester. Became Thames waterman. Wrote lively verse and prose. Walked from London to Braemar. Tried to journey from London to Queenborough in a brown-paper boat and narrowly escaped drowning.

REV. HENRY TEONGE (1621–1690), of Spernall, Warwickshire, naval chaplain. Sea diary; aboard the *Assistance* and the *Royal Oak*; lively details of naval conditions.

RALPH THORESBY (1658–1725), of Leeds, antiquary. Diary giving careful notes on antiquities, churches, travels, Bible studies, and scholars of the time.

THOMAS TRAHERNE (1638?–1674), poet and mystic. Rector of Credenhill near Hereford. Religious poetry and prose in *Centuries of Meditation.* Poems found in manuscript on a bookstall in 1896, thought to be the work of Henry Vaughan.

SIR SAMUEL TUKE (*d.* 1674), dramatist, his *Adventures of Five Hours*, admired by Pepys, shows the adaptation of Spanish dramas to the English stage.

SIR EDMUND VERNEY (1590–1642), a Royalist standard-bearer, who fell at Edgehill. A member of the distinguished family in Buckinghamshire.

SIR RALPH VERNEY (1613–1696), son of Sir Edmund, fought for the parliament, but refused the covenant, and in exile at Blois, was created a baronet in 1661.

THOMAS VINCENT (1634–1678), helped Thomas Doolittle at Islington academy, started in 1662 as a boarding-school in Moorfields. Edmund Calamy and Thos. Emlyn were pupils. Vincent wrote vividly of the Great Fire of London.

IZAAK WALTON (1593–1683), angler and biographer; friend of Donne, of Sir Henry Wotton, and of Bishops Morley, Sanderson, and King. Lived latterly much at Winchester. Chiefly known by the *Compleat Angler*, full of humour, wisdom and charity. Also renowned for his *Lives.*

NED WARD (1667–1731), tavern-keeper, wrote coarse, humorous prose and doggerel verse, remarkable for sketches of London life. Written in the easy style of the trained reporter, the *London Spy* is the tale of two school-fellows who range about the town noting 'the stink of sprats and the untenable clamours of the wrangling society'.

SIR PHILIP WARWICK (1609–1683), secretary to Charles II. Wrote *Memoires of the Reigne of King Charles I: with a Continuation to the Happy Restauration of King Charles II.*

SIR ANTHONY WELLDON (*d.* 1649?), wrote *The Court and Character of King James I.*

ADAM WHEELER (*fl.* 1685), of Salisbury; drummer. A military diarist describing the marches of the Wiltshire Regiment.

GEORGE WILKINS (*fl.* 1607), dramatist. His plays include *The Miseries of Inforst Mariage*, and *The Travailes of the Three English Brothers.*

ARTHUR WILSON, historian; his *History of King James I* is 'all new writ by a learned and impartial hand'.

EDWARD WINSLOW (1595–1655), one of the Pilgrim Fathers, sailed in the *Mayflower*; from 1624 was assistant-governor or governor of the Plymouth colony, described in *Good Newes from New England*, and *New England's Salamander.*

GEORGE WITHER (1588–1667), poet and pamphleteer. Wrote pungent satire, *Abuses Stript and Whipt*, and five pastorals *The Shepherd's Hunting.* Raised a troop of horse for parliament. Lost position and property at the Restoration.

ANTHONY WOOD (1632–1695), antiquary and historian. Antiquities, history, heraldry, genealogies and music occupied most of his time. His *Autobiography* is very detailed.

JOHN WOODALL (1556?–1643), surgeon; of Peirse Ithell, North Wales. Surgeon at St Bartholomew's; surgeon-general, East India Company. Wrote *Viaticum, Being the Pathway to the Surgeon's Chest*; *The Surgeon's Mate.*

HANNAH WOOLLEY (*fl.* 1670), writer of works on cookery. Adept at needlework, medicine, cookery, household management. Lived at Newport Pond near Saffron Walden. Wrote *The Queen-like Closet, The Ladies Delight, The Cook's Guide*.

JOHN WORLIDGE (*fl.* 1669–1698), agricultural writer; of Petersfield, Hampshire. Compiler of the first systematic treatise of husbandry on a large scale. Wrote *Systema Agriculturae, Vinetum Britannicum or a Treatise on Cider, The Complete Bee Master*.

DR JAMES YONGE (1647–1721), of Plymouth, medical writer. His sea diary tells of his work as a naval surgeon, and gives description of foreign towns and countries.

INDEX

Figures in **bold** refer to illustrations.